www.wadsworth.com

wadsworth.com is the World Wide Web site for Wadsworth and is your direct source to dozens of online resources.

At *wadsworth.com* you can find out about supplements, demonstration software, and student resources. You can also send email to many of our authors and preview new publications and exciting new technologies.

wadsworth.com
Changing the way the world learns®

From the Wadsworth Series in Mass Communication and Journalism

General Mass Communication

Biagi, Shirley, *Media/Impact: An Introduction to Mass Media,* 5th Ed.
Bucy, Erik, *Living in the Information Age: A New Media Reader*
Craft, John, Frederic Leigh, and Donald Godfrey, *Electronic Media*
Day, Louis, *Ethics in Media Communications: Cases and Controversies,* 3rd Ed.
Dennis, Everette E., and John C. Merrill, *Media Debates: Great Issues for the Digital Age,* 3rd Ed.
Fortner, Robert S., *International Communications: History, Conflict, and Control of the Global Metropolis*
Gillmor, Donald, Jerome Barron, and Todd Simon, *Mass Communication Law: Cases and Comment,* 6th Ed
Gillmor, Donald, Jerome Barron, Todd Simon, and Herbert Terry, *Fundamentals of Mass Communication Law*
Hilmes, Michele, *Only Connect: A Cultural History of Broadcasting in the United States*
Jamieson, Kathleen Hall, and Karlyn Kohrs Campbell, *The Interplay of Influence,* 5th Ed.
Kamalipour, Yahya K., *Global Communication*
Lester, Paul, *Visual Communication,* 2nd Ed.
Lont, Cynthia, *Women and Media: Content, Careers, and Criticism*
Sparks, Glenn G., *Media Effects Research: A Basic Overview*
Straubhaar, Joseph, and Robert LaRose, *Media Now: Communications Media in the Information Age,* 3rd Ed
Surette, Ray, *Media, Crime, and Criminal Justice: Images and Realities,* 2nd Ed.
Whetmore, Edward Jay, *Mediamerica, Mediaworld: Form, Content, and Consequence of Mass Communication,* Updated 5th Ed.
Zelezny, John D., *Cases in Communications Law,* 3rd Ed.
Zelezny, John D., *Communications Law: Liberties, Restraints, and the Modern Media,* 3rd Ed.

Journalism

Adams, Paul, *Writing Right for Today's Mass Media: A Textbook and Workbook with Language Exercises*
Anderson, Douglas, *Contemporary Sports Reporting,* 2nd Ed.
Bowles, Dorothy, and Diane L. Borden, *Creative Editing,* 3rd Ed.
Catsis, John, *Sports Broadcasting*
Chance, Jean, and William McKeen, *Literary Journalism: A Reader*
Dorn, Raymond, *How to Design and Improve Magazine Layouts,* 2nd Ed.
Fischer, Heintz-Dietrich, *Sports Journalism at Its Best: Pulitzer Prize Winning Articles, Cartoons, and Photographs*
Fisher, Lionel, *The Craft of Corporate Journalism*
Gaines, William, *Investigative Reporting for Print and Broadcast,* 2nd Ed.
Hilliard, Robert L., *Writing for Television, Radio, and New Media,* 7th Ed.
Kessler, Lauren, and Duncan McDonald, *When Words Collide,* 5th Ed.
Klement, Alice M., and Carolyn Burrows Matalene, *Telling Stories/Taking Risks: Journalism Writing at the Century's Edge*
Laakaniemi, Ray, *Newswriting in Transition*
Rich, Carole, *Workbook for Writing and Reporting News,* 3rd Ed.
Rich, Carole, *Writing and Reporting News: A Coaching Method,* 3rd Ed.

Photojournalism and Photography

Parrish, Fred S., *Photojournalism: An Introduction*

Public Relations and Advertising

Hendrix, Jerry A., *Public Relations Cases,* 5th Ed.
Jewler, Jerome A., and Bonnie L. Drewniany, *Creative Strategy in Advertising,* 7th Ed.
Newsom, Doug, and Bob Carrell, *Public Relations Writing: Form and Style,* 6th Ed.
Newsom, Doug, Judy VanSlyke Turk, and Dean Kruckeberg, *This Is PR: The Realities of Public Relations,* 7th Ed.
Sivulka, Juliann, *Soap, Sex, and Cigarettes: A Cultural History of American Advertising*
Woods, Gail Baker, *Advertising and Marketing to the New Majority: A Case Study Approach*

Research and Theory

Babbie, Earl, *The Practice of Social Research,* 8th Ed.
Baran, Stanley, and Dennis Davis, *Mass Communication Theory: Foundations, Ferment, and Future,* 2nd Ed.
Rubenstein, Sondra, *Surveying Public Opinion*
Rubin, Rebecca B., Alan M. Rubin, and Linda J. Piele, *Communication Research: Strategies and Sources,* 5th Ed.
Wimmer, Roger D., and Joseph R. Dominick, *Mass Media Research: An Introduction,* 6th Ed.

Media Effects Research

A Basic Overview

Glenn G. Sparks
Purdue University

WADSWORTH

THOMSON LEARNING

Australia • Canada • Mexico • Singapore • Spain
United Kingdom • United States

WADSWORTH

THOMSON LEARNING ™

Publisher: Holly Allen
Assistant Editor: Nicole George
Editorial Assistant: Mele Alusa
Marketing Manager: Kimberly Russell
Signing Representative: Lori Grebe
Project Manager, Editorial Production: Mary Noel
Print/Media Buyer: Rebecca Cross
Permissions Editor: Robert Kauser

Production Service: G & S Typesetters, Inc.
Copy Editor: Carolyn Russ
Cover Designer: Lisa Langhoff,
One Good Dog Design
Cover Printer: Webcom, Ltd.
Compositor: G & S Typesetters, Inc.
Printer: Webcom, Ltd.

Wadsworth / Thomson Learning
10 Davis Drive
Belmont, CA 94002-3098
USA

For more information about our products, contact us:
Thomson Learning Academic Resource Center
1-800-423-0563
http://www.wadsworth.com

International Headquarters
Thomson Learning
International Division
290 Harbor Drive, 2nd Floor
Stamford, CT 06902-7477
USA

UK / Europe / Middle East / South Africa
Thomson Learning
Berkshire House
168-173 High Holborn
London WC1V 7AA
United Kingdom

Asia
Thomson Learning
60 Albert Street, #15-01
Albert Complex
Singapore 189969

Canada
Nelson Thomson Learning
1120 Birchmount Road
Toronto, Ontario M1K 5G4
Canada

**Library of Congress
Cataloging-in-Publication Data**
Sparks, Glenn Grayson.
    Media effects research : a basic overview / Glenn G. Sparks.
        p.   m.—(Wadsworth series in mass communication and journalism)
    Includes bibliographical references and index.
    ISBN 0-534-54586-6 (pbk. : alk. paper)
    1. Mass media—Social aspects.   2. Mass media—Research—Methodology.   I. Title.
II. Series.
HM1206 .S66 2001
302.23—dc21

2001045317

Dedicated to Cheri Wilcox Sparks
The love of my life

Contents

Preface   xv
Acknowledgments   xvi

Chapter 1 A Scientific Approach to
                the Study of Media Effects   1

Ways of Knowing   2
    Experience   2
    Authority   3
    Science   4
Goals of Science   4
    Prediction   4
    Explanation   5
    Understanding   6
    Control   6
How Are the Goals of Science Achieved?   8
    Falsifiability   9
The Nature of Science   10
    Science Is General   11
    Science Acknowledges the Existence of Objective Truth   13
    Science Assumes a Skeptical Attitude   14
    Science Can't Answer Certain Kinds of Questions   15
Summary   16
Key Terms and Concepts   16
Key Names   17
Web Links   17
Notes   17

Chapter 2 Scientific Methods in Media Effects Research   19

Analyzing Media Content   19
    What Is Content Analysis?   20
    An Example: The Content of TV Commercials   21
The Sample Survey   23
    An Example: The Effects of Talk Show Viewing on Adolescents   24
The Search for Causal Relationships   27
    Criteria for Causal Relationships   27

The Experimental Method   32
    Manipulation of a Key Variable   33
    Random Assignment to Experimental Conditions   33
    Identical Treatment Except for the Manipulation   33
    Control Groups   34
    An Example: The Effects of Realistic Versus Reenacted Violence   35
Controversy About Research Methods   36
Summary   36
Key Terms and Concepts   37
Key Names   37
Web Links   37
Notes   38

Chapter 3 A Brief History of Media Effects Research   39
Setting the Stage   40
    1898—Congress Declares War on Spain   40
    1917—Propaganda in World War I   41
    The 1920s—Movies Explode as Mainstream Entertainment   41
1929–1932—The Payne Fund Studies   42
    What Was the Content of Movies?   42
    The Emotional Impact of Movies   42
    Does Watching Movies Affect Behavior?   43
    The Aftermath of the Payne Fund Studies   45
The Invasion From Mars   45
    The Research at Princeton   46
Early Theory of Media Effects: The Magic Bullet Model   47
The People's Choice Study: The "Limited Effects" Model   48
    Why Use Control Groups?   48
    Media Impact in the 1940 Campaign   48
    The Limited-Effects Perspective   49
The Evils of Comic Books   51
The Dawn of Television   52
Many Types of Media Effects   52
Summary   54
Key Terms and Concepts   55
Key Names   55
Web Links   55
Notes   56

Chapter 4 Time Spent With Mass Media:
            Reasons and Consequences   57
The Uses and Gratifications Perspective   58
    Why Do Children Watch TV?   58
The Problem With Self-Reports   62
Time Spent With Media   63
    The Displacement Hypothesis   64
    Television Viewing and Obesity   67

Summary   69
Key Terms and Concepts   69
Key Names   69
Web Links   70
Notes   70

Chapter 5 Effects of Media Violence   72

The Presence of Violent Content   74
The Causal Link Between Viewing Violence and
  Behaving Aggressively   76
  The Research of Albert Bandura   76
  The Long-Term Studies of Leonard Eron and Rowell Huesmann 79
  The Research of Brandon Centerwall   81
  The Catharsis Hypothesis   81
  A Priming Analysis of the Effect of Media Violence   83
Desensitization to Violence   84
Why Do People Like Media Violence?   85
Concluding Comments   86
Summary   87
Key Terms and Concepts   87
Key Names   87
Web Links   87
Notes   88

Chapter 6 Sexual Content in the Media   90

Human Sexuality Brings Out Passionate Opinion   90
Sorting Out Definitions and Terms   92
The Commission on Obscenity and Pornography   93
  Major Finding   93
  A Reexamination of the Commission's Findings   94
Research Following the Commission Report   95
  Content Available   96
  Perceptual Consequences of Viewing   96
  Behavioral Consequences of Viewing   97
The Meese Commission Report on Pornography   99
  Major Conclusion   99
Sex on Prime-Time TV   100
  The Dynamics of Excitation Transfer   101
  Content Analyses   102
  Sexual Behavior and Viewing   104
Control over Media Content   104
  Sex and the Internet   104
  Legal Control   105
  Social or Economic Control   105
  Control Through Education   106
Summary   106
Key Terms and Concepts   107

Key Names 107
Web Links 107
Notes 107

Chapter 7 Frightening Media 109
Fright Reactions to Media Are Prevalent 111
What Scares One Child May Not Scare Another 112
Experimenting with the Incredible Hulk 113
Why Is the Paranormal So Scary? 116
Poltergeist 117
The Nightmare on Elm Street Series 118
The Exorcist 119
What's a Parent to Do? 120
Is it Fun to Be Scared? 122
Frightening Films and Roller-Coaster Rides 122
The Sexual Dynamic in Viewing Frightening Films 123
Summary 124
Key Terms and Concepts 125
Key Names 125
Web Links 125
Notes 125

Chapter 8 Persuasive Effects of the Media 127
What Is Persuasion? 127
Subliminal Persuasion: The Magic Key? 128
Early History 128
The Presumed Mechanism 129
Two Important Questions 129
How Media Messages Persuade Without Even Trying 131
The Theory of Media Cultivation 133
Do Media Messages About the Paranormal Influence Paranormal Beliefs? 135
Intentional Persuasion in the Media 137
The Great American Values Test 137
How Does an Advertiser Determine Success? 139
Some Evidence for the Effectiveness of Advertising 139
The Third-Person Effect 140
Some Key Principles of Media Persuasion 140
The Power of the Source 142
Message Features: Simplicity and Repetition 143
More Message Features: Fear, Guilt, and Humor 143
The Health Campaign 145
Summary 147
Key Terms and Concepts 147
Key Names 147
Web Links 148
Notes 148

Chapter 9 The Effects of News and Political Content   151

Do Certain News Reports Cause More People to Die?   151
  Imitative Suicides and the News   152
Thinking About the News   153
  Need for Cognition   154
  Political Sophistication   154
  Agenda-Setting Theory: A Theory About Thinking   155
  The Spiral of Silence   157
  How Much of the News Do We Remember?   158
The Role of Emotion   160
Summary   164
Key Terms and Concepts   164
Key Names   164
Web Links   165
Notes   165

Chapter 10 The Effects of Media Stereotypes   167

What's in a Face?   167
Stereotypical Representations in the Media   171
  Sex Role Stereotypes   172
  Effects of Sex Role Stereotypes   173
  Media Images of Thin Bodies and Effects on Body Image   175
  Racial Stereotypes   177
  Overrepresentation of African Americans as Lawbreakers   177
The Imbalance in Media Research on Stereotypes   180
Summary   182
Key Terms and Concepts   182
Key Names   182
Web Links   183
Notes   183

Chapter 11 The Impact of New Media Technologies   185

The Revolution in New Media Technology   185
Computers and the Internet: Connection or Alienation?   187
  The Carnegie Mellon Study   187
  Applying the Lessons of History   190
Are Video Games Really Training Kids to Kill?   192
  An Opinion on Video Games from an Expert on "Killology"   193
  What Does the Research Say?   194
Summary   198
Key Terms and Concepts   198
Key Names   198
Web Links   198
Notes   199

Chapter 12 Meet Marshall McLuhan:
          A Less Scientific Approach to Media Impact   200

Is There Any Value to Considering Marshall McLuhan?   200
Meet Marshall McLuhan   201
The Eras of Communication History   202
    The Tribal Age   202
    Moving from the Tribal Age to the Print Age   203
    Moving on to the Current Electronic Age   204
The Medium Is the Message   206
The Effects of Electronic Media on Human Beings   207
    Education in the Electronic Age   208
    War in the Electronic Age: Not So "Hot"   209
    Politics in the Electronic Age:
      Was Bill Clinton "Cooler" Than George Bush?   211
    Drugs in the Electronic Age   212
McLuhan's Influence   212
Some Final Reflections   213
Summary   214
Key Terms and Concepts   215
Key Names   215
Web Links   215
Important Sources on Marshall McLuhan   216
Notes   216

Names Index   217
Subject Index   219

Preface

I never intended to write a textbook. I have always identified myself as a researcher and teacher of mass-communication effects—not a textbook writer. My intentions changed after teaching university undergraduates for over two decades. In my course at Purdue University on mass-communication theory, I watch semester after semester as my students gradually sink into the dry-sand prose of most texts that attempt to present theories of mass media. Once the sinking starts, I am almost never able to rescue them. I finally grew tired of this routine.

Compounding my frustration was the fact that my main desire was to teach about media impact rather than about mass-communication *theory*. Theory is fully realized when it meets the soil of observation. I have found that students can digest incredible doses of theory in the context of discovering what research says about media impact. So, this book is focused on the research instead of the theory that motivates the research. Nevertheless, if you use this text, I am betting that you will find plenty of theory to keep your students occupied—but the theory is presented in the context of research findings.

I became convinced to write a book for undergraduate students when I realized that it *was* possible to write a text that was not dry and boring. My two primary exemplars are Robert Cialdini's classic text on persuasion, *Influence,* and Em Griffin's best-selling introduction to communication theory, *A First Look at Communication Theory.* Since Em asked me to advise him about what to include in the mass-communication section of his book, I began thinking more seriously of trying to write a text of my own. This book represents my first attempt to do so. All of the chapters have been pretested on my own classes, and the results have encouraged me to make the material available to more people. Before you dive in, let me outline just a bit about the guiding philosophy of the book and how I think the text can be used.

Above all else, I have tried to write plainly and in a style that will engage the typical undergraduate student. This means that I often share personal anecdotes and refer to myself in the first person. I am committed to this style. I think students respond better if they can sense that there is a living, breathing human being behind the words. The reactions of my own students have helped to convince me that this is truly the case.

As you evaluate the text, keep in mind that I have attempted only to *introduce* the topic of media effects—not to write everything known by the research community. I believe that textbook writers make a tragic mistake when they

try to cover the whole terrain of their topic. This might satisfy textbook reviewers and serve as a valuable reference for scholars, but I don't think it does
much good at generating genuine interest among the students who ultimately
have to pay for and read the text. Because of my commitment to limiting this
textbook to an introduction to media effects, I am certain that some professors
will examine this text and spot crucial omissions that simply *must* be included.
I am well aware that the book fails to cover everything. I planned it that way. One
of my goals is to keep the material manageable so that students will actually read
the chapters. I also want students to finish the book and still be interested in
finding out more about media effects. I have decided to sacrifice a little breadth
on the altar of student interest. I think it is a sacrifice well worth making.

How can this book be used? I think the text can fit into two different
kinds of courses. First, it can obviously be used in a mass-communication theory course or a mass media research course. Second, the book can be used as a
secondary text in a basic introduction to mass communication. Most of the
texts for the basic course have little or no coverage of media effects research.
For professors who want their students to develop a deeper understanding of
the effects literature, this book should not be too overwhelming as an accom-
panying volume in the basic introductory course. I have deliberately held the
presentation of material to 12 chapters in order for the book to fit comfortably
into different course formats. In the 15-week semester, I have found that students would rather ease in and ease out. For years, I attempted to fight that attitude; now I find myself subscribing to it. Once again, my philosophy here is to
meet the needs of the audience. If I don't assign a chapter of reading in either
the first or last week, I can still assign a chapter per week for the rest of the semester and have one week for some additional reading that I might select. If
there is a topic that a professor believes must be in the course that I don't cover,
the flexible week fills the need. The chapters are also short enough and easy
enough to read that more than one chapter *could* be assigned in a single week
for schools that are on a shorter semester. In the end, my primary goal is to have
students understand more about media research and still be interested in the
topic when they finish reading. The initial evidence suggests that I have succeeded. I am eager to discover if you agree.

ACKNOWLEDGMENTS

Writing a book of this type is not easy. Very simply, I could never have done
it without help from lots of people. My students over the years helped to shape
my thinking about a book of this type. To the extent that the book is successful at communicating well about media effects, I am indebted to my students'
willingness to share their reactions and insights. Before I ever started my work
at Purdue, I was fortunate enough to be mentored in graduate school by Joanne
Cantor. Her integrity and dedication to my training as a scholar were unparal-
leled. I could never have written this text without the kind of education that
Joanne provided. The book would never have been completed if I hadn't been
blessed with a working environment that was conducive to productive labor. I

have been in the Department of Communication at Purdue University for 15 years. It is a fabulous place to teach, conduct research, write, and generally enjoy life. For these things, I am thankful.

The people at Wadsworth have been fantastic to work with from the beginning. My editor, Karen Austin, has been particularly helpful. I also owe a debt of gratitude to the many reviewers on the first version of the manuscript: Andy O. Alali, California State University, Bakersfield; Lisa R. Barry, Albion College; Robert M. Brady, University of Arkansas; Travis Dixon, University of Michigan; Anita Fleming-Rife, Pennsylvania State University; Linda C. Godbold, East Carolina University; Bradley S. Greenberg, Michigan State University; Gerald Kosicki, Ohio State University; Annie Lang, Indiana University; Miriam J. Metzger, University of California, Santa Barbara; John Sumser, California State University, Stanislaus; and Wayne Wanta, University of Oregon.

If you're like me, you find it difficult to sustain work on a project over many months unless you have close friends who bear your burdens, share your joys and offer words of encouragement. I have a few choice friends who do all of these things. I could write several pages about each of them, but that would undoubtedly embarrass them. So, I will just extend a heartfelt thanks to Em Griffin, Will Miller, Bob Ogles, Stuart Robertson, and John Greene. These are the friends who nourish my soul.

Finally, I owe everything to my wife, Cheri Sparks. A Ph.D. in her own right, she has contributed to this project in ways too numerous to count. Most importantly, she offered her daily encouragement and support. It was Cheri who convinced me that I ought to try my hand at this project. She is also the mother of my three incredible children, David, Erin, and Jordan. To my family, both immediate and extended, I offer my deepest thanks for helping me in all of the little ways (and big ones too) to achieve whatever I manage to achieve.

Glenn Sparks
March 2001

1

■

A Scientific Approach to the Study of Media Effects

On April 13, 1999, two students at Columbine High School in Littleton, Colorado, stunned their classmates and the nation when they unleashed a horrible assault of gunfire and bombs, leaving many students and one teacher dead. In the national discussion that followed this tragic event, a persistent theme was sounded over and over again: The mass media must share a significant part of the blame for this incident and others like it. President Clinton called upon the producers of mass media messages to reduce gratuitous violence. The clear implication of Clinton's rhetoric was that exposure to violent entertainment images increased the probability of this type of violent behavior. But others disagreed. They charged that media messages were simply a convenient scapegoat distracting us from the real problem of poor parental oversight. In a Gallup poll published 2 weeks after the shootings in Littleton, only 2% of the respondents identified violent entertainment as the culprit in the crime. Only 1% identified the root cause of the problem as the unrestricted proliferation of guns.[1]

If you listened carefully to any of this national discussion, you may have heard viewpoints that seemed consistent with your own values or political positions. It may have seemed tempting to embrace one or more of the ideas that you heard about how to prevent similar events in the future. In the end, *opinions* about the events in Littleton were easy to come by. But if you were thinking carefully about the variety of opinions that were expressed about the causes of school shootings, you probably realized that opinions were limited in bringing you to an understanding of the truth. Despite the fact that President Clinton was in a position of national leadership, his opinion about the role of the mass media in the Littleton shootings was still only an opinion. You can read more about the actual effects of media violence in chapter 5 to see whether President Clinton's opinion has any scientific merit. In this chapter, you will learn something about how science is different from casual opinion.

WAYS OF KNOWING

Experience

There are many ways that we try to know things about the world around us. One way is through direct **experience.** This is sometimes called **empiricism.** Experience is often a very reliable way to knowledge. One morning, after leaving home from the Chicago area without a map, I found myself in Milwaukee, Wisconsin. The only problem was that I was trying to get to Muskegon, Michigan. If you consult a map, you will discover that I had gone up the wrong side of a rather large lake (Lake Michigan). I have now learned from my experience to consult a map before I travel long distances. This knowledge has often saved me from additional navigating disasters. But learning by experience can also be filled with many trials and errors. Progress can be painfully slow and lead down blind alleys. For nearly 300 years, the people of Europe were afraid to eat tomatoes, which had been introduced from Central America in the 1500s. Personal experience told them that any fruit from the nightshade family was unsafe.[2] Legend has it that someone may have eaten a tomato and died shortly thereafter. In this case, experience proved to be very misleading.

When it comes to our knowledge of media effects, many of us tend to rely upon our own personal experience to reach a conclusion. In class discussions about the media violence controversy, it is not uncommon for me to hear students expressing the following viewpoint:

> Well, I don't really think that media violence makes us more violent. After all, look at me. On Saturday mornings, I watched every violent cartoon that the networks put on. Today, I love movies like *The Terminator.* The more blood and guts, the better. My parents love violent movies, too. I grew up on them. But am I a violent person? Of course not! I have never even gotten into a fight. I don't own a gun. I've never been arrested for anything. I'm a peaceful and law-abiding citizen. In fact, my whole life is a personal testimony to the fact that media violence has no negative effect at all. Kids can tell the difference between real violence and fantasy violence. So, I'm sorry, I just don't buy it. Media violence is just fun entertainment. I don't see the harmful effects.

It shouldn't be difficult to recognize that this viewpoint is a great example of knowledge by personal experience. It should also be relatively easy to see that a person's individual experience may be a poor guide to the best general knowledge on a given topic. Just as people thought that tomatoes were poisonous for everyone, people might also think that media violence is benign for everyone. In both cases, personal experience might seem to point to a solid conclusion. But a more careful look might show such a conclusion to be solidly wrong. One possibility is that the conclusion from personal experience is valid for oneself but not for others. The fact that violent media might not trigger aggressive behavior for one individual does not necessarily imply that it functions the same way for everyone. Another possibility is that one's impression about being invulnerable to media impact is simply incorrect. Perhaps the effects of media violence are difficult for people to detect in themselves—even though the effects are definitely present.

Authority

Another way of knowing is to rely on **authority.** Obviously, we can't know everything there is to know. When we get sick, we usually consult a doctor and follow whatever advice he or she gives. We recognize that long years of study and practice tend to have qualified the doctor as an authority on medical diagnosis. Often the trust we place in medical authorities is rewarded with a cure. But as some have learned, medical authorities are only human. They make mistakes. Some doctors are better than others. Medical horror stories of incompetent physicians who ruin the lives of their patients are not difficult to find. Blind allegiance to authority can often have debilitating results on our search for reliable knowledge. Our knowledge that doctors generally know more than we do about medical cures can lead to a shortcut in our thinking that results in the conclusion that *any* doctor can be trusted as an authority. That kind of mental shortcut can be dangerous. Another dangerous mental shortcut that often occurs with authority figures is to transfer authority to an area that is unrelated to the area of expertise. My doctor might be an authority in prescribing medication, but there may be little reason to trust the doctor's advice when it comes to finding a good auto mechanic or trying to figure out the best way to motivate my children to do well in school.

Hundreds of years ago, religious authority figures were adamant that the earth was the center of the universe and that every celestial body revolved around it. However, new astronomical discoveries by **Copernicus** indicated that the earth actually revolved around the sun. Copernicus feared the actions of the church leaders so much that he kept his discoveries secret for over a decade before publishing them. Nearly 100 years later, Galileo was still confronting resistance from the church with regard to the Copernican model of the solar system.[3] Many people continued to reject the truth about the movement of the celestial bodies because they relied on the religious authorities for all knowledge. In this case, reliance upon authority resulted in wrong beliefs.

Over the years, executives from the TV networks have made various statements about the effects of media violence that tend to minimize the possibility of negative impact. Shouldn't these network executives be regarded as authorities on the topic? After all, they are in the day-to-day programming business. They sell advertising time on the basis of their understanding of the effects of commercials. If the network executives say that media violence isn't a problem, shouldn't we listen? As we shall see later, one of the problems with arriving at knowledge by appeal to authority is that the supposed authority figures often have various interests to protect. Just as the religious authorities rejected new views of the solar system to protect what they believed to be their religious interests, the TV networks can probably be blamed for issuing statements about media violence out of their concern for maintaining economic profits.[4]

Science

In the chapters that follow, I have attempted to summarize the scientific evidence on the question of media effects. **Science** is a particular way of knowing. One of the hallmarks of the scientific method is **systematic observation** as opposed to casual observation. Science combines empiricism with logical thought and is always pressing onward toward greater precision of observation.[5] One of the best arguments in favor of the power of the scientific way of knowing is the observation that *science works*. A commitment to science has brought us powerful antibiotics to cure our diseases. It has also put human beings on the moon. While science is a human activity that suffers from the multitude of human shortcomings, it is still the most powerful way of knowing that humans have at their disposal. One of the best ways to understand the scientific method of arriving at new knowledge is to understand the **goals of science.**[6] Whether one is doing natural science or social science, the goals are the same. Natural scientists attempt to achieve the goals of science in their study of biology, chemistry, physics, astronomy, and the like. Social scientists attempt to achieve the goals of science in their study of social and psychological phenomena that involve human beings.

GOALS OF SCIENCE

Prediction

Accurate predictions are one of the coveted goals of science. If you turn on the weather forecast tonight on your local TV news, you will discover that the meteorologist has employed a wide array of instruments, maps, and satellite photos in an attempt to provide an accurate prediction of tomorrow's weather. **Prediction** can be defined simply as foretelling the future. Over the years, the science of meteorology has produced increasingly accurate forecasts. Forecasts for a day in advance are usually ones that people can trust in planning their picnics. When the citizens of Oklahoma City experienced an onslaught of killer tornadoes on May 3, 1999, they had a full 30 minutes of advance warning. In this case, accurate prediction undoubtedly saved lives. But the state of the art is not advanced enough to accurately predict the weather over the long term. Science is in continual pursuit of better prediction.

In the area of media effects, accurate predictions are also one of the chief goals. For example, if researchers can predict ahead of time which children are most likely to imitate violent behavior seen in films, parents might be able to intervene to prevent film exposure. Likewise, if scholars can predict that certain types of characters will facilitate learning on programs like *Sesame Street,* then young children might have a better start upon entering elementary school.

Explanation

Science certainly has no monopoly on prediction. Insurance companies are also in the prediction business. When my son recently celebrated his 21st birthday, I received notice that my auto insurance rates would be getting cheaper. Data collected by the insurance industry led to the prediction that drivers who have reached their 21st birthday are much less likely to have accidents than those who are younger. The statistic is so dramatic that the insurance companies can pass on premium savings to the customer. The insurance companies don't really care much about *why* accidents drop off after drivers turn 21. You can probably identify several possible reasons without thinking too long (more years of driving experience, increased social maturity, and so on). The insurance companies care mainly about the fact that they can predict that the decrease will happen. It is on this point that the scientist and the insurance company may begin to part ways. They are both interested in prediction. But the scientist is also interested in **explanation**—knowing why something occurs the way it does.

What does it mean to say that something has been explained? Think about something simple like flicking a light switch. If someone asked you to explain why the lights go on and off each time you move the switch, what would you say? You would probably say something about the electric circuitry behind the switch, including wires, lightbulb filaments, and the flow of electricity. All of these ingredients provide a broader framework or pattern that you invoke to help uncover the "why" behind the phenomenon of the light switch. And this is usually what it means to explain something. **Explanations place the phenomenon to be explained into a broader framework or pattern that doesn't really require much additional elaboration.**

Scientists are always searching for the best explanation for why something happens the way it does. You can probably appreciate the fact that arguments will often erupt about the adequacy of specific explanations. A parent might answer a 3-year-old child's question about why the leaves turn colors in autumn by saying something like "That's the way God made trees." In this case, "God" becomes the broader framework or pattern that requires no additional elaboration. Such an answer might satisfy the 3-year-old but seem increasingly inadequate as the child gets older. The child who discovers that asking "why" is appropriate regardless of what explanation parents may provide has actually discovered something very important about explanations. Explanations can continually be scrutinized and pressed until more detail emerges that seems more satisfying. One of the characteristics of science is that it always encourages additional scrutiny.

In media effects research, as in other sciences, scholars argue about how adequate certain explanations are for given research findings. For example, some researchers have located the primary explanation for people's increased tendency for aggression after seeing media violence in the aggressive images shown in the programs or films.[7] Other researchers have argued that these images are not the most important thing. Instead, they have identified the increased physiological arousal caused by exposure to violent images as the critical explanatory ingredient in the increase in aggressive behavior.[8] You will read more about these explanations in the chapter about media violence.

Understanding

Good explanations provide a sense of understanding. What does it mean to say that we understand how something works? Usually, **understanding has to do with knowing the particular sequence of causal events** that unfold in a given phenomenon of interest. An explanation that yields a high level of understanding of how the light switch turns the light on would be one that ordered the causal chain of events beginning with the flick of the switch and ending with the illumination of the bulb. Since good explanations provide understanding, these two goals of science are closely related and they tend to go hand in hand.

In the case of explanations for how watching media violence might increase aggressive behavior, our understanding would not be very deep if the explanation consisted simply in the statement that children watch the shows and then they copy what they see. Regarding this type of explanation, we might ask what really happens between the viewing and the copying. In other words, what is the exact causal sequence of events? Another hallmark of science is the constant quest for deeper levels of understanding.

Control

When scientists can accurately predict, explain, and understand some phenomenon, they are afforded greater **control** over that phenomenon. In the wake of the Oklahoma City tornadoes, a number of news features appeared on TV that explained how the science of meteorology has advanced over the last few decades. With the help of such developments as Doppler radar, satellite cloud images, and computer analyses of storm data, meteorologists are now much better able to forecast the occurrence of a tornado. While it is still far from perfect, the level of explanatory insight that scientists can claim for the tornado phenomenon is greater than it once was. In contrast to years ago, scientists now understand some of the causal forces that produce these extraordinary storms. Advances in prediction, explanation, and understanding provide a greater sense of control over the tornado event. People who live in areas that the data show are particularly susceptible can now be warned to take safety precautions. Broadcast practices can be modified to get the word out when meteorologists detect the early signs of a tornado.

Similar to the scientific investigation of tornadoes, the investigation of media effects also holds ramifications for controlling events. A good example

---

STUDY BOX 1-1   How Do Ratings Affect Children's Entertainment Choices?

In 1998, Volume 2 of the *National Television Violence Study* was released. The 3-year study was funded by the National Cable Television Association. One of the research teams participating in that study was led by Professor Joanne Cantor of the University of Wisconsin–Madison. Cantor and her associates (Kristen Harrison and Amy Nathanson) wanted to know whether children's interest in TV programs and movies was affected by the ratings that they saw prior to viewing. They tested children between the ages of 5 and 15 from cities in Wisconsin.

The children completed a background questionnaire and then read short descriptions for eight different programs. The program names were selected from old movies or were completely fictitious. The researchers selected the names in order to minimize the possibility that some children would think that they had already seen the programs. Each program description contained one of several different advisories—randomly assigned by the researchers. For example, one of the advisories called for parental discretion. Another called for viewer discretion. A third advisory followed the MPAA ratings (G, PG, PG-13, and R). A few other advisories were also tested.

The results of the study revealed that, in most cases, children's interest in the programs was not affected by the particular advisory that appeared. However, the MPAA rating system (the one that is actually in use by the movie industry) tended to produce a "forbidden fruit" effect. Older children were more likely to express interest in movies or programs that carried the PG-13 or R rating. In contrast, if a description carried the G rating, older children expressed less interest. After considering the new TV rating system that was adopted for use beginning in 1997, Cantor and her associates concluded:

[T]he industry's choice of a rating system is not only destined to be uninformative for parents, it is likely to make their job of protecting children harder by making restricted programs more attractive. The systems which merely provided content information, when subjected to the same test as the MPAA ratings, did not make programs containing violence more tantalizing. (p. 321)

SOURCE: Cantor, J., Harrison, K., & Nathanson, A. (1998). Ratings and advisories for television programming. In Center for Communication and Social Policy at University of California, Santa Barbara (Eds.), *National television violence study 2* (pp. 267–322). Thousand Oaks, CA: Sage.

---

of the control implications of media effects research is easily seen in a program of studies conducted by Professor **Joanne Cantor** (University of Wisconsin–Madison). Professor Cantor and her associates discovered that the film rating system (G, PG, PG-13, R, and so on) used by the Motion Picture Association of America (MPAA) actually tends to attract older children to the very film material that is, theoretically, not intended for their consumption. As a result of her studies, Cantor recommends a rating system that includes brief content descriptions rather than warning labels (see Study Box 1-1).[9] Just as in tornado prediction, an increase in the ability to predict and understand a given media effect results in increased control.

Sometimes the implications for control that may arise out of scientific research are controversial. The MPAA has resisted the policy suggestions that

spring from Cantor's research. This is not the first time that research has ultimately led to controversy about media policy. Back in 1974, researchers discovered that a short commercial message ("The Swing") that was designed
to promote sharing and turn-taking behavior in young children was effective
in modifying children's behavior. But the commercial caused great controversy
among some people who were concerned about its potential to "brainwash"
children. According to these critics, sharing a swing on the playground might
promote passive compliance among children who need to learn to stand up for
their rights.[10]

While lawmakers, organizations, and other policy makers might debate the
pros and cons of particular strategies for controlling a phenomenon, scientists
usually hesitate to become identified too closely with a particular policy. Instead, they are more comfortable pointing out the range of control strategies
that are available as a result of the increased ability to predict, explain, and understand a given phenomenon. While the goal of science is not necessarily to
push any particular remedy for controlling an event, scientific progress is generally oriented to providing greater measures of control over the things that are
studied.

HOW ARE THE GOALS OF
SCIENCE ACHIEVED?

When I teach the fundamentals of science to students and I ask them how they
think the goals of science are usually achieved, I typically get a variety of answers. Students often identify experiments, testing, observation, data analysis,
surveys, and so on. While these are all tools of the scientist, the most powerful
way to achieve the goals of prediction, explanation, understanding, and control
does not appear on that list. The thing that generates experiments, testing, data
analysis, and the like is **theory.**

Scientific theory is a bit different from the kind of theory that we might
refer to in everyday conversation. When my wife and I were driving home from
campus a few weeks ago, we noticed that there was much more traffic than usual
and we wondered about the reason for the increase. I announced that I had a
theory about the change, and I proceeded to speculate that road construction
in another part of town had caused traffic to divert to our usual route home.
Thus, we were now in a traffic jam—even though the road construction was
nowhere near our location. In this case, my casual use of the term *theory* was
really just a synonym for the word *idea*. I could just as easily have said that I had
an idea about the traffic change. The meaning would have been the same. But
in science, the word "theory" cannot easily be replaced with the word "idea."

There are several parts to the notion of scientific theory. First, a scientific
theory **consists of more than one statement.** My notion of why traffic had
increased on our route home was easily stated in a single sentence. But scientific
theories take much more than a sentence to state completely. Often, they involve an entire manuscript that might even be as long as a book. Darwin expli-

cated his theory of evolution in a book called *The Origin of Species*.[11] **Albert Bandura** took an entire book chapter to present his "social cognitive theory of mass communication."[12] You will read more about that theory in a later chapter. The point here is that scientific theories consist of a *set* of statements— not just a single statement.

One of the things that this set of statements does is to **identify the key concepts of the theory and specify how they are related.** In meteorology, a theory about tornado formation might include the concepts of warm air, cold air, and updrafts. The theory might describe how these concepts relate to each other to produce conditions that are favorable for tornadoes. A theory about how media violence affects viewers might describe how the concepts of attention, role models, identification, rewards, and punishments relate together to lead to the anticipation of viewers' aggressive behavior.

Perhaps the most important characteristic of scientific theories is that **they yield hypotheses that are testable by observation. A hypothesis is a specific prediction about what will happen under a certain set of well-specified conditions.** Hypotheses are not theories. They are produced by theories. Copernicus presented his heliocentric theory of celestial motion in the 1500s. The theory yielded a hypothesis that the earth rotates around the sun. One way to test this hypothesis was to look at the stars. As one scientist put it, "If Copernicus's theory were true . . . then stars nearer the Earth should seem to change their position relative to more distant stars as the Earth moved around the sun."[13] This change in position is called *parallax*. Once powerful telescopes were invented, parallax was actually observed, thus lending credence to Copernicus's theory. If parallax had never been observed, the heliocentric theory would have eventually been discredited and replaced by a theory that gave a better account of the data.

In media effects research, just as in research on physical theory, hypotheses are often proposed from theories and then tested with observations. Reading in chapter 5 about media violence, you will learn how researchers were able to test the hypothesis that angry individuals who watch violent films will actually behave *less* aggressively. In this case, the hypothesis turned out to be disconfirmed.

Falsifiability

What does it mean to say that a theoretical hypothesis must be testable by observation? A key aspect of the meaning of testability is that the hypothesis must be **falsifiable.** This does not mean that the hypothesis has to turn out to be false. Instead, it means that **it should be possible to specify ahead of time what sort of data, if observed, would make the hypothesis false.** If one is able to clearly specify in advance the data that would falsify the hypothesis, and that data is never observed in systematic tests, the hypothesis has to be taken seriously. But if one is unable to specify in advance the data that would falsify the hypothesis, then we will always be in a relatively weak position in terms of being able to say that the hypothesis has merit. Em Griffin illustrates this concept in his book about communication theory, using an analogy involving a trick basketball shot.[14] His description reminded me of my own experience from childhood that makes essentially the same point.

During the summer, I used to play a series of Wiffle-ball games with one of my friends. During that series, my friend boasted that he had found a way to throw a secret pitch that was impossible to hit. The first time he threw me the pitch, I swung and missed. "See," boasted my friend, "the pitch just can't be hit." When I swung and missed a second time, I started to wonder if he might be right. But the third time he gave me the secret pitch, I hit it down the left field line. Before I could say a word, my friend announced, "That wasn't my secret pitch. I didn't have my fingers lined up right." For several more innings, my friend tried to protect his thesis that the secret pitch could not be hit. Each time I swung and missed, he declared that he had thrown the secret pitch. But when I managed to hit a double or a home run, I discovered afterwards that it hadn't been the secret pitch.

What was wrong with my friend's claim? As he eventually discovered, I couldn't take his thesis about the secret pitch very seriously. If he had really wanted to convince me that the thesis was true, he needed to announce *ahead of time* what would have to happen to disconfirm his claim. He needed to say something like, "This is the secret pitch—and if you hit it, then I can no longer say that my secret pitch is impossible to hit." The fact that he couldn't make his claim a falsifiable one undermined his ability to have the claim taken seriously. This is exactly the case with scientific theory. If a theory yields a hypothesis that can never be falsified, the theory will not ultimately enjoy acceptance in the scientific community. Sometimes theories, including theories of mass communication, that sound very provocative are not able to contribute very much to the goals of prediction, explanation, understanding, and control.

THE NATURE OF SCIENCE

Theories that are falsifiable certainly form an important foundation for the achievement of the goals of science. Without research generated by such theories, there would be little progress toward those goals. A great deal of scientific activity is devoted toward the actual details of the research process. What methods can be used to actually test a hypothesis? Chapter 2 will introduce you to some of the methods used to investigate mass media effects from a scientific perspective. But before we move along to a consideration of these methods, it is important to understand some of the underlying commitments of the scientific enterprise. While we live in a culture that enjoys the numerous benefits of these commitments, the commitments themselves are not often articulated clearly—even by scientists.

At this moment, I am witnessing an event that people who lived 100 years ago would find unbelievable. My fingers are tapping on lettered keys, and words are instantly appearing on an illuminated screen. If, during this process, I get a headache, I know that I can take two aspirin tablets and my headache

---

STUDY BOX 1-2   Characteristics of Social Science

Social science is

Logical: Scientists use inductive and deductive logic to achieve their goals. Theories must not contain logical inconsistencies.

Deterministic: Scientists assume that events happen for reasons. Things do not "just happen."

General: The aim is to understand overall patterns of events. The larger the scope that is explained, the more useful it is.

Parsimonious: The aim is to gain the greatest amount of understanding from the smallest number of variables.

Specific: The scientist must be specific about the methods of measurement used to investigate a given phenomenon.

Empirically verifiable: Propositions and theories must be testable in the real world.

Intersubjective: Descriptions of observations are sufficiently detailed that other scientists should be able to replicate the observations.

Open to modification: As time passes, new evidence may be expected to revise existing ways of thinking about a phenomenon.

SOURCE: Babbie, Earl R. (1973). *Survey research methods.* Belmont, CA: Wadsworth.

---

likely will disappear in a matter of minutes. The application of science brought the benefits of my opportunity to use the computer and the relief of my headache. It is easy to take the benefits of science for granted while simultaneously remaining ignorant of how these benefits were derived. To the extent that we can understand the underlying nature of science, we will be in a better position to actually implement the scientific method, understand the outcomes of science, and make additional advances. In Study Box 1-2, you will find a brief list of qualities that a sociologist, Earl Babbie, identified as describing the nature of social science.[15] Below, I have expanded on one of the dimensions noted by Babbie, and I have also added a few other aspects of science that are important to grasp.

Science Is General

One of the important aspects of science that is often misunderstood is the quest for generality. Think back to the opening discussion about the shootings at Columbine High School. Most of the public discussion that followed this incident focused on uncovering the particular reasons why two young boys would turn guns on their classmates. Social commentators cited a wide range of possible explanations, including parental neglect, social isolation from peers, the influence of violent video games, the impact of a particular scene from the movie *Basketball Diaries,* and the impact of mood-altering drugs. You may have noticed that on the various news and talk shows that proliferated in the aftermath of the shootings, few scientists went before the cameras claiming that the cause of the shootings was easy to identify. Their reluctance to identify the specific causes may not have been very satisfying to the news media, but it made sense from the standpoint of what constitutes good science.

The predominant quest of the news commentators following the Columbine event was to find the particular reason(s) for why it had happened. In research, this would be analogous to a "case study" approach to knowledge. In such an approach, the investigator seeks to describe a given case with as much detail as possible—invoking as many variables as possible—so that a full and complete understanding of the event can be achieved. Once this understanding is reached, it *could* be helpful in generalizing to other cases—but the details of a given case are typically so idiosyncratic that generalizing is typically impossible. For example, one of the boys who did the shooting at Columbine was an avid participant in a fantasy baseball league. In the case study approach, this fact could turn out to be highly significant. Perhaps the boy had become disenchanted with his team's progress and his mood had sunk, thus contributing to his outrage.

Unlike the case study approach to knowledge, science searches for general patterns or principles. These patterns are usually stated in terms of probability and attempt to employ as *few* variables as possible. For example, researchers might know that the probability of antisocial behavior among youth increases with parental neglect. Or, media researchers might know that boys who play violent video games are more likely to exhibit aggressive behaviors. Notice that it might be difficult or nearly impossible for a scientist to connect these general findings with a specific case. In a given incident, violent video games or parental neglect may have had little to do with a specific crime. Even though scientific research on fantasy baseball leagues might reveal that such a hobby is generally healthy (this is purely speculative and hypothetical), it might turn out to be a significant culprit in a crime in any given case.

In the end, case studies do much more to inform us about idiosyncratic cases than they do to help us understand broader patterns. Scientific research does more to inform us about broad, general patterns across large groups of individuals than it does to help us understand the particulars of a given case. Scientists who did participate in the public discussions after the Columbine shootings tended to take the opportunity to discuss the general patterns found in research pertaining to playing violent video games or taking mood-altering drugs. The fact that they stopped short of claiming that these variables had anything to do with the actual shootings at Columbine may have frustrated some viewers. But the commitment of science to uncovering general patterns is viewed among scientists as more valuable to society than an emphasis on specific cases. You would probably appreciate the value of this emphasis if your doctor informed you that the drug you were about to take was effective in 99% of the cases. The information about this general pattern of effectiveness would undoubtedly be much more pertinent to your decision to take the drug than would the details of any single case study.

Science Acknowledges the Existence of Objective Truth

It is quite fashionable today to proclaim that there is no objective **truth** to be uncovered. My students can often be overheard saying that there is no such thing as truth—truth is relative. Something may be true for you but not true for me. When classroom discussions turn to the effects of the media, I can almost always count on at least one person saying something like the following:

> It is certainly OK for you to believe that media have bad effects on children. I mean, if that's true for you, then no one can really argue with you about that. And I'm certainly not going to argue with you. But for me, the media don't have bad effects on children. I grew up with TV and I don't think it hurt me at all. I kind of liked cartoons and then I got into science fiction for a while. So, no one will convince me that it has bad effects. But if it does for you, that's OK. You know—what is true for you is true for you and what is true for me is true for me. There is no such thing as something that's true for everybody.

If all of my students take this sort of perspective, it certainly produces great harmony in the classroom. It sounds very tolerant. But tolerance notwithstanding, there are certain features of the statement that make little sense when subjected to critical scrutiny. Let's start with the last statement: "There is no such thing as something that's true for everybody." The problem can be uncovered quite simply by asking this question about the statement itself: Is this statement true for everybody? If, on the one hand, the statement is true for everybody, then the existence of this fact stands as a complete disconfirmation of the statement itself. If, on the other hand, the statement is *not* true for everybody, then it might not be true for you or me. If it isn't true for you or me, then we can reject the statement as false. In either case, the statement runs into significant problems as a claim to be taken seriously. Two scientists, **Theodore Schick Jr.** and **Lewis Vaughn** have summarized the situation this way:

> Each time we assert that something is the case or we think that something is a certain way, we assume that there is objective reality. Each time a relativist denies it, he entangles himself in self-refutation and contradictions. In the very argument over the existence of objective truth, both those who accept it and those who deny it must assume it or the argument would never get off the ground. (p. 80)[16]

With respect to arguments about media effects, the assertion that the media affect children is incompatible with the assertion that they don't affect children. Both assertions cannot both be true. There is, in fact, an objective reality "out there" to be discovered by the media effects researcher. The fact that the truth is out there to be discovered is no guarantee that scientists will actually discover it. But when one takes a scientific approach, one is definitely committing oneself to the notion that objective truth exists.

Let's go back to the student's statement about media effects, just to make sure that we don't get things confused. It may well be that the media might affect two people differently. If that is the point the student is trying to make, then we surely have to grant it. But when this position gets articulated in a general way that results in the denial of the existence of an objective truth, the scientist would issue a correction. Look again at the student's statement. The actual effects of the media may, in fact, be relative. That is, the media may affect people differently. But the *fact* that they affect people differently is an objective truth for everyone. As Schick and Vaughn note, "Certain states-of-affairs . . . may be relative to individuals. *But the truth about those states-of-affairs isn't relative.*"[17] The point then is to recognize that **scientific activity is concerned with uncovering the truth about things.** In the area of media effects, scientists want to uncover the truth about media impact.

Science Assumes a Skeptical Attitude

If you zip through the channels of your local cable TV system, it probably won't be long before you come to a channel that advertises psychic advice. If you want advice about your future, a psychic will talk to you over the telephone and supposedly tell you things about your life that he or she knows only by some psychic process. After you become convinced (if you do) that the psychic knows the details of your life, he or she will proceed to give you advice about how to conduct your future affairs. Of course, this advice doesn't come for free. Each year, this telephone industry does literally billions of dollars of business.[18] Obviously, many people believe the psychics and take their advice. But should they?

A person with a **scientific attitude** would approach the phenomenon of psychic advice with great skepticism. If such a psychic process did actually exist, it would violate the current understanding of natural law. That is, scientists would have no current way to explain how such a process took place. This feature alone would not cause the scientist to rule out psychic phenomena. For years, scientists could not explain how the firefly lit up, but there was no disagreement that it did. Now, of course, scientists understand the chemistry of the firefly's light so well that they have been able to harness it. Children now carry luminescent sticks on Halloween and wear luminescent necklaces that became possible after the chemistry of the firefly was discovered and explained. However, upon examining the claims of the psychic's ability to see into the future, a scientist still has many unanswered questions. Unlike the firefly phenomenon, about which there was no disagreement, scientists are quite skeptical about the claim that psychics can know the future any better than the average person. If psychics can really see future events, why can't they purchase winning lottery tickets before a drawing for a huge jackpot? Psychics will inevitably dodge such questions with a variety of explanations about how the psychic process doesn't permit them to see lottery numbers. But it is harder for the psychic to deal with the fact that certain people who have studied their craft can seem to duplicate their amazing powers—without claiming any psychic ability.

Finally, remember the acid test of science—falsifiability. If the psychic's power is real, then why not offer a clear prediction about a future event that would clearly show their power? Actually, there is a rather large monetary award ($1 million) waiting for the first psychic who can meet this challenge successfully. It is offered by the professional magician and illusionist James Randi.[19] Ultimately, scientists are skeptical about psychic claims because no scientific evidence exists for their validity. Social scientists should likewise be skeptical about claims of media impact until the evidence in favor of those claims is clear. As you will read in some of the later chapters, plenty of ideas have been offered about media effects that turn out not to be supported.

Science Can't Answer Certain Kinds of Questions

Some people think that a scientist is a person who believes that all things are knowable and that scientists know nearly all of them. Some people think of scientists as "know-it-alls" who look down on others as "know-nothings." Some scientists don't do a lot to combat this image. This is unfortunate. One of the things that a good scientist will readily admit is that there are certain kinds of questions that fall outside the purview of scientific investigation. Scientists may have invented the atom bomb, but science can never give a definitive answer about how the bomb should be used. In the area of media effects research, science can tell us how viewing violent images is likely to affect children, but it can't answer what the federal government should do about them—or whether it should do anything at all.

There are other kinds of mass communication theory and research that won't be presented in this book because they are not really concerned with documenting the effects of the media. These other theories (e.g., critical and normative theories) address questions that scientists can't answer by applying scientific methods. At the same time, these other theories can't answer questions about media impact by applying the methods of criticism or interpretation. In their book *Mass Communication Theory,* two media scholars, **Stanley Baran** and **Dennis Davis,** present a number of questions that scientific theory is ill equipped to answer, for example,[20]

> Should media do something more than merely distribute whatever content will earn them the greatest profits in the shortest time?
>
> Should media become involved in identifying and solving social problems?

Likewise, questions such as the following are most appropriately addressed within a scientific framework:

> Does viewing media violence cause people to become desensitized to violence in real life?
>
> Are the outcomes of political elections affected by the news media's projections of winners prior to the closing of the polls?

Scholars who take different perspectives in their search for knowledge may be trying to answer different questions. Sometimes the tension that exists between scholars who identify with different traditions of inquiry can be alleviated a bit by recognizing the difference in the kinds of questions that are capable of being addressed from each perspective. Scientists do themselves no favors when they give the impression that their perspective can be used to answer every kind of question. It can't. But the general power of science as a mode of inquiry can hardly be denied. Without the knowledge that has been generated about media effects from a scientific perspective, we would be left with little else but opinion and speculation. Science is not after opinion and speculation. It is after truth. As **Ralph Estling,** a writer from the United Kingdom, has recently argued in an essay,

> In science, pluralism and tolerance will imperceptibly fade into relativism where there is no such thing as external truth, objective facts, intrinsic, self-sustaining reality, where there is only "my truth" and "your truth." There is never any need to compare, contrast, question, doubt, argue, seek to learn from what the data say and what the Universe tells us. When this happens, truth—for there is such a thing—is in dire peril. And science ceases to function. (p. 55)[21]

SUMMARY

This chapter began with a discussion of the tragic events at Columbine High School. Many opinions about the causes of those events were expressed in the popular press, but it is often difficult to determine the truth from sifting through a host of opinions. Personal experience and appeal to authority are different ways of knowing—but they don't apply the systematic observation and logic that is included in a scientific approach. The goals of science are prediction, explanation, understanding, and control. Scientists achieve these goals by advancing theories and testing theoretical hypotheses that are falsifiable. There are a number of important ingredients that characterize a scientific approach. Science is concerned with uncovering truth. But it maintains a **skeptical attitude** and acknowledges that it can't answer every question. Ultimately, the scientific method seeks to make general statements about the way variables are related. Consequently, while scientists may have much to contribute to a general discussion about an event such as the one at Columbine High School, they will probably refrain from making statements about the particular causes involved in an isolated incident.

KEY TERMS AND CONCEPTS

Empiricism 2

Experience 2

Authority 3

Science 4

Systematic observation 4

Goals of science 4

prediction 4

explanation 5

understanding 6

control 6

Theory 8

Hypothesis 9	Truth 13	Skeptical attitude 16
Falsifiability 9	Scientific attitude 14	

KEY NAMES

Copernicus 3	Albert Bandura 9	Stanley Baran and
Joanne Cantor 7	Theodore Schick and	Dennis Davis 15
	Lewis Vaughn 13	Ralph Estling 16

WEB LINKS

1. For more on the controversy about violent video games, try . . . http://www.usatoday .com/life/cyber/tech/review/games/cgg105.htm

2. For more on the goals and nature of science, try . . . http://www.libfind.unl.edu/ rhames/courses/current/sciencegoals.htm

3. For a humorous point about scientists and the research on spiders, try . . . http://www .geocities.com/CollegePark/6174/science_spider.html

4. For information on the standing reward of $1 million if you think you are a psychic, try . . . http://www.randi.org/

To learn more about the topics in this chapter, enter the Key Terms and Concepts and Key Names found in this chapter as subject and keyword searches on your InfoTrac College Edition.

NOTES

1. Curry, T. (1999, April 30). *Politicians take on Hollywood* [Online]. Available: http://www.msnbc.com/news/264365 .asp#BODY

2. Rhodes, D. (1999). *Tomatoes: General introduction* [Online]. Available: http:// www.hort.purdue.edu/rhodcv/hort410/ tomat/to00001.htm

3. Schick, T., & Vaughn, L. (1995). *How to think about weird things: Critical thinking for a new age.* Mountain View, CA: Mayfield.

4. Liebert, R. M., & Sprafkin, J. (1988). *The early window: Effects of television on children and youth.* New York: Pergamon Press.

5. Graziano, A. M., & Raulin, M. L. (1989). *Research methods: A process of inquiry.* New York: Harper & Row.

6. Although I have not consulted my notes from graduate school in writing about the goals of science, I am certainly aware that my thinking on this and other topics I discuss in this chapter was crystallized in a course that I took from Professor Joseph Cappella at the University of Wisconsin–Madison in 1981.

7. Jo E., & Berkowitz, L. (1994). A priming effect analysis of media influences: An update. In J. Bryant & D. Zillmann (Eds.), *Media effects: Advances in theory and research* (pp. 43–60). Hillsdale, NJ: Erlbaum.

8. Zillmann, D. (1991). Television viewing and physiological arousal. In J. Bryant & D. Zillmann (Eds.), *Responding to the screen: Reception and reaction processes* (pp. 103–133). Hillsdale, NJ: Erlbaum.

9. Cantor, J., Harrison, K., & Nathanson, A. (1998). Ratings and advisories for television programming. In Center for Communication and Social Policy at University of California, Santa Barbara (Eds.), *National television violence study 2* (pp. 267–322). Thousand Oaks, CA: Sage.

10. Liebert, R. M., & Sprafkin, J. (1988). *The early window: Effects of television on children and youth*. New York: Pergamon Press.

11. Darwin, C. (1900). *The origin of species*. New York: Burt.

12. Bandura, A. (1994). Social cognitive theory of mass communication. In J. Bryant & D. Zillmann (Eds.), *Media effects: Advances in theory and research* (pp. 61–90). Hillsdale, NJ: Erlbaum.

13. Schick, T., & Vaughn, L. (1995). *How to think about weird things: Critical thinking for a new age*. Mountain View, CA: Mayfield.

14. Griffin, E. (2000). *A first look at communication theory*. Boston: McGraw-Hill.

15. Babbie, E. R. (1973). *Survey research methods*. Belmont, CA: Wadsworth.

16. Schick, T., & Vaughn, L. (1995). *How to think about weird things: Critical thinking for a new age*. Mountain View, CA: Mayfield.

17. Schick, T., & Vaughn, L. (1995). *How to think about weird things: Critical thinking for a new age*. Mountain View, CA: Mayfield.

18. Nisbet, M. (1998). Psychic telephone networks profit on yearning, gullibility. *Skeptical Inquirer, 22,* 5–6.

19. Special announcement [Online]. Available: http://www.randi.org

20. Baran, J., & Davis, D. K., (1995). *Mass communication theory: Foundations, ferment and future*. Belmont, CA: Wadsworth.

21. Estling, R. (1998, July/August). Is science concerned with truth? *Skeptical Inquirer*.

2

■

Scientific Methods in Media Effects Research

When I was about 14 years old, my grandmother came to visit for the summer. She loved to watch soap operas in the middle of the afternoon. My father didn't think much of soap opera content, and he didn't hesitate to voice his opinion that soap operas affect viewers in a negative way. The main gist of his complaint was that he thought they encouraged viewers to see their own lives as a constant melodrama. I was never sure that I agreed with my dad about the impact of soap operas on viewers, but his strong opinions on the subject made me wonder. **How would one ever go about discovering the effects of media content?**

Having read chapter 1, you may suspect that a good general answer to this question is to use a scientific approach. But what would this approach entail? One of the main goals of this chapter is to introduce three specific methods that social scientists use to answer questions related to media impact. Taken together, these methods comprise the main arsenal of the media effects researcher. The three methods are the **content analysis,** the **survey,** and the **experiment.**

ANALYZING MEDIA CONTENT

In general, the first step in scientific investigation is to **describe** the phenomenon of interest with precision. **Content analysis** allows a researcher to describe the nature of the content of communication in a systematic and rigorous fashion. Content analysis can be applied to almost any type of communication, but it is particularly appropriate for mass media messages because it permits us to describe precisely a vast diversity of message content that might prove to be elusive otherwise. Content analysis is a logical beginning point for the investigation of media effects because it helps us to discover what content is present that might be bringing about various effects. The controversy about the impact of media violence on children would hardly capture our attention if all of the programs and movies that were made contained no violent scenes. On the other hand, it is important to understand that **the results of a content analysis do not permit one to make inferences about the effects of that content.**

I carry a card in my wallet that was distributed by a group called TV Tune-In, located in Cleveland, Ohio. One of the "TV Awareness Facts" that appears on the card is particularly striking: "More guns are fired on TV in one evening than are fired in the course of an entire year by a metropolitan police force of 504 officers!" This fact is based on content analyses of prime-time TV. Researchers arrived at this figure after counting the number of guns fired during an average evening of prime-time offerings. It may seem like an easy jump to move from this fact to the inference that TV influences people to shoot guns. But such an inference would be unjustified. It could be the case that people become disgusted with all the guns fired on TV and consequently use them less frequently than they would otherwise. The facts themselves that come from a content analysis don't ever permit us to answer the question about the *effects* of the content. In order to answer that question, other research methods need to be used. Before we examine some of those other methods, let's take a closer look at the method of content analysis and examine the role that it can play in mass-communication research.

What Is Content Analysis?

One researcher, **Bernard Berelson,** defined content analysis in the following way: "Content analysis is a research technique for the *objective, systematic,* and *quantitative* description of the *manifest* content of communication."[1] Essentially, content analysis is a method that allows the researcher to describe messages in quantitative terms even though those messages are essentially verbal or non-quantitative in nature.

Content analysis is **objective** in the sense that the method permits multiple researchers to examine the same content and come to identical conclusions. This is possible because the method is **systematic.** That is, it specifies an unambiguous set of rules or procedures for coding the message content. Theoretically, any **coder** (a person who examines the content and classifies it into categories) who understands the rules or procedures will arrive at the same coding of the message content as any other coder. The data that result from content analysis are **quantitative.** That is, certain aspects of the content are coded and tallied in some quantitative way. This aspect of content analysis is important because it permits the researcher to conduct various statistical tests on the results of the coding.

Finally, content analysis is concerned with the coding of **manifest content** rather than **latent content.** Manifest content refers to the material that actually appears, uninterpreted, in the message. Latent content is content that might become apparent after a coder has interpreted or "read between the lines" of the message prior to coding. For example, a coder might classify the following statement in a TV sitcom as a compliment: "Gee, Jerry, that's a real attractive outfit you're wearing." The actual statement is the manifest content. The surface meaning of the statement suggests that it should be coded as a compliment. However, it might be apparent from other cues in the program that the statement was uttered with great sarcasm and was not actually intended as a compliment. If the coder classified the statement as an insult instead of as a compliment, that would be an example of coding the latent content. As you can probably begin to appreciate, the issue of manifest versus latent content is somewhat controversial among content analysts. Some researchers are content to code only the manifest content and discuss alternative interpretations after the data have been analyzed. Other researchers might be interested in coding the latent content directly, so long as agreement among different coders can be established.

While the above introductory overview may provide a general conceptual description of the method of content analysis, the chances are good that your understanding of this method is still a little vague. An example is in order.

Suppose you believe that TV commercials potentially influence the culture by setting certain expectations, norms, or standards for a wide variety of behaviors. In particular, suppose you have noticed that the voice-overs in TV commercials (the voice that narrates the commercial message) tend to be male rather then female. Perhaps you also think that, based on the commercials you have seen, very few elderly people ever appear. You want to study TV commercials in some systematic fashion to determine if your casual observations have any merit, but you aren't sure how to proceed. Content analysis is the method that can answer your questions.

An Example: The Content of TV Commercials

Actually, if you had really wondered about these particular questions, you wouldn't be alone. In 1985, two researchers wondered about these same questions with respect to TV commercials on Canadian TV. In order to get some answers, **Timothy Moore** and **Leslie Cadeau** decided to design a content analysis.[2] A closer look at their study will reveal the essential steps that one goes through in designing this sort of research.

The Sample Every content analysis has to be done on a particular sample of messages. In this case Moore and Cadeau selected the commercials that appeared on three networks over an 8-week period. Their final sample contained 1,733 TV commercials.

Sometimes, the population that a researcher wants to draw from is so large that a smaller **random sample** of the messages is chosen. A random sample is one that permits every member of the population to have an equal chance of being selected in the sample. It is a crucial technique if the researcher wants to be able to generalize the results of the sample back to the larger population. In many content analysis problems, the population of interest is so large that it simply wouldn't be worth the time and expense to use each member. In fact, Moore and Cadeau could probably have randomly sampled far fewer ads from their population of over 1,700 and still have arrived at the same general conclusions about the content of advertising over the 8-week period.

Units of Analysis After the sample is selected, the researchers must decide what units of the content will be coded. For example, in a newspaper article, the researcher might code each paragraph for certain attributes. Thus, the paragraph would be the **unit of analysis.** If each sentence were coded, then the sentence would be the unit of analysis. Sometimes TV shows are broken into scenes and each scene is coded. In this case, the scene is the unit of analysis. In Moore and Cadeau's study of Canadian TV commercials, each commercial was the unit of analysis, that is, each commercial was coded for various attributes.

Categories In every content analysis, the content of the message is coded according to a **category scheme.** Moore and Cadeau wanted their coders to code the TV commercials in several ways. For example, the coders decided whether the voice-over in the commercial was male or female. They also decided what type of product was being advertised and whether or not elderly and minority characters appeared in the ads.

Coding Agreement After the data have been coded by more than one coder, some statistical index of agreement among the coders is computed. Sometimes this statistic is simply the number of times the coders agree, divided by the number of coding decisions they made. For example, if two coders watched 10 commercials and decided for each one whether the narrator was a male or female, they might agree 9 times out of 10. The percentage agreement in this case is 90% or .90. While this may seem like pretty good agreement, consider the fact that there were only two possible categories in this case: male or female. The possibility of agreeing just by chance was 50%. Because of the possibility of chance agreements, many researchers compute coding agreement (often referred to as **coding reliability**) with a special formula that makes an adjustment for the chance hits. A rule of thumb in content analysis is that coding reliability must be at least .70 (lower levels are accepted if a formula that adjusts for chance agreements is employed). Moore and Cadeau achieved this level in their study of TV commercials for each of the categories being coded (sex of voice-over, appearance of elderly people, and so on).

Statistical Analysis Once the researchers establish coding reliability, the data from the study can be described in statistical terms. In Moore and Cadeau's study, it turned out that 88% of the voice-overs in commercials were male. Only 35% of the central characters in the TV ads were female, and fewer than 2% of all the commercials featured elderly people as central characters. As it turns out, these findings are fairly typical of content analyses that have examined TV advertising. In fact, when Moore and Cadeau compared their findings with ones from 10 years earlier, they found little change.

Interpretation of Findings After the results are summarized, the authors of a content analysis usually discuss the implications of the study. Moore and Cadeau discussed the possibility that the systematic under-representation of females and the elderly in TV commercials might cause viewers to adopt negative attitudes toward these groups. But they stopped short of making any claim for the effects of these under-representations. As good content analysts, they understood that their study did not establish any *effects* of media content. Instead, their study helped us to understand the nature of the content of the media.

Although the results of a content analysis cannot be used to document the effects of the media, these types of studies often have implications for claims about media effects. Suppose that a researcher wanted to investigate the possibility that viewing commercials caused viewers to attribute greater authority and expertise to females due to the females' tendency to serve as voice-overs in the ads. The presumed media effect in this case would be based on an assumption about the content of commercials that Moore and Cadeau's study reveals to be false. Females do not tend to serve as voice-overs. This example illustrates an important relationship between content analyses of media content and research on media effects. Ideas about media effects are usually based on some assumptions about the presence or absence of certain kinds of media content. Content analyses are often an excellent way to begin research on media effects because they can confirm or disconfirm these assumptions.

THE SAMPLE SURVEY

Content analysis in mass-communication research focuses on message content. But there are a host of interesting research questions that can't be answered with this method. Many of the most important questions require researchers to investigate *people* instead of message content. One of the best ways of investigating people is to ask them questions directly. The method that is designed particularly for this purpose is the survey. It is often referred to as the **sample survey** because in most cases, it is based on a random sample of some larger population of interest.

The survey method is probably the one that is most familiar to the average citizen. If you haven't actually participated in a survey as a respondent in the last month, you have almost certainly heard the results of at least one survey reported by the mass media. The quest by politicians and government officials for an accurate gauge of public opinion has served to refine the methods of survey research over the years. Today, sample surveys play a vital part in the governmental process. The U.S. Census Bureau relies heavily on sample surveys to reveal information about the changing demographics in the population.

In mass-communication research, surveys are invaluable in helping us to understand people's media habits. Through survey research, scholars now have a good sense of how much TV the average person watches, what types of content are most popular, and what people report about their own reactions to that content. The survey, as it turns out, is an excellent method for getting descriptive insight into a given phenomenon.

Beyond simple descriptive data, the survey is an excellent way of exploring relationships between different variables. Suppose, for example, a researcher thought that children who tend to watch lots of television during a typical week also tend to be more obese. This relationship could be uncovered in a sample survey. Phone numbers in a given area might be selected randomly, and parents who answered the phone might be asked a number of questions about their child's weekly TV viewing. After getting estimates of the child's daily viewing, estimates of each child's weight might also be solicited. After the researcher collected this data, a statistical analysis could be applied to the data to see if the children who watch more TV during the week also tend to be the children who weigh more. Studies similar to the one described have actually been conducted. Two researchers, **Larry Tucker** and **Marilyn Bagwell,** surveyed nearly 5,000 adult females and found that obesity was twice as likely among those who viewed 4 or more hours of TV per day as compared to those who viewed less than 1 hour of TV per day.[3] Statistical analyses that reveal this type of finding are an important tool of the mass-communication researcher. This chapter will introduce you to a few of the basic concepts that are important to grasp. First, let's take a closer look at an example of an actual survey that was conducted to study media effects.

An Example: The Effects of
Talk Show Viewing on Adolescents

At some point in your TV viewing experience, the chances are good that you have watched at least a brief clip from *The Jerry Springer Show.* This program regularly features physical attacks by one guest on another. In some markets, the show airs during the afternoon when young adolescents have arrived home from school and may be interested in watching TV before beginning their homework. Programs like Jerry Springer's have prompted considerable controversy among parents, educators, and political leaders. Senator Joseph Lieberman complained that some of the TV talk shows "make the abnormal normal."[4] Politicians in the city of Chicago, where the program is taped, have considered various measures against the show. One possibility includes having police officers arrest anyone who engages in physical assault in the studio. Assault, after all, is against the law. Jerry Springer's show is only one of many talk shows that air daily on TV. There are a total of approximately 20 shows with an estimated 10 million viewers.[5] Two researchers, **Stacy Davis** and **Marie-Louise Mares,** decided to move beyond the popular rhetoric about the impact of talk shows. They decided to conduct a survey of adolescents to explore the possibility that watching TV talk shows has negative effects.[6]

The Sample Davis and Mares chose 292 students from two public high schools and one private high school in North Carolina. Since their sample was not randomly selected, the reader must be careful about extending the results to a larger population of high school students. It is always possible that the particular group of students surveyed was different in some way from the larger population of high schoolers. To their credit, the researchers recognized this limitation and cautioned the reader about extrapolating the results to all adolescents.

The Questionnaire The questionnaire itself took about 30 minutes to complete and included a number of questions about attitudes toward social issues that are featured on TV talk shows (such as teen runaways, teen pregnancy, and guns in schools). The second part of the questionnaire included questions about the talk shows that the students watched. These questions were placed later in the survey so that the students were not thinking about talk shows when they answered the questions about their attitudes.

Descriptive Findings One of the chief advantages of a sample survey is that the researcher can often generate a brief statistical summary that provides a descriptive glimpse of the phenomenon under investigation. This descriptive glimpse can often reveal things that no amount of speculation could ever produce. For example, in this case the results revealed that during the school year 46% of the students reported watching a talk show either sometimes or every day. This percentage increased to 68% during the summer. *Ricki Lake* (41% watching sometimes or every day) was the most frequently watched program, followed by *Oprah Winfrey* (36%) and *Montel Williams* (31%).

Statistical Relationships When Davis and Mares examined the relationships between social attitudes expressed by the adolescents and their reported viewing of TV talk shows, they made a number of interesting findings. First, as they expected, there was a tendency for heavy viewers of the talk shows to overestimate the real-world frequency of phenomena like teen sex, teen pregnancy, and teens running away from home. While most of the adolescents who completed a survey tended to overestimate the frequency of these happenings, the respondents who were heavy talk show viewers overestimated them to a greater extent than did the adolescents who were light viewers.

A second question that Davis and Mares wanted to answer concerned the relationship between talk show viewing and perceptions of the importance of social problems. Do heavy viewers tend to trivialize these problems? The data on this point seem to suggest that trivializing does not take place. In fact, the opposite tendency was uncovered. Especially among older adolescents, heavy talk show viewers were *more* likely to perceive the various problems depicted as significant.

Interpretation of the Findings Davis and Mares stated their conclusions succinctly: "Overall, we conclude that the sweeping condemnation of talk show viewing is rather extreme. Although talk shows may offend some people, these data do not suggest that the youth of the U.S. is corrupted by watching them." Of course, being the careful researchers that they are, Davis and Mares reminded the reader that no direct tests of adolescent *behaviors* were measured in this survey. As they stated, "For example, we do not know whether talk show viewers were more likely to have had sex or become pregnant than non-viewers." But their data did show that the heavy viewers were just as intolerant as the light viewers of the sorts of behaviors that were regularly featured on the shows. "They were equally as likely as light viewers to believe that the victims in the vignettes had been harmed and to think that the antisocial behavior described was wrong."

Types of Surveys The survey conducted by Davis and Mares is one of the most common types of surveys reported in social science research. It was a survey of a single sample of some population. This kind of survey is commonly referred to as a **cross-sectional** survey. The distinguishing characteristic of a cross-sectional survey is that it occurs at a single point in time and involves a single sample. Often, researchers are not satisfied with a single sample. The research questions that they have cannot be answered unless a separate questionnaire is administered at more than one point in time. When a researcher designs a survey project that includes more than one sample taken at different points in time, the survey design is referred to as **longitudinal.** There are three kinds of longitudinal survey designs.

The first type of longitudinal design is a **trend study.** Suppose that 5 years after Davis and Mares finished their survey on talk show viewing among high school students, they wondered whether there had been some change in the viewing habits among the students at the three respective high schools used in their study. In order to answer this question, they might return to the same high schools years later and readminister their questionnaire to another sample of students. By comparing the results of this second questionnaire with the initial results, they would be able to detect changes in the viewing trends among high school students. Notice that in a trend study, the individuals who are surveyed the first time are not the same individuals who are surveyed the second time. The only similarities between the two groups would be their enrollment in the same high school, and their same station in life at the time of the survey.

A second type of longitudinal survey is a **cohort** study. Again, suppose that Davis and Mares were interested in any change in the viewing habits among the students in the first study. Instead of surveying different students from the same high schools, the researchers might choose another sample of individuals who were the same age as the individuals in the first sample. For example, they might choose to visit a college campus 4 years after the first survey and administer the questionnaire to college students. These college students would be members of the same age cohort as the high school students in the first survey. But they wouldn't be the same students. Perhaps you have seen the news reports on how the attitudes of "baby boomers" have changed over the last decade. These changes are typically detected with a cohort design. If people between the ages of 40 and 50 were surveyed in 1990, then people between the ages of 50 and 60 would be surveyed in 2000. The cohort survey allows the researcher to assess changes in a general cohort group—but not in the exact same individuals.

The final type of longitudinal survey design is a **panel study.** If the researchers actually wanted to measure the changes in viewing habits in the exact same individuals, then a panel design would be used. Long-term panel designs are relatively rare because of the time and effort it takes to keep track of the same individuals. In the chapter about media violence, you will learn about a long-term panel study that followed young children into their adult years. While such studies are rare in mass-communication research, the results are usually very important in revealing trends that no other method is capable of detecting. Short-term panel designs are used more frequently. Researchers often design short-term panels during political campaigns to track attitudinal changes that might take place in response to media messages and other political events.

THE SEARCH FOR CAUSAL RELATIONSHIPS

Before considering the third general research method used by researchers in mass communication, it is important to understand that one of the principal goals of doing research on media effects is to explore the possibility that media messages bring about some change in people's thoughts, attitudes, emotions, behaviors, and so on. That is, the researcher is interested in documenting **causal relationships** between media and people. Documenting causal relationships is not nearly as easy as one might suspect. There are three general criteria that need to be met before a researcher can make the claim that one thing (the media message) is causing another (a change in attitude or behavior, for example).

Criteria for Causal Relationships

The first thing a researcher needs to establish before making a claim that one thing causes another is that the two things in question are **empirically related to each other.** Recall the study mentioned above that investigated the relationship between TV viewing and obesity. In order to document that watching TV *caused* people to become more obese, Tucker and Bagwell first needed to establish that these two variables (TV viewing time and level of obesity) were actually related to each other. As it turned out in their study, the two variables were empirically related. That is, there was a tendency for the people who spent more time watching TV to also be the people with higher body weights. Researchers need a specific tool to detect an empirical relationship like this one. They can't simply eyeball the data and make a casual declaration that two variables either seem to be related or unrelated. The methods of science are more precise than that. The most common statistical tool used to determine relationships between two variables is the technique of **correlation.**

Correlation Coefficients When researchers want to know whether two variables are related to each other, they often apply a statistical formula to the

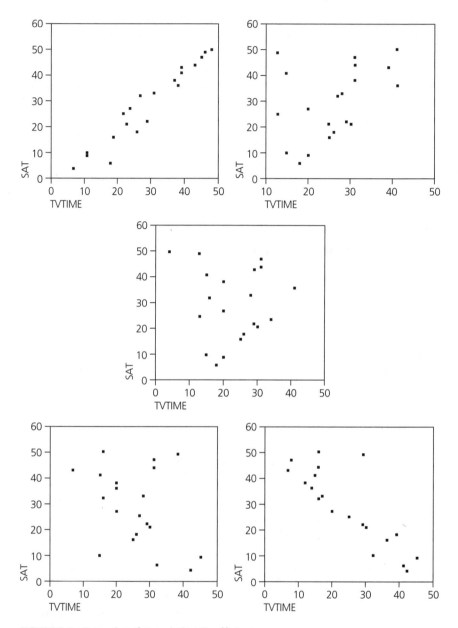

FIGURE 2-1 Examples of Correlation Coefficients

Above, there are five different scatterplots that illustrate hypothetical
relationships between the number of hours that 20 high school students
spent watching TV during the week before their Scholastic Achievement Test (SAT). Moving from left to right, the two plots on the top
show correlation coefficients of .97 and .48 respectively. As TV time increases, SAT scores tend to increase. The graph in the middle shows a
correlation coefficient of .03 or nearly zero. The variables are unrelated.
The bottom two graphs show correlation coefficients of −.38 and −.85
respectively. As TV time increases, SAT scores tend to decrease.

data and compute a **correlation coefficient.** The particular formula for the correlation coefficient is commonly available in introductory statistics texts, and you don't need to be concerned with formulas here. But because of their importance in documenting empirical relationships between variables, it is helpful to know how to interpret correlation coefficients. Correlation coefficients are computed between two variables. The data in the obesity study conform nicely to the sort of situation where correlation can be useful. The researchers had a measure of two different variables for each person in the sample. If increases in one of the variables tended to go along with increases in the other variable, then the two variables would have a **positive correlation.** This was actually the case in the obesity study. People who had higher TV viewing times tended to weigh more. Sometimes, increases in one of the variables tend to go along with *decreases* in the other variable. When this situation arises, the two variables have a **negative correlation.** Some studies have documented a negative correlation between income level and TV viewing. People who make more money tend to watch less TV. Of course, it is not always the case that the two variables being correlated are related to each other in a positive or negative way. The two variables might be unrelated. In order to get a picture of relationships between variables, check out Figure 2-1. This figure displays graphs of five different correlation coefficients.

Interpreting Correlation Coefficients When researchers compute correlation coefficients between two variables, the result is a specific number that provides an index of how strongly the variables are related. The formula for the correlation coefficient is designed so that variables that are perfectly related have an index of $+1.0$ (if the relationship is positive) or -1.0 (if the relationship is negative). No correlation coefficient can exceed $+1.0$ or -1.0. The smallest correlation that could exist between two variables is no relationship at all—indicated by a coefficient of zero (0.0). Most relationships between two variables fall somewhere between 0.0 and 1.0. The statistical symbol for the coefficient is r. Typically then, when correlation coefficients are reported, you might read something like $r = .34$ (if the relationship between the variables is positive) or $r = -.21$ (if the relationship between the variables is negative).

Once a correlation coefficient has been computed (usually by a computer), its meaning must be interpreted. Suppose the correlation between two variables is indicated by $r = .45$. What do we know? While we know that the two variables have some association, we still don't know how likely it is that this result occurred by chance alone. If the correlation between two variables is very likely to occur by chance, then we wouldn't want to attach too much importance to the particular coefficient that was computed. Fortunately, statisticians have determined how likely it is that correlation coefficients of given magnitudes occur by chance, given samples of various sizes. These probabilities appear in statistical tables and are built right into the computer programs that compute correlation coefficients. Scientists have agreed by consensus to adopt a particular standard for determining a chance occurrence. If a statistical result could happen by chance more than 5 times in 100, it is generally considered to be a chance finding. If, on the other hand, a statistical result could happen by chance 5 times in 100 or less, the result is considered unlikely to be due to chance. A statistical result that is unlikely to be due to chance is referred to as a **statistically significant** result. When correlation coefficients are reported in the scientific literature, they usually look something like this: $r = .32, p < .04$. The first part of this expression reports the magnitude of the correlation coefficient. The second part of the expression reports how likely it is that a correlation this large would occur by chance alone. In this case, it would be expected by chance less than 4 times in 100 and would be considered statistically significant.

Once a researcher determines that a correlation is statistically significant (that is, unlikely to be due to chance), the first criterion for documenting a causal relationship has been met (see Study Box 2-1 for more detail on interpreting correlation coefficients). The researchers who documented that there was a significant positive correlation between TV viewing and obesity met this first criterion. But recall that there are three criteria for establishing causal relationships. Unless all three are met, the researcher is on faulty ground in declaring a causal relationship between the two variables. The fact that TV viewing and obesity are positively correlated is only the first step.

The second criterion that must be met in order to establish a causal relationship is the **time-order** of the two variables. One thing can't cause another thing unless it precedes it in time. A bullet leaving the chamber of a gun cannot be the cause of the trigger-pull that fired it. In order to clearly establish causality, researchers must document the fact that **the variable doing the causing precedes the variable that is caused.**

This second criterion is often more challenging than it appears initially. Think about the survey that documented an empirical relationship between TV viewing and obesity. We learned that people who watch a lot of TV tend to have higher body weights. But do we know from the survey data that TV viewing *preceded* body weight in the sequence of time? The answer to this question is quite clearly no. Since all the data in this survey were collected at the same point in time in a cross-sectional survey design, the researchers have no way of sorting out which variable came first. Could body weight cause TV viewing instead of the reverse? If you think about it, that possibility is perfectly plausible. Perhaps, for whatever reasons, some people weigh more than others. Perhaps these heavier people prefer to lead a more passive lifestyle because exercise is an extra effort that strains the body. In their passivity, they might naturally turn to TV as a form of entertainment more frequently than physical exercise. In this case, a cross-sectional survey is simply an inadequate tool for establishing the time-order between the two variables.

One of the advantages of longitudinal surveys is that they can establish the time-order between variables. In the chapter on media violence, you will read about a panel study that found that early viewing of TV violence was significantly correlated with aggressive behavior much later in life. Longitudinal surveys of this type are capable of establishing empirical relationships between two variables as well as establishing the time-order between the variables. For the sake of our example, let's suppose that the researchers studying TV viewing and

---

STUDY BOX 2-1 **Interpreting Magnitudes of Correlation Coefficients**

Correlation coefficients can range in value from -1.0 to $+1.0$. Coefficients are treated as if they were zero (indicating no relationship between the variables), unless the statistical test for significance reveals that the magnitude of the correlation is not likely due to chance. It is important to keep in mind that even in the case of no correlation, the variables still could be related in a **nonlinear** fashion. That is, correlation coefficients test only for linear relationships—not nonlinear ones. Imagine a situation where people who watch no TV at all are very high on knowledge of current events, perhaps from reading a lot. In the same scenario, people who watch heavy amounts of TV are also well informed, because they watch many news programs. A third group, with the lowest knowledge of current events, consists of moderate users of TV. While this example is completely hypothetical, it does illustrate a nonlinear relationship between TV viewing and knowledge of current events. In such a case, the correlation coefficient would be a poor test of a relationship between the two variables. Fortunately, researchers are able to apply special statistics to cases where variables are related in nonlinear ways.

When a statistical test does indicate that a correlation is not likely to be the result of chance ($p < .05$), then the magnitude of the relationship is important to examine. One statistician, J. P. Guilford,* suggested that correlation coefficients between 0 and .20 were very slight and should be viewed as indicating nearly no relationship at all. Coefficients between .20 and .40 should be considered small but definite relationships. Moderate relationships are indicated by coefficients between .40 and .70. Coefficients above .70 (rare in the social sciences) are considered to be substantial and large.

Another way of judging the size of the relationship between two variables is to simply square (r^2) the value of the correlation coefficient. This value, the **coefficient of determination,** provides a statistical indication of how much information or variance in the dependent variable is explained or accounted for by knowing the values of the independent variable. For example, if the correlation between TV viewing and obesity was $r = .30$, $p < .05$, you would know that the relationship was not likely due to chance. In addition you would know that TV viewing was able to account for 9% ($.30^2 = .09$) of the variance in the measure of obesity. In this example, 91% of the variance in obesity would be unexplained by TV viewing. This is a valuable tool to apply because it tells us something about the relative **statistical importance** of the relationship between the two variables.

---

*Guilford, J. P. (1956). *Fundamental statistics in psychology and education* (3rd ed.). New York: McGraw Hill.

---

obesity had conducted a longitudinal survey and established that reports of TV viewing in the first survey were significantly correlated to weight gains reported in the second survey. In such a case, both of the first two criteria for establishing causal relationships would have been met. But this is still not enough evidence to establish the causal claim. There is a final criterion that also needs to be met.

After empirical relationships and time-order have been established, a researcher must also establish that the observed relationship is not due to some unmeasured variable causally related to both of the others. All possible **third-variable explanations must be eliminated.** In the study on TV viewing and obesity, one plausible third-variable explanation for the relationship might be socioeconomic status. People with low incomes may only be able to afford housing in poor, urban areas. Such areas may not provide many opportunities for recreation and physical exercise. People living in these neighborhoods may perceive that they are in danger when they go outside, so they prefer to stay indoors for their recreation—thus burning fewer calories and gaining more weight. TV viewing is the predominant entertainment available indoors and so these folks also watch more TV. In this scenario, low income would be causing both TV viewing and obesity. If a researcher examined TV viewing and obesity without including a measure of income, the empirical relationship might emerge and lead the researcher to think that watching TV causes obesity—but this would be a mistaken conclusion. The true cause of the relationship in this case (low income) would remain hidden.

From the above discussion, it might seem impossible to design a study that simultaneously meets all three criteria for establishing a causal relationship. If an unmeasured variable might be responsible for the relationship between two measured variables, then clearly a sample survey (whether cross-sectional or longitudinal) can never provide the definitive evidence needed for a causal relationship. Since no survey can measure every possible variable, there is always a chance that a variable that went unmeasured is precisely the one that explains why two measured variables are related to each other. A good survey design can anticipate some of the obvious variables that might play the role of explanatory third variable. Once these variables are measured, they can be tested to see if they might be responsible for an observed relationship between two other variables of interest (this was done in Tucker and Bagwell's study on TV and obesity). But no matter how clever the survey design, no survey can measure everything. Consequently, the survey is, in principle, not capable of satisfying all three of the criteria needed to say that one thing causes another.

Where does this leave us? If the sample survey is only capable of establishing two of the three criteria for causal relationships (empirical relationships and time-order), is there an alternative method that might allow us to meet all three criteria simultaneously? The answer to this question leads to the last of the three fundamental methods used to study media effects: the experiment.

THE EXPERIMENTAL METHOD

Like the survey method, **experiments** in mass communication gather data directly from people. But unlike the survey, the experiment seeks to gather these data under controlled conditions. If an experiment is carefully executed, a researcher is often able to make a case that all three of the criteria for documenting causal relationships have been met. What are the key ingredients that make this possible?

Manipulation of a Key Variable

Once an experimenter has identified a variable (usually called the **independent variable**) that is thought to be a potential cause of another variable (usually called the **dependent variable**), the strategy is to manipulate the independent variable in order to create more than one experimental condition. The purpose of this manipulation is to be able to observe the impact of various levels of the independent variable on some dependent variable. My daughter has always been concerned about drinking too much diet soda. Her concern stems from reports she has heard from her friends that too much of the sugar substitute in diet soda might cause cancer. We did a little investigating and discovered that researchers have completed many experiments on this topic. In this case, the sugar substitute is the potential causal variable. Consequently, researchers manipulated this variable and created a number of experimental conditions. In one condition of a typical experiment, laboratory animals might be injected with very large doses of the substance over a period of weeks. In a second condition, moderate doses might be administered. A third group of animals might get very light doses. The animals in each of these conditions can then be compared for their incidence of cancer.

Random Assignment to Experimental Conditions

One crucial feature in experiments is **random assignment** of people (or animals) to experimental conditions. In experiments on the impact of sugar substitutes, laboratory animals are randomly assigned to one of the doses. Why is random assignment so important? The answer to this question should be clear upon thinking about the population of the laboratory animals. Suppose that one of the cages where a group of the animals is housed resides in a corner of the building that contains cancer-causing asbestos. If all the animals in that cage were placed in the same experimental condition, the researchers might erroneously conclude that the experimental treatment was responsible for more cancer in this condition. Or suppose that some of the animals are already developing the early stages of cancer. If those animals are spread evenly across the experimental groups, then researchers can still detect the impact of the sugar substitute. Random assignment to experimental conditions theoretically makes the experimental groups equivalent just prior to their exposure to the experimental manipulation. Consequently, any difference that emerges after the manipulation can be confidently attributed to the manipulation itself.

Identical Treatment Except for the Manipulation

Random assignment to experimental conditions makes the experimental groups equivalent at the beginning of the experiment. Random assignment must be followed by identical treatment in all ways except for the **manipulation of the variable.** In the sugar substitute experiment, the animals in all three conditions should have identical diets except for the difference in the dose of sugar substitute. They should be housed in identical cages with equal amounts of light and dark, equal numbers of other animals in their cages, and so on. In short, *anything* that introduces a difference in the experimental conditions except the manipulated variable must be avoided. Otherwise, once the experiment is over, the researchers can't be confident that differences in the manipulated variable among the experimental groups caused the dependent variable of interest (in this case, incidence of cancer).

Recall the discussion on the three criteria for establishing causal relationships. Survey designs are capable of meeting two of the three: revealing the presence of a relationship and establishing the time-order of the variables. But as we saw, the survey design could not eliminate all third variables that might present themselves as possible alternative causes to consider in a given relationship. The experimental method, however, is able to meet all three criteria at once. Consider the experiment on sugar substitutes. If one of the conditions shows a higher incidence of cancer, then a relationship between consumption of the substitute and cancer has been found. That's the first criterion. If the experimental groups were equivalent at the beginning of the experiment, then time-order has also been established. The increased incidence in cancer in one of the groups occurred *after* consumption was manipulated. That's the second criterion. Finally, if the experimental groups were equivalent at the beginning of the experiment and they were treated equally throughout the experiment except for the manipulation, then there are no third variables that can offer a rival account for how differences in cancer emerged in one of the groups. The experiment theoretically controls all possible third variables that might compete with the manipulation to explain the outcome of the experiment. It is this feature of the experiment that makes it such a valuable tool for investigating questions of media effects.

Control Groups

In order to properly assess the impact of a manipulated variable in an experiment, some sort of **control group** is typically used. Suppose that, in the experiment on sugar substitutes, animals in the large-dose group were more likely to develop cancer than animals in the small-dose group. Such a finding might be interpreted to mean that the sugar substitute is dangerous and consumption should be avoided. However, notice that the experiment described earlier did not contain a control group that received no sugar substitutes. The inclusion of a control group in the experiment might completely change the interpretation of the results. What if, in an experiment that included a no-substitute control group, animals in the control group had the *highest* incidence of cancer? In this case, the interpretation of the results is completely changed. With the inclusion of the control group, it now appears that consumption of any level of the sugar substitute *reduces* the incidence of cancer. Heavy consumption reduces it less than light consumption, but both doses reduce it. These results are completely hypothetical, but they help to illustrate how the inclusion of a control group in an experimental design can often aid the researcher in interpreting the results of an experiment clearly. In order to get a more concrete sense of how the experimental method is applied in mass-communication research, let's look briefly at a real example of a published experiment.

An Example: The Effects of
Realistic Versus Reenacted Violence

Over 20 years ago, scholars who studied the effects of media violence recognized that it might be important to distinguish between realistic violence and reenacted violence. Two researchers, **Leonard Berkowitz** and **Joseph Alioto,** designed more than one experiment to see if there was a difference between these two types of content and the tendency for viewers to behave aggressively after watching a film.[7] A closer look at one of these experiments should help you to see how this method works to document media effects.

Participants For this study, the authors recruited 51 college males to participate in the study. Typically, the recruits participate in order to satisfy a course requirement or to earn extra course credit. They were randomly assigned to one of the two experimental conditions.

Independent Variable All participants in the study viewed an aggressive film depicting scenes of combat in a war setting. The researchers manipulated the realism of the film by telling half of the participants that the combat was real; the remaining half were told that it was only a reenactment.

Dependent Variable Prior to viewing the movie, each participant was angered or annoyed by one of the experimenters. This was done in order to provide some motivation for later aggressive behavior, which generally does not occur without provocation. The researchers had to provide such provocation in order to observe the behavior under study. The dependent variable measured in this study was the severity of electric shocks that participants delivered after the movie to the person who had annoyed them earlier. Although the participants believed the shocks were real, no actual electrical shocks were delivered to anyone. The researchers wanted to see if the level of realism in the movie affected the level of shocks that the participants delivered after the movie was over.

Experimental Results As the researchers suspected might be the case, the men who believed that the combat movie was "real" were more likely to deliver severe shocks than the men who thought they were watching a reenactment. The difference in the two groups was statistically significant (that is, the probability that the difference occurred by chance was less than 5 times in 100).

Interpretation of Results Research results must always be interpreted. In this case, the authors of the study concluded that the men who watched the film in the "reenactment" condition probably disassociated themselves from the aggression in the film in comparison to the men who watched "real" combat. The authors believed that this disassociation carried over to response tendencies immediately after the movie and tended to curtail the impulse to behave aggressively. In the chapter on media violence, you will learn more about the specific processes that researchers believe occur after watching media violence.

CONTROVERSY ABOUT
RESEARCH METHODS

This chapter has introduced you to the research methods used in media effects studies. Perhaps, as you read about each of the methods, you wondered about the extent to which we should rely upon them for our understanding about the effects of the media. For example, maybe it occurred to you that when people are asked questions on a survey, they might not respond with truthful answers. Or maybe you wondered about whether a carefully controlled laboratory experiment can really tell us very much about behavior that happens in more natural environments—are laboratory experiments too artificial? Questions like these are important ones that researchers have debated for years. A full consideration of each potential problem of a particular research method is beyond the scope of this text. If you are interested in these problems, your instructor should be able to point you to additional reading on research methods or even recommend a good course on the topic.

In spite of the difficulties with individual research methods, media effects researchers gain confidence in the results of research studies by examining the same research problem in a number of different ways. If a particular finding seems to show up again and again in studies of different types, scientists would refer to this as replicating a research result with convergent evidence. **Replication** refers to the fact that the same result can be observed over and over again. **Convergence** refers to the fact that the use of different methods still leads to the same general conclusion. In the end, researchers are reluctant to declare that they know anything about media effects until they have results from more than one or two studies. While no single research method is perfect or beyond criticism, the careful application of the three methods discussed in this chapter provides a powerful arsenal of tools for learning about the ways that media messages affect people.

SUMMARY

In this chapter, you have been introduced to three major research methods used by media effects scholars: content analysis, the sample survey, and the experiment. Each method yields valuable information that may be pertinent to documenting a media effect. Content analysis reveals what content the media contain. Surveys can reveal valuable descriptive information as well as important relationships between variables. They are capable of meeting two of the three criteria for causal relationships: documenting the presence of a relationship and documenting time-order.

Relationships between variables are often documented with the technique of correlation. Correlation coefficients can range in value between −1.0 and +1.0. Coefficients that are unlikely to occur by chance any more than 5 times in 100 are declared to be statistically significant. While correlation coefficients can be computed from survey data, and time-order between two variables can often be established, surveys always measure a finite set of variables. Consequently, they are incapable of eliminating all possible third variables that might be responsible for a relationship. The third research method, the experiment, has the advantage of being able to meet all three of the criteria for causal relationships. Taken together, these three research methods constitute an invaluable set of tools for exploring the effects of the mass media.

KEY TERMS AND CONCEPTS

Content analysis 19

  coder 20

  manifest content 20

  latent content 20

  units of analysis 22

  categories 22

  coding reliability 22

Random sample 21

Sample survey 23

  cross-sectional 26

  longitudinal 26

    trend study 26

cohort study 26

  panel study 27

Causal relationships 27

Correlation coefficient 29

  positive correlation 29

  negative correlation 29

Statistical significance 30

Time-order 30

Third-variable explanation 32

Experiment 32

  independent variable 33

  dependent variable 33

  random assignment to conditions 33

  manipulation of a variable 33

  control group 34

Replication 36

Convergence 36

KEY NAMES

Bernard Berelson 20

Timothy Moore and Leslie Cadeau 21

Larry Tucker and Marilyn Bagwell 24

Stacy Davis and Marie-Louise Mares 24

Leonard Berkowitz and Joseph Alioto 35

WEB LINKS

1. For a brief note on content analysis, try . . . http://www.uiowa.edu/~commstud/adclass/research/content_analysis.html

2. For a pictorial representation of the criteria for causality, try . . . http://instruct.uwo.ca/fim-lis/504/504cau.htm

3. For an interesting discussion of an unusual social science experiment that sought to determine if arresting people deterred crime, try . . . http://www.rit.edu/~jmkgcj/October%2014%201998.html

To learn more about the topics in this chapter, enter the Key Terms and Concepts and Key Names found in this chapter as subject and keyword searches on your InfoTrac College Edition.

NOTES

1. Berelson, B. (1952). *Content analysis in communication.* Glencoe, IL: Free Press.

2. Moore, T. E., & Cadeau, L. (1989). The representation of women, the elderly and minorities in Canadian television commercials. *Canadian Journal of Behavioural Science, 17,* 215–225.

3. Tucker, L. A., & Bagwell, M. (1991). Television viewing and obesity in adult females. *American Journal of Public Health, 81,* 908–911.

4. Alter, J. (1995, November 6). Next: "The revolt of the revolted." *Newsweek,* 46–47.

5. Alter, J. (1995, November 6). Next: "The revolt of the revolted." *Newsweek,* 46–47.

6. Davis, S., & Mares, M. L. (1998). Effects of talk show viewing on adolescents. *Journal of Communication, 48,* 69–86.

7. Berkowitz, L., & Alioto, J. T. The meaning of an observed event as a determinant of its aggressive consequences. *Journal of Personality & Social Psychology, 28,* 206–217.

3

■

A Brief History of
Media Effects Research

When I was in graduate school at the University of Wisconsin–Madison, I became interested in the study of children's fright reactions to mass media messages. As I started to read the current research literature in the area of media effects, it became apparent that virtually no one who conducted studies on media impact was doing any research on this topic except my graduate advisor, **Joanne Cantor.** She was something of a pioneer in opening up this new area of research to the current community of scholars. You will read more about her and the research on frightening media in chapter 7. The impact of frightening media was not a mainstream research topic when we started to study it in the late 1970s. However, when we turned our attention to research done 15, 30, and even 50 years earlier, we were intrigued to find evidence of prior interest in our topic. In fact, one of the early research teams in the area investigated physiological changes in the body while people watched scary movies, a technique that would become a standard component in studies done 50 years later.[1] Another research team even attempted a systematic study of how exposure to scary movies could affect one's sleep—a topic that is still studied today.[2] It was important for us to read this past research so we wouldn't run the risk of "reinventing the wheel," or duplicating research that had already been done. It was also enlightening to see how research interests had changed over time and interacted with the technologies that were available. This experience convinced me that a solid understanding of any research area must include an understanding of its development over time. As it turns out, the history of media effects research is a fascinating field to study in its own right. An understanding of that history will give you an appreciation of the scholarly tradition reflected in the subsequent chapters of this book. The questions that you will raise about the study of media effects will almost certainly be different as a result of knowing some of the history behind the topic. With that in mind, the rest of this chapter takes you on a quick tour through the history of research on media effects. What follows is not complete in any sense. It will highlight some of the most important moments and provide a basic framework for thinking about past studies on media effects—especially those that occurred before television came into its own. It also provides you with some of the names and citations that could take you farther back on the road to the past, if you ever decide to take that journey in a more leisurely fashion.

SETTING THE STAGE

In the wake of the tragic shootings at Columbine High School in Colorado in the spring of 1999, a number of social and political commentators observed that the country would never be quite the same. The incident seemed to crystallize a number of issues on the public agenda (for example, debate about the easy availability of guns, parental responsibility, social isolation, the effects of violent video games, and incivility). Perhaps, years from now, scholars will look back and identify this event as a significant one that helped to shape a particular research agenda in sociology or family studies. Today, in mass communication, scholars have identified a number of early events that seem to have set the stage for public and scholarly concern about the impact of mass media. While there is no universal agreement about these precipitating events, most would acknowledge that each of the situations outlined below played a role in stirring interest in the study of media effects.

1898—Congress Declares War on Spain

Why did Congress declare war on Spain in April 1898? Although a complete answer to this question would require reading through several book-length manuscripts, many historians would point to the famous newspaper publisher, **William Randolph Hearst,** as a prominent player in the decision to go to war. When Hearst's illustrator, **Frederic Remington,** wrote him a memo from Havana that there was no trouble there and there would be no war, Hearst responded with the now infamous words, "Please remain. You furnish the pictures and I'll furnish the war."[3] The fact that Congress eventually did declare war may have had something to do with the newspaper coverage in Hearst's *New York Journal;* many believe Hearst stirred up public opinion in favor of war and helped to provide Congress with a public mandate.

1917—Propaganda in World War I

President Woodrow Wilson certainly recognized the potential of newspaper-men like Hearst to influence public opinion. He appointed one of those men, **George Creel,** to lead the **Committee on Public Information.** This committee helped to advise President Wilson on how public relations could be used to influence public opinion about the war. As one scholar in mass communication noted, "It [the Committee on Public Information] engaged in public relations on a scale never before seen, using movies, public speakers, articles in newspapers and magazines, and posters."[4] The use of **wartime propaganda** sensitized the public to the fact that mass media might be used to influence public opinion on a large scale.

The 1920s—Movies Explode as Mainstream Entertainment

If you ever think about what life was like in the United States nearly 80 years ago, you probably think of the daily routine then as being very different from your own routine today. Certainly life is different in many respects. But in one respect, it might be similar. If you go to the movie theater regularly for your entertainment, you are no different than millions of people who lived in the 1920s. Shearon Lowery and Melvin DeFleur characterize the situation with respect to movies in their book, *Milestones in Mass Communication Research:*

> Going to the movies was a frequent event for most families—they were great fun. Also, there were very few alternatives for inexpensive recreation. Homes had neither radios nor television sets. Some had pianos and windup victrolas; a few even had books. But for the majority of families with limited means, taking in a motion picture was an enjoyable and affordable evening out . . . Data on movie attendance were not systematically gathered before 1922. During that year, some 40 million tickets were sold every week in the United States. By the end of the decade, the figure had more than doubled to 90 million! Among the moviegoers in 1929 were an estimated 40 million minors, and among those were approximately 17 million children under the age of fourteen. (p. 32)[5]

With so many people visiting the cinema every week, it was inevitable that people would begin to think about the effects of movies on attitudes and behaviors. Parents undoubtedly became aware that their children were picking up certain behaviors from the movies they saw on Saturday afternoons. With movies as the primary source of public entertainment, researchers started to become interested in documenting the effects of movies toward the end of the 1920s. Fortunately, the development of social science research techniques converged with the appearance of movies, and researchers were able to launch a series of studies that focused on the effects of film.

1929–1932—THE PAYNE FUND STUDIES

In 1928, in response to the growing public concern about the effects of movies on children, a private foundation known as **The Payne Fund** agreed to fund a series of studies that were conducted by the leading researchers of the time. The purpose of these studies was to discover the real impact of movies on children and adolescents. The studies represent the first systematic attempt to discover media impact scientifically. A total of 13 studies were published in 10 volumes on various topics pertaining to the impact of movies. One interesting aspect of these studies is that they introduced many themes that persist in the media effects literature to this day.

What Was the Content of Movies?

A researcher named **Edgar Dale** studied the content of 1,500 films made between 1920 and 1930.[6] Although Dale did not have the advantage of today's more sophisticated techniques of content analysis, he did attempt to categorize the films in different groups according to their major themes. Imagine that you were to do such a study on today's movies and had to use the 10 categories that Dale used in 1930. His categories were children, comedy, crime, history, love, mystery, sex, travel, social propaganda, and war. Which categories do you think would see the most use today? It might be interesting to repeat Dale's study with current films to see what changes have taken place, if any. His results revealed that over 75% of all the films he studied could be classified with only 3 of the 10 categories: crime, love, and sex. If this result were released for current films, it probably wouldn't surprise many people. These same themes often provoke controversy in today's entertainment market, yet they remain prominent and readily available for consumers.

The Emotional Impact of Movies

Of course, the *effects* of movies cannot be gauged just by looking at content. Researchers involved with the Payne Fund studies wanted to collect information about how these themes actually affected viewers. In one line of investigation, children and adults were monitored with physiological electrodes to see how they reacted to romantic or sexy content.[7] One measure that was used in this investigation was **galvanic skin response.** When a person has an emotional reaction to some event, the reaction is often reflected in a sweat response. Perhaps you have discovered that before you are called upon to give a speech or visit your professor to talk about your grade, your fingers and palms get sweaty. Because moisture conducts electricity, researchers are able to measure the intensity of the emotional reaction by shooting a small (undetectable) electric current through two electrodes that are typically attached to the inner pads of two fingers. The more moisture coming off the skin, the better the conductivity in the electric circuit. The conductivity can be measured precisely in units called **micromhos.** When the researchers involved with the Payne Fund studies employed this technique, they found that young children were not much affected by romance movies. But older adolescents had dramatic increases in their physiological responses. This research foreshadowed two ideas that are clearly present in current research. First, as you will discover in chapter 7 (scary media), today's media scholars make important theoretical distinctions between younger and older children in their attempts to predict and explain the effects of media messages. Second, measuring physiological responses to media messages, including skin conductance responses, is an integral technique employed in many current studies of media impact.

Does Watching Movies Affect Behavior?

One of the key questions addressed in the Payne Fund studies dealt with the impact of movies on actual behavior. Once again, this emphasis back in the late 1920s on the impact of movies seems just as relevant today. Public discussion about the V-chip and the possible effects of violent video games is just a contemporary version of the same concerns that were voiced 70 years ago. One study that addressed the issue was conducted by a prominent scholar named **Herbert Blumer.**[8] Blumer collected responses from questionnaires and interviews with children, adolescents, and young adults. In these questionnaires and interviews, the respondents were encouraged to reflect on how exposure to media messages had affected their behavior. Many of the responses indicated that people definitely believed that they had been influenced by the media. For example, one 19-year-old male said:

> In my childhood it was common for one to imitate consciously heroes of the screen. For instance, I would climb the lone tree that was in the yard of the Catholic school near us and hang by one hand or hammer my chest shouting, "Tarzan" and the like. Jumping over fences on a run as did the heroes of the screen was usual in my young life. Fighting with one another, and after conquering him, placing one foot on his chest and raising our arms to the sky as Tarzan did was also common. (p. 22)

Responses like these were typical in Blumer's study, and in retrospect, they raise a number of interesting issues. First, the behavior described by the 19-year-old male fits very nicely with the **theory of social learning** that you will encounter in a later chapter. According to **Albert Bandura,** the author of this theory, children are more likely to imitate characters that receive rewards for their behavior and are perceived as attractive. Certainly, Tarzan fits the bill.

Second, as appealing as it might be to embrace Blumer's results and take the autobiographical comments at face value, it is important to recognize that his technique would come under criticism today (as it did in the 1930s) as a valid technique for assessing media impact. The technique assumes that people are aware of how media affect them. While this assumption might be valid in some instances, it turns out to be misguided in many others. There are at least two kinds of problems. One problem is that people may be mistaken about the effects that they attribute to the media regarding their own behavior. Perhaps the young man in Blumer's study heard some of his friends talking about the impact of the media on children and used this idea to selectively reconstruct his past experiences. Maybe he did engage in the behavior described, but he may have been imitating other friends who were playing with him more than he was copying the actual behaviors on the TV show. A person's own introspections about the causes for behavior may or may not be accurate. Another problem is that by relying on people's own reports about media impact, researchers run the risk of missing effects that occur quite unconsciously. As you will see in later chapters, most of the effects of the media that are well documented in research studies are not ones that people are capable of reporting on a conscious level. People are not necessarily aware when media messages affect their attitudes and behavior. If researchers relied exclusively on introspective reports, they would miss a rich world of very significant media impact.

One example that shows the potential problems with relying on self-reports for assessments of media impact comes from the recent annals of criminal behavior. Ted Bundy was an infamous serial killer who raped and killed women. He was eventually brought to trial and executed. Before his death, he issued a public statement containing his own analysis of his actions. What had caused him to engage in such atrocious behavior? According to Ted, it was the mass media. Specifically, it was exposure to volumes and volumes of pornography. As you will read in chapter 6, pornography certainly has been studied and associated with antisocial effects. But to what extent should we rely on Ted Bundy's own assessment of what caused his behavior? According to Paul Wilson, former research director at the Australian Institute of Criminology, it probably isn't a good idea to indict pornographic media as the culprit on the basis of Bundy's own self-analysis. Wilson noted:

> In Ted Bundy's case, no serious social scientist or law enforcement officer takes the explanation that "pornography made me do it" seriously. Well before Bundy turned the pages of a sexually explicit magazine or watched an adult video he was exhibiting bizarre behavior. Dr. Dorothy Lewis, who conducted multiple interviews with the killer just after his arrest, reported that Bundy was a highly disturbed child at the age of three. When Bundy was first arrested in 1978, early interviews with police and psychiatrists reveal that the killer referred to popular sexually explicit magazines as "normal healthy sexual stimuli." It was only in the 1980s, when a court refused to certify him insane and to save him from the electric chair, that Bundy became a born-again Christian and reiterated the party line on pornography. (p. 40)[9]

The Bundy case illustrates that in addition to being unaware of media impact upon themselves, people may deliberately articulate a view of media effects for personal reasons. In the final analysis, although Blumer's work on the Payne Fund studies was critical for its time and helped to launch the formal scientific examination of media effects, scholars are reluctant to attach too much weight to the introspective self-reports that Blumer's methodology generated.

The Aftermath of the Payne Fund Studies

The Payne Fund studies played a huge role in the development of the study of media effects. In terms of the public consciousness, Lowery and DeFleur noted that the conclusions of the studies helped to establish a **legacy of fear**—widespread beliefs that the media were dangerous and that the effects of media messages might pervert and upset the proper social order.[10] Earlier concerns about propaganda and the role of newspapers in shaping political events helped to reinforce the attitude of public concern following the publication of the Payne Fund studies. Subsequent events in American life only tended to fuel the fire of concern about the pernicious impact of the media. In the end, one thing that inevitably impresses the student of media effects about the Payne Fund studies is how many of the themes and rhetorical tidbits from the 1930s resonate with those of the modern day. As Lowery and DeFleur point out in their excellent review of the studies, a summary document of the major findings concluded that "the commercial movies are in an unsavory mess," and "the producers ought to have heart" over their bad influences on children.[11] The current Hollywood film industry has endured many similar attacks that call upon filmmakers to exercise a greater sense of social responsibility.

THE INVASION FROM MARS

In the late 1930s, the dominant communication medium in America was radio. If there was any doubt about the potential of radio to influence people quickly and in large numbers, those doubts ended on the night of October 30, 1938. On that particular evening, the CBS radio network broadcast a radio drama as part of its *Mercury Theatre on the Air*. A young man by the name of **Orson Welles** narrated a radio adaptation of "War of the Worlds," a science fiction story written by H. G. Wells. An estimated audience of about 6 million listeners tuned in. Of all the programs that the producers at CBS might have thought would have an impact on the audience, this particular program was not one of them. In an article written for *Harper's* by John Houseman, one of the cofounders of *Mercury Theatre* along with Orson Welles, we learn that virtually no one thought that this production was going to be anything special. In the week preceding the broadcast, the production crew even contemplated scrapping the whole idea.[12] But they didn't. The show went on as planned and stirred the public as nothing before it ever had.

The premise of the show was very simple. Listeners would be lulled into a sense of relaxation and even boredom as the show began with classical music. Then, a radio announcer would interrupt and refer to an atmospheric disturbance that had been reported over Nova Scotia. Listeners were returned to the light music until the announcer interrupted again. Over the course of the hour program, what started as an atmospheric disturbance turned into an alien invasion by Martians who landed their invading craft in Grover's Mill, New Jersey. In retrospect, one would think that the discerning listener would easily recognize that the reported events were nothing more than a fictional drama. But the realistic format of cutting away from the music to feature what sounded like live news reports apparently fooled about one million people in the show's audience. In some cases, random events helped along the illusion of reality. In the town of Concrete, Washington, there was a power failure that corresponded with the radio announcer informing Americans that the Martians were disrupting power and communications across the country. Needless to say, the people who lived in Concrete didn't need any more reason to believe the broadcast was true. But even without such events, people up and down the eastern seaboard went into a panic. CBS eventually apologized to the public for its miscalculation. The morning after the broadcast, a bewildered Orson Welles was shown fielding questions about the broadcast from a crowd of reporters that must have seemed to him like an attack mob. Welles was still trying to figure out exactly what had happened.

The Research at Princeton

Orson Welles was not the only one who wondered what had happened on that October night. A research team at Princeton University led by **Hadley Cantril** did a quick postmortem of the whole affair in a study that included an analysis of newspaper accounts of the incident as well as data from surveys and personal interviews.[13] Lowery and DeFleur summarized the findings of the research.[14] As to why so many listeners found the show believable, the Princeton research team cited the fact that most Americans had tremendous confidence in radio as a news medium. They never expected that their most trusted medium would mislead them into a hoax. They also noted that the show used the brilliant creative technique of on-the-spot reporting and sounded convincing in introducing various scientific experts to the public. Also contributing to the panic was the fact that many listeners missed the announcement at the beginning of the show that told the audience that the program was a dramatic adaptation.

The Princeton research also focused on the characteristics of people who believed the program was real. According to the results, these were people who had less critical ability, less self-confidence, and less emotional security. People with strong religious beliefs were also more likely to believe that earth was being invaded by Martians. These results may not be particularly surprising, and they didn't exactly startle the scholarly community. But the broadcast and the subsequent research were important in the history of media effects. The broadcast itself demonstrated that the media could trigger widespread, intense responses in the audience. The research pointed the way to future studies that would employ a variety of personality and demographic variables to predict media impact. In terms of the legacy of fear, the "War of the Worlds" broadcast did little to dispel the notion that media messages were potentially dangerous for society. Entering the 1940s, this assumption was widespread.

EARLY THEORY OF MEDIA EFFECTS:
THE MAGIC BULLET MODEL

In the wake of the Payne Fund studies and Cantril's study of the "War of the Worlds" broadcast, the view among scholars was that the mass media were indeed powerful agents for change and influence. The studies that were done were typical of studies in a new area of research. They were essentially exploratory studies that attempted to discover any new information. The studies were not characterized by well-developed theory and the testing of specific hypotheses.

Contemporary scholars often look back on this early period of media effects history and see a general theoretical view that seemed to prevail, even though it wasn't stated formally. This view has come to be known as the **magic bullet model** or the **hypodermic needle model** of mass communication. According to this view, the communication of a message in a mass medium can be compared to shooting a gun that contains a magic bullet or to injecting someone with a hypodermic needle. Once the message reaches the audience, it will exert powerful, relatively uniform effects on everyone who processes it. It would probably be difficult to find a single scholar in 1940 who articulated this particular viewpoint of media impact. It seems too extreme and overly simplistic. Nevertheless, it does capture something of the general outlook that many scholars held at the time regarding the media's tremendous power.

Part of the explanation for this outlook had to do with the psychology of the time, with its emphasis on the uniform physiological mechanisms common to every human being. There was little consideration given to the possibility that people might respond differently to the same message. The theoretical framework that permitted individual differences in responding was not yet in place. The public tended to concur with the view of great media impact. The Orson Welles affair was still fresh in their minds, and the public debate about movies in the aftermath of the Payne Fund studies had resulted in an attitude of self-censorship on the part of Hollywood that only served to highlight the power of movies.

The convergence between the scholarly and public view of media impact, though, was about to change. In 1940, a team of researchers from Columbia University undertook an exhaustive study of the role of radio messages on voter behavior in the presidential election. Their results had a great impact on how scholars came to think about the theoretical underpinnings of media effects. More than any other study up to that point, *The People's Choice* advanced the study of media effects both theoretically and methodologically.[15]

THE PEOPLE'S CHOICE STUDY:
THE "LIMITED EFFECTS" MODEL

The 1940 presidential election was between Wendell Wilkie, the Republican, and the Democratic incumbent, Franklin Roosevelt. As the two candidates prepared to do battle at the polls, a team of researchers from Columbia University, **Paul Lazarsfeld, Bernard Berelson,** and **Hazel Gaudet,** set out to study "how and why people decided to vote as they did." The study took place in Erie County, Ohio, using a sample based on visitations to every fourth house in the county. The researchers decided to employ a longitudinal **panel study** design (see chapter 2). That is, they followed a main panel of 600 people throughout the campaign and interviewed them repeatedly (seven times). One of the methodological innovations of this very ambitious study was the use of large **control groups** of 600 respondents each.

Why Use Control Groups?

Upon reflection, it is easy to see why control groups were used. Imagine that you were one of the 600 people selected for repeated interviewing during the campaign. The fact that you knew ahead of time that you were likely to be interviewed again about your voting preferences and behavior might cause you to modify your behavior or your answers in the next round of questions. That is, the panel design itself might have an effect on the data collected—an effect quite separate from the responses that people might make if they were untarnished by the repeated interviews. In order to determine if this was actually happening, when the researchers went back to the main panel of 600 people to interview them for a third time, they also interviewed a separate group of 600 people for the first time. Theoretically, if interviewing the main panel three times had no impact on their responses, then there would be no difference between them and the control group of 600 people that had been interviewed for the first time. The researchers selected another control group of 600 people to interview when the main panel was interviewed for the fourth time. They repeated this procedure on the sixth interview. In general the main finding from this procedure was that the responses of the control groups did not differ significantly from the responses of the main panel. This was a very important finding. It indicated that the longitudinal panel design was a viable method to study change. Concerns that multiple interviews would alter the nature of people's responses proved to be unfounded in this case. The longitudinal survey design is still a very important technique in research today.

Media Impact in the 1940 Campaign

One of the surprising results of *The People's Choice* study was that the impact of media exposure to campaign messages was rather negligible in terms of **conversion**—changing voters from an intention to vote for one candidate to an intention to vote for the other. A more significant effect of media exposure was

reinforcement—assuring voters that their current intention was worthwhile and correct. The data showed that half of the voters had already decided by the first survey who they were going to vote for. It was important that media messages over the coming months keep these people in the fold. Although the effect of reinforcement doesn't appear in the data as a great change, it is nonetheless a very important media effect.

In today's modern age of computing technology, it is a little tough to appreciate the monumental task that the researchers from Columbia had after they gathered their data. They had no personal computers on their desktops. There was no large mainframe computer at Columbia that could be called upon for number crunching. It is little wonder then that it took the researchers nearly 8 years to synthesize their data and bring it to publication. Consequently, the theoretical impact of *The People's Choice* study did not appear to take hold until the end of the 1940s or the beginning of the 1950s. Combined with several other significant studies of media impact in the 1950s,[16] *The People's Choice* served to usher in a new perspective on media impact. Far from the view that media effects were powerful and comparable to a magic bullet, the newer research seemed to indicate that the media had **limited effects.**

The Limited-Effects Perspective

One of the chief spokespeople for the new limited-effects perspective was a communication consultant who worked for the General Electric Company, **Joseph Klapper.** In 1958, Klapper published a book that had wide influence. It argued that the effects of mass media were small to negligible.[17] Klapper's position is captured in remarks that he made as part of a program on mass media presented in New York City by the Child Study Association of America on March 21, 1960. He said:

> I think it has been pretty well demonstrated that the mass media do not serve as the primary determinant or even as a very important determinant of any of the basic attitudes or the basic behavior patterns of either children or adults. This is not to say that they have no influence at all, but only that their influence seems to be incidental to other forces; or if it is not incidental, to pertain to rather superficial aspects of attitude or behavior rather than to basic attitudes and behavior. (p. 48f)[18]

Ironically, Klapper's comments about the minimal influence of the media came at just the time when scholars were starting to explore the impact of the new medium that had virtually exploded on the scene in the 1950s: television. Just as the limited-effects perspective was starting to take hold in the scholarly community, a new wave of research would call the perspective into question. As it turned out, the advent of the limited-effects model of mass communication is a good example of how theories pertaining to social phenomena can change as society changes. In an era of relatively high political stability, strong party identification, and straight-ticket voting, it isn't surprising that the Columbia researchers found that radio messages didn't change many votes. Today, however,

STUDY BOX 3-1   The Principle of Selective Exposure to Communication

In an amazing interview captured on videotape (Episode 9 of *A Walk Through the 20th Century With Bill Moyers*), the well-known journalist Bill Moyers interviewed Fritz Hippler, one of the men who helped produce Nazi propaganda films during World War II. As Moyers listened attentively, Hippler explained that the Germans had discovered a very important principle of mass propaganda: **People only want to see things that they find to be agreeable.** The Germans capitalized on the principle by showing the mass audiences images of military might, but never focusing on the problems associated with warfare. They were busy practicing a powerful principle of communication before that principle had been formally uncovered in the annals of communication research.

Today, the principle of selective exposure is so well known and well documented that in 1985, Dolf Zillmann and Jennings Bryant edited an entire book on the subject, *Selective Exposure to Communication.* Their volume contains overviews of how the dynamic of selective exposure enters into the mass-communication process at multiple points. People are motivated to expose themselves to messages that they already agree with or to messages that make them feel good. Similarly, they are motivated to avoid messages that they find disagreeable or messages that make them feel bad.

One interesting line of research on selective exposure reported in the volume by Zillmann and Bryant is described by Jacob Wakshlag. Wakshlag reports how the principle of selective exposure should inform the work of TV producers who work on educational TV programs. In a study with first- and second-grade children, Wakshlag and his colleagues made different versions of an educational TV program available on different channels. The children were free to watch whichever channel they wished for as long as they wished. They were also free to turn the TV off. The researchers discovered that the children strongly preferred to watch the educational programs that contained humorous content. Wakshlag summarized the implications of this research in the following way:

[T]he findings suggest that nonentertaining educational television programs are not likely to compete very well with other educational programs, such as *Sesame Street,* which contain humor and other embellishments. Furthermore, when faced with programs whose principal function is entertainment, such as those typically available from the networks, nonentertaining educational programs would probably fare even worse. (p. 194)

In today's competitive media environment, programmers would undoubtedly do well to consider carefully the wisdom of media effects research on this point of selective exposure. In general, audiences will not voluntarily expose themselves to messages that they find to be unpleasant.

SOURCES: (1) Wakshlag, J. (1985). Selective exposure to educational television. In D. Zillmann & J. Bryant (Eds.), *Selective exposure to communication* (pp. 191–201). Hillsdale, NJ: Erlbaum. (2) World War II: The propaganda battle. *A walk through the 20th century with Bill Moyers* (Episode 9). Alexandria, VA: Public Broadcasting Service. (3) Wakshlag, J. J., Day, K. D., & Zillmann, D. (1981). Selective exposure to educational television programs as a function of differently paced humorous inserts. *Journal of Educational Psychology, 73,* 27–32.

political scientists work with a concept called **voter volatility.** The political system is more unstable. There are fewer people who identify strongly with a single party, more people who call themselves independents, and more people splitting their ticket at the polls. In such a volatile climate, scholars expect that the media might have more impact on the political process than it did in the 1940s. One important principle to emerge from the limited-effects perspective that remains important today is the notion of **selective exposure** to communication. According to this idea, people are motivated to expose themselves voluntarily to messages that they already agree with. Likewise, they will tend to avoid messages that they find disagreeable. Study Box 3-1 focuses on this principle and discusses some of the research over the years that supports the principle.

THE EVILS OF COMIC BOOKS

During the 1950s, the public's view of media effects probably didn't change very much from the one reflected by the phrase "legacy of fear." One reason why public attitudes didn't change was because of the research of **Frederic Wertham,** a famous psychiatrist. Wertham took his case right to the people in the form of articles in popular magazines like *Collier's* and the *Ladies' Home Journal.* His book, *Seduction of the Innocent,*[19] was a virtual diatribe against the evils of comic books. (If you are lucky enough to find a genuine 1954 edition of this book, it might make sense to buy it. The book is becoming somewhat rare and is highly valued among comic book enthusiasts.) Wertham's research was based on selective analyses of comic book content—not random samples. He tended to highlight the most offensive material and characterized the entire comic book industry on the basis of the material he examined. He also studied a variety of young people who had been referred for behavioral difficulty. Wertham was convinced on the basis of his interviews and testing that comic books played an important role in corrupting the behavior of the adolescents he studied. One of the more incredible claims that Wertham made in his analysis of comic books was that the heroes Batman and Robin were homosexual lovers. He wrote:

> Only someone ignorant of the fundamentals of psychiatry and of the psychopathology of sex can fail to realize a subtle atmosphere of homo-erotism which pervades the adventures of the mature, "Batman" and his young friend "Robin." (pp. 189–190)[20]

Wertham also warned the public about Superman. Apparently, he was concerned about the large "S" that Superman wears on his shirt. According to him, this symbol was uncomfortably close to the famous Nazi "SS." Wertham believed that exposure to the messages of these comic books could corrupt juvenile behavior and lead to a life of reckless crime and self-abuse. Many lawmakers and ordinary citizens agreed. On the basis of "research" procedures that were hardly scientific, Wertham managed to convince many that comic books had powerful effects on young people. His content analysis procedures were not systematic and did not rely on random samples. And the youth that he based his conclusions upon were from a population that had already been referred for problems of various sorts. They did not represent the larger population of comic readers in any sense.

THE DAWN OF TELEVISION

As the public became worked up over comic books, a new medium was exploding on the scene. In 1950, only about 10% of American homes had a TV set. Neither the scholarly community nor the public could have imagined how the next 10 years would change the media effects landscape. By the end of the decade, 90% of homes had a TV. From the very beginning, it seemed like something new had started to take place on a regular basis. Reports of imitative crimes, particularly among young people, proliferated. Robert Liebert and Joyce Sprafkin documented some of these crimes in their book about the effects of television on children.[21] One example that they cite from the *New York Journal-American* was reported in the following way:

> [P]olice arrested an 11-year-old who admitted having burglarized Long Island homes for more than $1,000 in cash and valuables. His accomplice was identified as a 7-year-old friend. The boy said he learned the technique of burglary by seeing how it was done on television. (p. 8)

This type of report tended to stir public and government concern. A number of government reports in the mid-1950s and 1960s called attention to the large amount of violence on TV, but the reports also noted that scientific studies that would establish a cause-effect relationship between exposure to violence and aggressive behavior were lacking in the literature.

As the government continued to keep media violence in the spotlight, it also started to make grant money available for scientists who wanted to study the media's impact on human behavior. The 1960s and 1970s were years of new theories and research about media impact. The limited-effects perspective started to give way to a new paradigm based on more sophisticated scientific techniques. In particular, the laboratory experiment was a critical method that was used repeatedly to study the issues surrounding the impact of media violence. Chapter 5 provides a closer look at that research.

MANY TYPES OF MEDIA EFFECTS

Today, media scholars understand **media effects** as being more complicated than either the "magic bullet" or the "limited-effects" view would imply. Depending on the message, the medium, the audience, and the type of effect focused on, researchers have found the effects of media to be either strong or weak. In one of the classic essays written on media effects, **Jack McLeod** and **Byron Reeves** outlined a number of ways to think about media effects.[22] Their analysis reveals that there is no simple answer to the question of whether the media affect people. It depends on what type of effect you may be talking about. According to McLeod and Reeves, media effects can be classified in many ways using some of the category schemes that appear below. The appearance of their essay in 1980 signaled a major move toward conceptualizing media effects in a much more sophisticated way than had been typical only 20 years earlier. Today, research on media effects makes use of all the distinctions alluded to by McLeod and Reeves.

Micro-Level or Macro-Level Effects **Micro-level effects** involve effects on individual media consumers. Studies that rely upon the experimental method might be classic examples. Studies that monitor physiological arousal while viewers watch a horror movie are concerned with how media messages affect individual body physiology. On the other hand, research on **macro-level effects** might examine media impact on large communities. Some researchers are concerned that in the age of media mergers and large corporate ownership of media outlets, the quality of news coverage in a given area might suffer and communities may not have adequate exposure to certain issues. Researchers might want to investigate the pattern of media ownership in a given community and attempt to relate it to general community awareness by studying the kinds of social programs or political action groups that citizens have available. Notice that in this case data are not gathered from individuals. Instead, the data are gathered on communities.

Content-Specific or Diffuse-General Effects One way to think about media effects is to ask whether they might result from exposure to particular kinds of content. People who watch media violence may adopt very different attitudes or behaviors than people who watch nature programs. Researchers who study this type of effect are interested in how **specific content** affects viewers. But another possibility is that the media bring about very general effects, quite apart from the content of the messages. In the next chapter, you will read about research that links TV viewing to obesity. The presumed effect in this case doesn't arise from exposure to any particular content; it is a much more general effect of time spent with the medium. Watching TV may replace physical exercise and give rise to more frequent eating. Such an effect would be referred to as a more **diffuse or general effect** than the effect of media violence on aggressive behavior.

Attitudinal Versus Behavioral Versus Cognitive Changes In 1980, when McLeod and Reeves wrote their article, they indicated that the history of media effects research "is very nearly the history of attitude change research." Up to that point, the main focus of study was the extent to which exposure to the media produced **changes in people's attitudes.** Certainly, this is an important effect to study. However, attitude change does not always produce **behavior change.** And sometimes changes in what people think about (that is, **cognitive changes**) might also be of great interest. Since McLeod and Reeves published their essay, the study of media effects has moved beyond the narrow focus on attitudes to include more studies on the media's impact on people's behavior and thoughts. You will encounter some of this newer research in later chapters.

Alteration Versus Stabilization Most people think of media effects in terms of change. Exposure to media messages might produce an **alteration** in public opinion or in a decision about whether to buy a particular product. In contrast to an emphasis on change, another way to think about media effects is to emphasize how media messages reinforce the status quo and exert a powerful force for **stability.** *The People's Choice* investigation discussed earlier in the chapter revealed that exposure to radio commercials tended to reinforce prior voting dispositions. People tended to listen closely to the ads for their own candidates and became even more committed in their intent to vote for those candidates. The absence of dramatic change might not indicate the lack of media impact. Instead, it might indicate that the media exert a force for maintaining things as they are. In the chapters that follow this one, you will learn about the results of current research in a number of important areas. This research reflects a number of different types of media impact, including some of the varieties that are mentioned by McLeod and Reeves.

SUMMARY

Examples of media effects extend back to the last century when the impact of newspapers on political affairs seemed obvious. With the Payne Fund studies, the research community generated the first systematic attempt to study the impact of media. These studies revealed that exposure to movies did have various effects on children. These results, combined with the obvious impact of the infamous "War of the Worlds" radio broadcast, introduced the "legacy of fear" —the idea that media were extremely powerful and could bring about effects that were often harmful. The research on comic books in the 1950s tended to reinforce the legacy of fear and the "magic bullet model" of mass communication. A study of voting behavior, *The People's Choice,* revealed a much more limited impact of mass media and ushered in the limited-effects perspective. As this perspective took hold in the 1950s, television exploded on the scene and attracted research attention in the 1960s and 1970s. This early research led to a more sophisticated view of media effects that prevails to the present day. Part of that sophistication is reflected in the number and different types of media effects that scholars now recognize.

KEY CONCEPTS AND TERMS

The Committee on
Public Information
41

Wartime propaganda 41

The Payne Fund Studies
42

Galvanic skin response
42

micromhos 43

Theory of social learning
43

Legacy of fear 45

Magic bullet or hypo-
dermic needle model
of media effects 47

Use of control groups
in a panel survey 48

Conversion and re-
inforcement in *The
People's Choice* study
48

Limited-effects perspec-
tive 49

Voter volatility 51

Selective exposure to
communication 51

Types of media effects
52

Micro-level versus
macro-level effects
53

Content-specific ver-
sus diffuse-general ef-
fects 53

Attitudinal versus be-
havioral versus cogni-
tive changes 53

Alteration versus sta-
bilization 54

KEY NAMES

Joanne Cantor 39

William Randolph
Hearst 40

Frederic Remington
40

George Creel 41

Edgar Dale 42

Herbert Blumer 43

Albert Bandura 43

Orson Welles 45

Hadley Cantril 46

Paul Lazarsfeld, Bernard
Berelson, and Hazel
Gaudet 48

Joseph Klapper 49

Frederic Wertham 51

Jack McLeod and Byron
Reeves 53

WEB LINKS

1. For a discussion of the current controversy over the effects of media violence, try . . .
   http://www.salon.com/mwt/feature/2001/02/02/kid_violence/index.html
2. For information on the infamous "War of the Worlds" broadcast, try . . . http://www
   .dartmouth.edu/~library/Library_Bulletin/Nov1998/KriegerInvasion.html
3. For information on Frederic Wertham and his "research" on comic books, try . . .
   http://www.comic-art.com/bios-1/wertham1.htm

To learn more about the topics in this chapter, enter the Key Terms and Concepts and Key Names found in this chapter as subject and keyword searches on
your InfoTrac College Edition.

NOTES

1. Dysinger, W. S., & Ruckmick, C. A. (1933). *The emotional responses of children to the motion picture situation.* New York: Macmillan.

2. Renshaw, S., Miller, V. L., & Marquis, D. P. (1939). *Children's sleep.* New York: Macmillan.

3. Straubhaar, J., & LaRose, R. (2000). *Media now: Communications media in the information age.* Belmont, CA: Wadsworth.

4. Baran, S. (1999). *Mass communication: Media literacy and culture.* Mountain View, CA: Mayfield.

5. Lowery, S. A., & DeFleur, M. L. (1983). *Milestones in mass communication research.* New York: Longman.

6. Dale, E. (1935). *The content of motion pictures.* New York: Macmillan.

7. Dysinger, W. S., & Ruckmick, C. A. (1933). *The emotional responses of children to the motion picture situation.* New York: Macmillan.

8. Blumer, H., & Hauser, P. M. (1933). *Movies, delinquency, and crime.* New York: Macmillan.

9. Wilson, P. (1995). *Dealing with pornography: The case against censorship.* Australia: University of New South Wales Press.

10. Lowery, S. A., & DeFleur, M. L. (1983). *Milestones in mass communication research.* New York: Longman.

11. Charters, W. W. (1933). *Motion pictures and youth: A summary.* New York: Macmillan.

12. Houseman, J. (1948). The men from Mars. *Harper's, 168,* 76.

13. Cantril, H. (1940). *The invasion from Mars: A study in the psychology of panic.* Princeton, NJ: Princeton University Press.

14. Lowery, S. A., & DeFleur, M. L. (1983). *Milestones in mass communication research.* New York: Longman.

15. Lazarsfeld, P. F., Berelson, B., & Gaudet, H. (1948). *The people's choice.* New York: Columbia University Press.

16. See the following for some of the most important studies during this time period: (1) Katz, E., & Lazarsfeld, P. F. (1955). *Personal influence: The part played by people in the flow of mass communication.* Glencoe, IL: Free Press of Glencoe. (2) Lewin, K., & Grabbe, P. (1948). Conduct, knowledge, and acceptance of new values. *Journal of Social Issues, 1,* 53–64. (3) Stauffer, S. A. (1948). *The American soldier: Studies in social psychology in World War II* (Vols. 1 and 2). Princeton, NJ: Princeton University Press.

17. Klapper, J. T. (1960). *The effects of the mass media.* Glencoe, IL: Free Press of Glencoe.

18. Klineberg, O., & Klapper, J. T. (1960). *The mass media: Their impact on children and family life.* Comments presented to the Study Association of America. New York: Television Information Office.

19. Wertham, F. (1954). *Seduction of the innocent.* New York: Rinehart.

20. Wertham, F. (1954). *Seduction of the innocent.* New York: Rinehart.

21. Liebert, R. M., & Sprafkin, J. (1988). *The early window: Effects of television on children and youth.* New York: Pergamon Press.

22. McLeod, J. M., & Reeves, B. (1980). On the nature of media effects. In S. B. Withey & R. P. Abeles (Eds.), *Television and social behavior: Beyond violence and children.* Hillsdale, NJ: Erlbaum.

4

■

Time Spent With Mass Media: Reasons and Consequences

In a documentary about the history of radio that was made for Home Box Office,[1] a young child's fascination with listening to radio drama was captured with a question that he directed to his parents: "Gee, Mom and Dad, what did people do before the days of radio?" The parents hesitated as they reflected on their past and finally answered, "Well, we *talked*." As the young child started to express his incredulity at how boring life must have been before radio, the parents ordered him to stop talking so they could listen to the radio. In the 1970s, this same conversation might easily have taken place with respect to television. When I was a teenager, I might well have been tempted to ask my own parents, "What did you ever do before the days of TV?" For my generation, growing up without TV was simply unimaginable. Today, the question I am likely to get from my own children is "What in the world did you ever do before the days of computers and the Internet?"

One thing that these parent-child conversations reveal is that, quite apart from the effects of media content, the mass media have had a profound impact on the way people use their time. In the 1940s, children spent time listening to their favorite radio heroes. In the 1970s, they were glued to the TV screen watching all sorts of shows, ranging from sporting events to sitcoms. Today, they are surfing the Internet, downloading MP3s, and chatting with their friends across town or across the country. They have been integrated into a more complex media environment. And radio and TV are not gone; they still occupy significant amounts of our time. Most of the chapters that follow this one will deal with the effects of particular kinds of media content. But this chapter deals with a different issue. Quite apart from the actual content of the media, why do we elect to spend so much of our time with media messages, and what are some of the consequences of those decisions?

Before we take a look at the research on how much time we spend with the media and how that time influences who we are as human beings, this is a good place to take a step back from the idea that the media influence people. Can we gain any insights from reversing the typical logic of media impact? Instead of thinking about the media first and impact on people second, what happens when we start with people and move to the media? It is certainly true that media messages influence us, but this influence does not take place in some sort of static environment of one-way communication. The time that people spend with mass media is often the result of a deliberate choice. Before we study the impact of the media messages that we consume, it is important to understand what leads people to the media in the first place. Why would people choose to spend their time going to a movie, watching a TV show, or reading a magazine or newspaper?

THE USES AND GRATIFICATIONS PERSPECTIVE

Recall from chapter 3 that in the 1950s and 1960s, there was a shift among scholars about how to think about media effects. The idea of limited effects became popular. This perspective emphasized that audience members are not all the same. Since individuals react to media content in very different ways, the idea of emphasizing uniform, powerful effects on a wide audience fell out of favor. It was only natural that the limited-effects perspective, which emphasized individual differences, would spawn a new interest in why individuals use media in the first place. This new emphasis, **the uses and gratifications perspective,** was formalized in an article by **Elihu Katz, Jay Blumler,** and **Michael Gurevitch.**[2] This perspective was designed to lend insight into the ways that people use media to meet their needs. It focused heavily on individual motivations for media use. Since the time of the article by Katz, Blumler, and Gurevitch, an entire tradition of studies in uses and gratifications has grown up and matured in the mass-communication literature. We now know a great deal about the various reasons people have for choosing media exposure of particular kinds.

Why Do Children Watch TV?

You might want to pause before you read the following paragraphs and take out a pen and paper. Why do *you* think children watch TV? Jot down as many reasons as you can think of, using your own childhood as an example. How many reasons were you able to come up with? How does your list compare with the one that follows? This list of **motivations** was developed by **Bradley**

STUDY BOX 4-1   Jordan's Reasons for Using the Internet

Glenn: Hi. I have a question for you.

Jordan: shoot

Glenn: List as many reasons as you can for why you use the Internet.

Jordan: Okay . . . It's a form of communication between my family members and me [COMPANIONSHIP]

Jordan: It's a way to express some things I "hold dear" to the rest of the world, or views I am interested in.

Jordan: It's a source of information for school [LEARNING]

Jordan: It's a source of information for other "facts" [LEARNING]

Jordan: It provides things to do, like play card games [RELAXATION]

Jordan: It's a hobby . . . like, my homepage . . . something to do when I'm bored [PASS TIME] (Note: Jordan's homepage is at http://www.geocities.com/. She learned how to write her own html code when she was 12 years old.)

Jordan: It's "vast" . . . it won't get boring easily [AROUSAL]

Jordan: It's a way to stay informed about issues in the world [LEARNING]

Jordan: It's a way to stay informed about ANYTHING, I guess . . . music, TV, etc. [LEARNING]

Jordan: It's a way to meet people—chat, email pen pals, blah blah [COMPANIONSHIP]

Greenberg in one study of British children[3] and was replicated by **Alan Rubin** in a study of children from the United States.[4]

Learning Not surprisingly, children turn to TV to learn things. Occasionally, I hear a very small minority of students say that when they have children, they won't permit TV in their homes. Inevitably, the rationale for this intention is that there is simply too much objectionable material on TV today. I am somewhat sympathetic with the position of these students, but having raised three children in a home with multiple TV sets, I also usually ask about the missed opportunities to use TV for **learning.** Cable TV has expanded the number of possible programs to object to. But it has also expanded the opportunities for learning that could never have taken place years ago. In our family, we love *PBS,* the *Discovery Channel,* and the *History Channel.* The data from the uses and gratifications research suggests that children do use TV deliberately to learn things. Perhaps not much has changed in terms of children's motivations for media use even in the age of the Internet. In Study Box 4-1, I have reprinted the text of an Internet chat that I had with my 14-year-old daughter Jordan about why she uses the Internet. As you will discover, learning things is an important motivation. Remember, though, that the scientific approach does not permit me to make any generalizations about children from just one child. If I really wanted to introduce evidence for this point, I would have to do a formal study with a random-sample survey of many children. Going back to the Payne Fund studies reviewed in the last chapter, there is no shortage of scientific evidence for the notion that children learn from the media. Researchers who study uses and gratifications note that some of this learning is motivated—not just an accidental by-product of media exposure.

Habit Watching television may be habit forming. The research studies reveal that children are conscious of the fact that they may view out of **habit.** If it's there, kids like to watch. Related to the habit motive is the suggestion in the literature that TV, like a drug, encourages behavior that looks like a full-blown addiction.[5] The literature on television addiction is somewhat mixed. One early survey of adults conducted by **Robin Smith** failed to find much evidence of a true addiction to TV.[6] But several later studies seem to indicate that **TV addiction** is a real phenomenon. One very recent study that appeared in the journal *Addictive Behaviors* found that while women tend to be more addicted to caffeine and chocolate, men are more likely to be addicted to alcohol, cigarettes, gambling, and television.[7] Research by **Robert McIlwraith** indicates that some college students endorse the statement "I'm addicted to television," and those who do tend to be more easily bored, more introverted, and more likely to suffer from neurosis.[8] The area of television addiction as well as possible addictions to video games deserves more attention from scholars, especially as it pertains to children. At present, it seems safe to say that there may be a tendency for some individuals to develop a psychological dependence on TV that resembles addictive behavior in some respects.[9]

Companionship Children watch TV because it gives them a sense of connection to other people—a sense of **companionship.** As it turns out, the same is true for adults. Why should this be? Where the Internet is concerned, the concept of companionship is easier to understand. People can actually communicate with other people in chat rooms and use email to keep in touch. But how does TV foster a sense of companionship? Researchers **Byron Reeves** and **Clifford Nass** may have some insight on this question. According to them, the human brain does not easily separate media images from reality. The title of their book summarizes their thesis rather well: *The Media Equation: How People Treat Computers, Television, and New Media Like Real People and Places.*[10] If Reeves and Nass are right, when children see people on TV, some primitive part of the brain is tricked into thinking that those people are physically present. Higher-order cognitive processes might tell them that the images are not real, but the images stimulate real emotional reactions just the same. A more complete confirmation of the Reeves and Nass thesis must await further testing and more complete understanding of brain functions. But the basic theoretical idea may be useful for explaining the sense that some people have of relationships with media personalities. Media researchers **Elizabeth Perse** and **Rebecca Rubin** refer to the feelings and attachments that people have toward media characters as **"parasocial relationships."**[11] There seems to be no doubt that such relationships do exist.

Arousal Some children watch TV because it stimulates them, excites them, and increases their **arousal** level. Arousal refers to the physiological system and involves responses like heart rate, blood pressure, sweat, respiration rate, and so forth. Back in the 1950s, **Donald Hebb** introduced the idea that each human being was wired with an **optimal level of arousal.** For some individuals, their natural baseline **set point** of arousal was over their optimum. Consequently, these people would seek out calm and boring activities. For other individuals, the natural set point of arousal is below their optimal level. As a result, these people would seek out stimulating and arousing activities. In support of this general notion, **Marvin Zuckerman** has documented the presence of a personality trait known as **sensation seeking.**[12]

Sensation seekers are individuals who tend to seek out arousing activities. Unlike individuals who are low sensation seekers, those high on sensation seeking express a much greater desire for activities like skydiving, riding roller coasters, attending wild parties, and using drugs for recreation. Zuckerman devised a simple measure of sensation seeking that consists of a number of statements about preferred activities. Respondents simply indicate whether each statement applies to them. Several studies show that high sensation seekers prefer to watch horror films.[13] One of the reasons why some children (particularly males) seem to seek out media content that is violent or frightening may have to do with the need for arousal. For such children, reading a book is not likely to be an adequate substitute for watching a movie. Riding a roller coaster may be a better alternative.

Relaxation Just as children use TV in order to raise their arousal levels, they also use it in order to **relax.** Today, when I talk to groups of parents about using TV effectively in the home, I often take a few minutes to talk about the transitional time between afternoon and evening activities. This is often a time of chaos in the household as people shift gears and change activities. For parents, the combination of winding down from the workday and preparing the evening meal can seem like a major challenge when young children are running around at a hyper pace. A carefully selected, nonarousing TV program or video can often be the perfect remedy to ease the household tension at this time of the day. Of course, in this case, the parents have control over the selection. But studies show that children do select relaxing shows themselves. Just as sensation-seeking behavior is a function of one's arousal set point, so too may be the tendency to use TV for relaxation. Of course, at any given time, any person may choose a TV program for the purposes of relaxation. But those who have high arousal set points that need to be lowered may be particularly likely to choose this kind of entertainment repeatedly.

Escape You have probably found yourself at one time or another using the media as an **escape** from the unpleasant duties and occupations that you have in real life. This escape behavior has been documented by uses and gratifications researchers in connection with TV. It may also be related to TV addiction discussed under the habit motive for TV use. Just as a drug addict seeks escape from reality through drug use, the TV addict may be seeking to find an escape from the stresses and strains of life through TV programs. While this motive has been documented by uses and gratifications researchers, not much is known about when such behavior may be healthy or unhealthy.

Passing Time A final motive for TV use is simply to **pass the time.** It is not uncommon today to find TV screens in a variety of public places where people have to wait for things to happen. When people sit in a doctor's waiting room, watching TV helps to pass the time if the doctor is running behind schedule. In the last 2 weeks, I have seen TV in two places where I had never encountered it before: in a hotel elevator and at the gas pump. As the pace of life seems to be increasing, people are less tolerant of situations in which they are forced to wait for something. Waiting creates frustration. If a person can catch up on the headlines while waiting for the gas tank to fill or waiting for the elevator to make it to the 20th floor, perhaps this frustration decreases a little. Major airlines caught on to this principle years ago when they started to offer movies on longer flights. They discovered that people would pay a few dollars for the headphones and watch a film that they might not order at home or rent at the local video store. Why? The reason is very simple. On an airplane, there is little else to do. Watching a movie helps to pass the time.

THE PROBLEM WITH SELF-REPORTS

One common criticism of the uses and gratifications perspective is that it relies heavily upon self-reports. Are people able to report accurately about the reasons they use the media? If they are able to report accurately, are they always motivated to do so? These are important questions that researchers can never answer definitively for all time. That is, whenever a given study is undertaken, these two questions must be considered. In answer to the first question, the chances of getting accurate answers about motivations improve with the recency of the behavior in question. You might be able to report quite accurately that the reason you watched the news last night was to find out how the weather would be for the football game today. But if you were called upon to report on your motivations for watching the news 6 weeks ago, you might have to resort to a reasonable speculation about your behavior. It may or may not be accurate.

The second question concerns whether or not people might deliberately misrepresent their viewing motives. One of the primary reasons that people might do this is because of **social desirability.** That is, they may want to make themselves look good for the researchers. As a professor, I might consider it more desirable to report that I watched TV in order to become better informed, instead of simply to pass the time or escape from life's stress. Passing the time doesn't sound quite compatible with the notion that as a professor, I should be concerned about learning things. In order to save face, I might be tempted to alter my response. Researchers can counter the tendency for people to respond out of social desirability by assuring them that their responses are completely confidential or even anonymous. These promises combined with an emphasis in the questionnaire's instructions that only honest answers are valuable to the researchers can be effective tools to combat social desirability. In the final analysis, researchers need to stay sensitive to the potential problems of self-report data. While these reports can sometimes be flawed, our knowledge about mass communication would be significantly impoverished without them.

TIME SPENT WITH MEDIA

When it comes to the topic of time spent with the media, it would be difficult to know much at all unless we relied on self-report data. You have probably read or heard about some of the statistics that are generated from surveys about media use. In fact, the data indicate that people spend rather large quantities of time processing media messages of one sort or another.

The most recent large-scale survey of media use was reported by the Kaiser Family Foundation.[14] The focus of this report was upon children and adolescents up to the age of 18. Included in the survey were questions about multiple media sources, including television, videotapes, movies, video games, print media, radio, CDs, and computers. What did the results show? First, regarding television use, it is important to note that viewing begins at a very young age. Even among children in the 2–4 age category, average viewing totals 2 hours daily. Children reach the peak of their TV watching by the time they reach the end of grade school (about 3½ hours daily). In later adolescence, viewing drops off to about 2¾ hours daily. One interesting finding that emerged from the study was that when all children (2–18 years old) and all media were considered together, the average amount of time spent with media was about 5½ hours. But during that 5½ hours, children were exposed to 6½ hours of media content! How is this possible? I need to think only of my own children to arrive at the answer. Too often, I have seen them surfing the Internet at the same time they are monitoring their favorite TV show. On the average, children use more than one medium at the same time for about 1 hour each day.

One major finding to emerge from the Kaiser Family Foundation survey was that reading time pales in comparison to time spent with TV. On the average, children between the ages of 2 and 18 spend only 25 minutes per day reading books, only 16 minutes per day reading magazines, and only 5 minutes per day reading newspapers. Many educators who are sobered by these meager reading statistics have placed their hope in the computer as the new educational tool for young people. But if this hope is to be realized, the findings from the survey will have to change radically in coming years. On the average, children between the ages of 2 and 18 only used the computer 34 minutes per day. And of those 34 minutes, 21 of them were devoted to recreational uses like games, chat rooms, and email. Only 8 minutes per day outside the classroom were devoted to schoolwork. The numbers for computer time will undoubtedly increase as more households acquire computers. But the survey showed that nearly 70% of households with children between 2 and 18 already own a computer, and nearly half have Internet access. Despite the explosive growth of computers, television is still the medium of choice for children and adolescents. During an average year, the average child spends the equivalent of nearly 2 solid months of 24-hour days doing nothing but watching TV.

When these statistics are combined with ones from the movie business, it all adds up to a large quantity of time watching moving images on a screen. The National Association of Theatre Owners recently reported that in 1999, 1.6 billion movie tickets were sold during the year in the United States and Canada.[15] The number of tickets sold annually in the United States has increased steadily over the last 5 years and is expected to continue in that direction for the next 5 years. This growth comes at the same time ticket prices are spiraling upwards. With all of this viewing time, it seems naïve to suggest that TV and movies are only innocuous sources of entertainment that have little or no impact on viewers. Starting with the next chapter, you will read about some of the effects associated with particular kinds of media content. But for now, let's focus on a different question: Apart from the content of TV and movies, does simply spending time watching the content have any unique effects that researchers have been able to document? The answer to this question seems to be yes. Let's look briefly at some of the effects that have been examined.

The Displacement Hypothesis

For a number of years, researchers have been concerned about the possibility that the large quantity of time spent with media (primarily television) was serving to displace time that would ordinarily be spent in other important activities. This general idea has become known as the **displacement hypothesis.** The basic notion is that people have a limited amount of time in their daily routines that can be allocated to different activities. If, as the data seem to show, the time spent watching TV and movies has increased over the years, then it would seem logical to suspect that the time spent in some other activities must necessarily have decreased. Depending upon what those other activities might be, there could be reason for concern. The symmetric version of the displacement hypothesis would suggest that if TV viewing decreased, the amount of time spent in other activities would correspondingly increase.

Relative to other areas, there are fewer studies that examine the displacement hypothesis directly. One study that was specifically designed to investigate this idea was a survey (panel design) of children in South Africa. The authors of the study, **Diana Mutz, Donald Roberts,** and **D. P. van Vuuren,** examined data on nearly 2,000 children over an 8-year period.[16] Each year, they questioned the children about the way they spent their time. The results of this study show that if a displacement effect exists, it isn't very large. The study began in 1974, and TV wasn't introduced to South Africa until 1976. Consequently, the authors were able to study the direct impact of TV in a way that can rarely be studied today. Initially, TV seemed to displace radio listening and movie attendance, but not other important activities. In fact, the authors reported that over 60% of children's viewing time came from activities that could be regarded as very marginal in terms of their overall importance.

Another major study that employed a longitudinal design (panel study) was reported by **Tannis MacBeth Williams** and **A. Gordon Handford.**[17] These researchers took advantage of a unique situation in Canada prior to the advent of TV in one of the towns they studied. Over a period of several years, the researchers studied three towns. One of the towns (referred to as "Notel") had no access to television at the study's outset. Another town ("Unitel") had access to only one TV station. Finally, a third town ("Multitel") had access to four stations. Just after the initial baseline data were collected from grade-school children in all three towns, Notel received access to a single TV station. Two years later, the researchers returned to each town and collected more data. At that time, Unitel had gained a second TV signal, and Multitel still had access to four stations. By studying the same children 2 years later and the kinder-garten children who had subsequently moved into grade school in the interim, the researchers could see if changes had occurred in the towns that increased their access to TV (Notel and Unitel). The results of the study revealed that television definitely had an impact on other activities. The authors concluded the following:

> Television apparently has little if any impact on the number of commu-
> nity activities available, but it has a noticeable negative effect on partici-
> pation in those activities. Involvement in community activities, summing
> across the categories, was greatest in the absence of television and fell sig-
> nificantly following its arrival in Notel . . . Television's negative impact
> was greatest for sports, and the effect was stronger for youths than for
> adults. There was also reasonably clear evidence to implicate television
> in decreased attendance at dances, suppers, and parties, and again, the
> effect was stronger for youths than adults. (pp. 182–183)

Displacement of Important Activities Of course, what constitutes a mar-ginal activity or an important activity may be debated. Should the effects from the Canadian study be regarded as ones that implicate TV in displacing impor-tant activities, or marginal ones? You may not tend to think that attending sup-pers and dances is very important. But sometimes, activities that seem trivial may not be so trivial when examined more closely. If TV viewing has a tendency to decrease opportunities for social interaction, perhaps people will lose the many benefits that come from close social ties. A psychologist, **David Myers,** has recently noted that in the United States, a number of disturbing social trends seem to point toward a decline in close connections between people.[18] For example, he discusses the decline in marriage, the reduction of social networks, the increase in individualism, a decline in civility, and so forth. Could these symptoms in society be related to increases in time spent with mass media? For the most part, these issues have yet to be explored by researchers.

Despite the lack of research in some areas related to the displacement hypothesis, researchers have examined certain issues. Child psychologists argue that developing children need to engage in a proper amount of fantasy play in order to maintain an optimum level of stimulation that encourages healthy growth. Does watching TV encourage such fantasy play or discourage it? In a major review on the research pertaining to this question, two researchers, **Tom van der Voort** and **Patti Valkenburg,** concluded that the best evidence suggests that TV viewing discourages fantasy play through a displacement effect.[19] The effect may depend upon the type of content viewed. In some rare cases, educational programs may actually stimulate fantasy play. Programs with high levels of violence reduce fantasy play, while nonviolent programs appear to have little impact either way.

One of the chief concerns among educators is that watching TV disrupts academic learning by displacing important educational activities such as reading. A team of researchers studied this issue by collecting diaries from preschool children over a 3-year period.[20] Once completed, the diaries contained information about the amount of time spent in a variety of different activities. In one sense, the results from this study show some support for the displacement hypothesis. As children spent more time watching TV, they tended to spend less time on activities related to education, talking to others, or playing video games. But the general relationship between TV viewing and these activities depended upon a number of other factors including the type of content viewed and the overall quality of the home environment. For example, watching educational TV programs did not result in any decrease in educational activities.

From these data, it appears as if the displacement hypothesis may not be a simple phenomenon. In a study conducted by **W. J. (James) Potter,** more data emerged in support of the idea that the displacement hypothesis probably didn't operate in a simplistic fashion.[21] While Potter did uncover a negative relationship between TV viewing and academic achievement (as viewing increased, achievement decreased), the relationship didn't appear to kick in until TV viewing had reached at least 10 hours per week. This kind of relationship is referred to as a **threshold effect.** In this case, no negative impact from TV viewing was observed until the 10-hours-per-week threshold had been crossed.

Educators generally agree that one of the most important skills learned during the educational process is reading. How does television viewing affect the acquisition of reading skill? Is there a negative impact and, if so, is that impact due to a displacement effect? Do children read less because they watch TV more? The available data on these questions do not permit a strong conclusion. The issue was examined extensively by the researchers who conducted the study of Notel, Unitel, and Multitel in Canada. They concluded that there was a small negative correlation between TV viewing and reading skill, but they argued that this relationship was probably not evidence of a direct impact of TV viewing. Instead, in the opinion of these authors, "[C]hildren who are more fluent readers tend to be more intelligent, to read more, and to watch television less." Consequently, it may be that the negative relationship between television viewing and reading skill has more to do with the fact that both of these things are related to intelligence, amount of reading, and other third-variable explanations.

Television Viewing and Obesity

Before I began writing this section of the chapter, I noticed that there was an exciting football game on TV. I also noticed that it was getting late in the afternoon and that I had not yet gone out for my 30-minute jog around the neighborhood. As I became more involved in the game, I found myself thinking that I might put off my jog until the next day. Fortunately, I resisted this temptation—partly because I knew that if I jogged, I would find it easier to read through the research for this section when I came back. The notion that television viewing might lead to obesity seems like a pretty reasonable conjecture. If TV displaces other activities, then perhaps it displaces activities like jogging and other forms of physical exercise that help keep extra pounds off. TV viewing may also encourage extra eating that could also lead to additional pounds. Obesity has recently attracted public attention as a health problem. On October 27, 1999, the *Journal of the American Medical Association* devoted an entire issue to obesity, which the editors noted was a major risk factor for heart disease. An estimated 97 million American adults (over half the population) are considered to be overweight. Is it possible that the large quantities of media use documented earlier in this chapter have something to do with the nation's proclivity toward being overweight? Is there any evidence that watching television may be playing a negative role in this national health problem? The current evidence is pretty intriguing.

Over 20 years ago, a sample of 1,000 respondents solicited through a questionnaire in the *National Enquirer* answered questions about their weight and their TV viewing.[22] The results of the study revealed that TV viewing was indeed positively correlated with snacking behavior. When the sample was broken down into subgroups, the results showed that 52% of the people who watched more than 28 hours of TV each week were overweight, compared to only 33% of those who watched fewer hours of TV. In another study of nearly 400 adolescent males whose average age was around 16, it turned out that those who watched less TV were not any less obese than those who watched more TV, but they were in much better physical condition.[23]

The most recent evidence on TV viewing and obesity establishes a positive relationship between these two variables. In a large-scale survey of nearly 5,000 women over the age of 19, those who watched 3–4 hours of TV per day were compared to those who watched less than 1 hour per day.[24] Those who watched 3–4 hours each day had twice the rate of obesity. It is important to remember that any correlation such as this one could be the result of some other variable that is related, in this case, to both obesity and TV viewing. But

> **STUDY BOX 4-2   Compute the Relationship Between Body Mass Index and Daily TV Viewing for Your Class**
>
> You can calculate the correlation between body mass index and daily TV viewing for your own class. Have your instructor coordinate the following exercise. First, have each student estimate the number of hours spent watching TV on a daily basis. Second, have each student compute his or her own body mass index. Body mass index is computed according to the following formula:
>
> 1.   Multiply weight in pounds by 700 (e.g., 190 lbs × 700 = 133,000)
> 2.   Divide that number by height in inches (e.g., 133,000 / 66 in. = 2,015)
> 3.   Divide the result by height in inches again (e.g., 2,015 / 66 in. = 30.53)
>
> The resulting BMI = 30.53.
>
> Your instructor can take the average hours of TV viewing and the BMI from each member of the class and compute a correlation coefficient using some statistical software. (If the class is relatively small, a hand calculator could be used after consulting any statistics text for the computational formula for the correlation coefficient.) What did you find? Were TV viewing and BMI related for your class? What do you think these results mean?

the authors of this study considered several variables like age, level of education, and weekly amount of exercise. Even controlling for the impact of these variables on the relationship, TV viewing was still positively correlated with obesity levels.

In the study that included more respondents than any other on this topic, a team of researchers studied over 20,000 males in the health profession who were between the ages of 41 and 78.[25] The results of this study showed a clear relationship between TV viewing and obesity. Some of the men reported watching TV over 41 hours per week. Others reported watching a maximum of only 1 hour per week. The men in the first group were over four times more likely to be obese than the men in the second group. The authors of the study concluded that watching TV (or the VCR) contributed to men's obesity.

One final study of interest in this area was conducted on nearly 2,500 Pima Indians.[26] The researchers in this study concluded that physical activity and watching TV were both related to body mass index—a new measure of obesity (see Study Box 4-2). The preponderance of the evidence on the relationship between TV viewing and obesity shows that the two variables are related. Many of the researchers have concluded that the relationship is causal in that TV viewing displaces physical activity and consequently leads to more obesity. While this may well be true, recall from chapter 2 the cautions about interpreting correlations as evidence for causality. What seems to be missing from the current literature on this topic is an experimental-type design that manipulates TV viewing and measures its impact on obesity. Until such a study is done, we have to settle with the knowledge that TV viewing and obesity are related, and there is good reason to suspect that the relationship is partly due to the fact that TV viewing displaces physical activity.

SUMMARY

This chapter started by reviewing some of the reasons that people have for using the media. With so many different reasons, it isn't surprising to find that daily media use is quite substantial. With people spending so much time with mass media, the question about the effects of all this time has occupied the attention of researchers for years. Apart from the content that people are processing, some research has focused on the impact of the time spent in and of itself. The major focus of this research is upon the displacement hypothesis—the idea that time spent on media use displaces other activities. Some research does indicate that TV viewing displaces social activities, reduces children's fantasy play, and leads to obesity by reducing physical activity. In the final analysis, mass-communication researchers need to study this topic with renewed vigor. The possibility that heavy media use decreases social interaction and contributes to higher levels of social isolation is one hypothesis that deserves to be taken seriously. The consequences of such a possibility are profound. Perhaps your course instructor may want to lead a classroom discussion on this topic and provide you with an opportunity to express your views.

KEY TERMS AND CONCEPTS

The uses and gratifications perspective 58

Motivations for media use 58

learning 59

habit 60

companionship 60

arousal 61

relaxation 61

escape 62

pass time 62

TV addiction 60

Parasocial relationships 61

Optimal level of arousal 61

set point 61

Sensation seeking 61

Social desirability in the problem of self-reports 62

The displacement hypothesis 64

Threshold effect 66

KEY NAMES

Elihu Katz, Jay Blumler, and Michael Gurevitch 58

Bradley Greenberg 58

Alan Rubin 59

Robin Smith 60

Robert McIlwraith 60

Byron Reeves and Clifford Nass 60

Elizabeth Perse and Rebecca Rubin 61

Donald Hebb 61

Marvin Zuckerman 61

Diana Mutz, Donald Roberts, and D. P. van Vuuren 64

Tannis MacBeth Williams and A. Gordon Handford 65　　　David Myers 65

Tom van der Voort and Patti Valkenburg 66　　　W. J. (James) Potter 66

WEB LINKS

1. For information on the Kaiser Family Foundation Research on Children & Media, try . . . http://www.kff.org/content/1999/1535/

2. For information on what the American Academy of Pediatrics says about TV and the developing brain, try . . . http://www.aap.org/advocacy/chm98nws.htm

3. For information on the relationship between television use and obesity, try . . . http://www.mercola.com/1998/mar/30/tv_and_obesity_in_children.htm

To learn more about the topics in this chapter, enter the Key Terms and Concepts and Key Names found in this chapter as subject and keyword searches on your InfoTrac College Edition.

NOTES

1. Cohn, B. (Producer), & Barry, M. (Writer). (1981). *Remember When.* Home Box Office.

2. Katz, E., Blumler, J. G., & Gurevitch, M. (1973). Uses and gratifications research. *Public Opinion Quarterly, 37,* 509–523.

3. Greenberg, B. S. (1974). Gratifications of television viewing and their correlates for British children. In J. G. Blumler & E. Katz (Eds.), *The uses of mass communication: Current perspectives on gratifications research* (pp. 71–92). Beverly Hills, CA: Sage.

4. Rubin, A. M. (1979). Television use by children and adolescents. *Human Communication Research, 5,* 109–120.

5. Winn, M. (1977). *The plug-in drug.* New York: Bantam.

6. Smith, R. (1986). Television addiction. In J. Bryant and D. Zillmann (Eds.), *Perspectives on media effects* (pp. 109–128). Hillsdale, NJ: Erlbaum.

7. Greenberg, J. L., Lewis, S. E., & Dodd, D. K. (1999). Overlapping addictions and self-esteem among college men and women. *Addictive Behaviors, 24,* 565–571.

8. McIlwraith, R. D. (1998). I'm addicted to television: The personality, imagination, and TV watching patterns of self-identified TV addicts. *Journal of Broadcasting & Electronic Media, 42,* 371–386.

9. Kubey, R. W. (1996). Television dependence, diagnosis, and prevention: With commentary on video games, pornography, and media education. In T. M. MacBeth (Ed.), *Tuning in to young viewers: Social science perspectives on television* (pp. 221–260). Thousand Oaks, CA: Sage.

10. Reeves, B., & Nass, C. (1996). *The media equation: How people treat computers, television, and new media like real people and places.* Cambridge: Cambridge University Press.

11. Perse, E. M., & Rubin, R. B. (1989). Attribution in social and parasocial relationships. *Communication Research, 16,* 59–77.

12. Zuckerman, M. (1979). *Sensation seeking: Beyond the optimal level of arousal.* Hillsdale, NJ: Erlbaum.

13. Zuckerman, M. (1996). Sensation seeking and the taste for vicarious horror. In J. B. Weaver III & R. Tamborini (Eds.), *Horror films: Current research on audience preferences and reactions* (pp. 147–160). Hillsdale, NJ: Erlbaum. Lawrence, P. A., & Palmgreen, P. C. (1996). A uses and gratifications analysis of horror film preference.

In J. B. Weaver III & R. Tamborini (Eds.), *Horror films: Current research on audience preferences and reactions* (pp. 161–178). Hillsdale, NJ: Erlbaum.

14. Roberts, D. F., Foehr, U. G., Rideout, V. J., & Brodie, M. (November, 1999). Kids & media @ the new millennium. Henry J. Kaiser Family Foundation [Online]. Available: http://www.kff.org/content/1999/1535/KidsReport%20FINAL.pdf

15. Madigan, N. (1999, November 18). Moviegoers to hit 1.6 billion in 1999. Entertainment Headlines [Online]. Available: http://dailynews.yahoo.com/h/nm/1999 1118/en/film-admissions_1.html

16. Mutz, D. C., Roberts, D. F., & van Vuuren, D. P. (1993). Reconsidering the displacement hypothesis: Television's influence on children's use of time. *Communication Research, 20,* 51–75.

17. Williams, T. M., & Handford, A. G. (1986). Television and other leisure activities. In T. M. Williams (Ed.), *The impact of television: A natural experiment in three communities.* Orlando, FL.: Academic Press.

18. Myers, D. G. (1999). Close relationships and quality of life. In D. Kahneman, E. Diener, & N. Schwarz (Eds.), *Well-being: The foundations of hedonic psychology* (pp. 374–391). New York: Russell Sage Foundation.

19. van der Voort, T. H. A., & Valkenburg, P. M. (1994). Television's impact on fantasy play: A review of research. *Developmental Review, 14,* 227–251.

20. Huston, A. C., Wright, J. C., Marquis, J., & Green, S. B. (1999). How young children spend their time: Television and other activities. *Developmental Psychology, 35,* 912–925.

21. Potter, W. J. (1987). Does television viewing hinder academic achievement among adolescents? *Human Communication Research, 14,* 27–46.

22. Forrest, D. V., & Ryan, J. H. (1977). The National Enquirer TV poll. *Journal of Biological Psychology, 19,* 16–20.

23. Tucker, L. A. (1986). The relationship of television viewing to physical fitness and obesity., *Adolescence, 21,* 797–806.

24. Tucker, L. A., & Bagwell, M. (1991). Television viewing and obesity in adult females. *American Journal of Public Health, 81,* 908–911.

25. Ching, P. L. Y. H., Willett, W. C., Rimm, E. B., & Colditz, G. A. (1996). Activity level and risk of overweight in male health professionals. *American Journal of Public Health, 86,* 25–30.

26. Fitzgerald, S. J., Kriska, A. M., Pereira, M. A., & DeCourten, M. P. (1997). Associations among physical activity, television watching, and obesity in adult Pima Indians. *Medicine & Science in Sports & Exercise, 29,* 910–915.

5

■

Effects of
Media Violence

Most people know Rod Serling's name because of his brilliant creativity in the hit TV series *The Twilight Zone*. Fewer people know about Serling's unfortunate venture into the world of made-for-TV movies. In a way, Serling's movie, *The Doomsday Flight* (1966), was his own journey into the Twilight Zone. The premise of the film was a sure winner for the NBC network. It promised to be a suspense-packed adventure from beginning to end. After a routine passenger jet took off and established its flight path, a report came in that the plane was carrying an altitude bomb. A terrorist had set the bomb to explode if the plane descended below 5,000 feet.

As planned, the movie was a ratings success. In the end, the plane managed to land in Denver, which was barely 5,000 feet above sea level. The plane averted disaster and everyone lived happily ever after. Well, almost everyone. Those who worked in the airline industry on the evening that *The Doomsday Flight* made its debut were not so happy. Even before the movie ended, there was a bomb threat phoned in to one of the major airlines. Four more were phoned in during the next day and eight more were reported by week's end. In some cases, the threats were for exactly the same kind of altitude bomb depicted in the movie.

Fortunately, none of these threats turned out to be real. Still, it was a time of tension and high anxiety for airline pilots, crew members, executives, and family members waiting for loved ones. They had been the victims of what media researchers know as the **copycat phenomenon.** People sometimes imitate the exact behaviors that they see depicted in the media. When those behaviors are violent or illegal, this translates into a significant social problem. Rod Serling felt such regret at this unanticipated effect of his movie that he issued a public apology to the nation and requested that the movie never be shown again.[1]

Rod Serling was not the first person—or the last—to feel the unanticipated effects of the copycat effect. Several years before the O. J. Simpson trial turned a spotlight on domestic violence, the ABC network aired a movie depicting spouse abuse. *The Burning Bed* (1984) starred Farrah Fawcett Majors as a battered housewife who felt so desperately trapped by an abusive husband that she did the unthinkable. In what she believed was her only avenue of escape, she soaked her husband's bed in gasoline while he slept. Then, she set the bed—and her husband—ablaze.

In the drama based on a real-life occurrence, she escaped a murder conviction. The court held that she had acted in self-defense. Many experts recognize this movie as one that encourages battered women to seek shelter in the professional help community. Unfortunately, researchers also recognize that the film triggered some rather nasty copycat consequences. In the days following the broadcast, several women around the country who were victims of abuse decided to copy the behavior of the main character in the televised drama. They murdered their husbands. In a few cases, the scenario for the crime was exactly the same as depicted in the movie. Women doused beds with gasoline and set their sleeping husbands on fire.

Scholars have documented the phenomenon of copycat crime regularly since the dawn of TV. Survey results indicate that as many as one third of the males convicted for felonies admit that they have imitated crime techniques shown on TV. Newspapers reported early copycat incidents back in the late 1950s and helped to trigger a massive effort to investigate the effects of television and movie violence. The controversy over media violence has raged ever since. One of the most recent incidents hit the news in February 2001 and stirred the controversy anew. According to one report, a young teen set his friend on fire after seeing the same stunt acted out on the MTV program *Jackass*. His friend suffered second- and third-degree burns over most of his body. Of the hundreds upon hundreds of studies that scholars have published on the effects of television and movies, violence is, by far, the most frequent topic of investigation.

The government's threat in 1996 to introduce a rating system for television programs designed to protect children from the unwanted effects of violence and other objectionable content spurred the networks to act. A new rating system went into effect amid great controversy. Manufacturers now produce TV sets with a V-chip that permits parents to block out programs that contain unwanted violence.

Should we be making all of this fuss over media violence? Is the murder and mayhem on television really to blame for the increased violence in society? Would copycat criminals eventually commit their crimes even if a TV program or movie never inspired them to act? The answers to these questions are not simple. The researchers who have conducted the studies over the years sometimes disagree among themselves. Nevertheless, if one examines the research carefully, it is possible to make some sense of the mountain of data.

What exactly do we know today about the effects of media violence? In the few pages that follow, I have tried to provide brief, accurate summaries of the many dimensions surrounding this complicated body of research.

THE PRESENCE OF VIOLENT CONTENT

George Gerbner, professor emeritus at Temple University and former dean of the Annenberg School of Communication, has directed a series of studies over the years that he designed in order to tell us something about how much violence there is on television. In short, Gerbner's finding was that there was a large amount of violence on prime-time TV, and that despite public controversy over the years, the level of violence had remained fairly constant.[2]

It isn't difficult to understand why our entertainment media contains a steady staple of violence. Good drama revolves around conflict, and violence is one of the common consequences of conflict. However, in the early days of the TV medium, the notion that people in the average home would have their set on for over 7 hours per day would have been incomprehensible. As recently as 1950, only one home in ten even had a TV. A decade later, only one home in ten was without one. The idea of having over 50 channels to select from— 24 hours a day—would have been laughable in 1950. Nevertheless, in the 1990s, it became a reality.

As the statistics on TV viewing changed, the sheer amount of violence being beamed into the average American household went beyond what anyone could have imagined. Today's estimates of viewing time, combined with what we know about how much violence is present, produces some very sobering numbers.

Newton Minow, former chairman of the Federal Communications Commission, noted in his recent book,[3] "By first grade, most children have spent the equivalent of three school years in front of the TV set." By age 18, time spent with TV exceeds time spent in school, time talking with teachers, time talking with friends, and time talking with parents. By age 70, today's average child will have over 7 years invested in TV viewing. Total viewing time varies with age, but the average child, regardless of age, spends over 3 hours each day in front of the tube. How much of that viewing time contains violence?

According to George Gerbner, children's shows contain more violence than any other type of programming. He estimates that shows designed for kids average about 32 violent acts per hour. Based on a study that spans 15 years, Gerbner estimates that crime is about 10 times more prevalent on TV than it is in the real world. According to the American Psychological Association, the typical child views over 8,000 murders and over 100,000 acts of TV violence over the course of a lifetime. These are conservative estimates.

So, there is little question about whether violence saturates our TV screens. No one can dispute this fact. The most recent studies have attempted to capture more than just the number of violent acts. In the recent *National Television Violence Study,*[4] researchers examined the context of violence. These data help to give us an even deeper understanding about what is happening on the screen.

According to these most recent content studies, nearly 60% of all television programming contains some violence. One third of all programs contain nearly 10 violent interactions. These statistics confirm what we knew from earlier research. Violence is prevalent on the tube. But how is it depicted? In nearly 75% of all of the scenes depicting violence, there is no punishment given for the violent actions. This finding takes on real significance when we consider it in the light of Albert Bandura's theory of social learning, which I discuss below.

How realistic are the portrayals of violence? The newest data show that in over half of all violent interactions, no character is depicted as experiencing pain. And fewer than half of the violent interactions result in negative consequences for the perpetrator of aggression. There is ample room for concern about the lessons that media violence might be teaching to TV audiences.

But we have to be careful at this point. While the content studies clearly show that there is a lot of violence, the studies have *nothing* to say about how that violence may be affecting people. Remember from chapter 2 that it isn't possible to make inferences about media effects just from the content alone. It is at least possible that all of that TV violence amounts to a kind of warning about how we ought *not* to behave. Maybe the best way to deal with the violent urges inside of us is to turn on the tube and purge these impulses by indulging our wildest violent fantasies. Over the years, a few scholars have suggested that this idea might have some merit. We will look at this idea in a later section in this chapter. The important point here is that we must resist the temptation to look at the content of the media and assume that there must be a particular effect on people. People can react to the very same content in a number of ways. A person could react by walking away from a program and forgetting that it existed. No matter how strong the tendency to think otherwise, it is important to recognize that **content does not equal effect.**

One of my favorite illustrations of this point about the difference between content and effect comes from the world of TV advertising. Several years ago, a clever person who was working on the ad campaign for Domino's Pizza invented a strange little cartoon character to star in the pizza commercials. This character was named the "Noid," probably because his name sounded like the word *annoy*. The Noid's sole purpose of existence was to find ways to make pizza cold before people could eat it. Domino's boasted fast delivery times and a special packing method that guaranteed the delivery of hot pizza. Their ad slogan was very simple: One could "avoid the Noid" by ordering from Domino's.

The people at Domino's loved the concept and the ads went on the air. Based on the content of the ad, it seemed easy to speculate about the effect: People would buy more pizzas. And that probably was one of the effects of the campaign. But the people at Domino's could not possibly have imagined in their most awful nightmare what was to happen next. Out there in the vast urban sprawl, there lived a little man named Mr. Noid. Mr. Noid was not playing with a full deck. He was a troubled person who had not yet figured out what TV was all about. Mr. Noid undoubtedly suffered from paranoia. When Mr. Noid slouched back on the couch one evening and saw the pizza commercial that told the whole world to avoid the Noid, he became furious. He couldn't believe the audacity of a major pizza chain taking out national advertising in order to tell the people of the world to avoid *him*. What had he possibly done to deserve such treatment? He searched his memory long and hard to try to remember if he had done something to make his local Domino's Pizzeria mad at him. He just couldn't understand why he was under personal attack. He had to do something drastic.

The next thing the people at Domino's knew, one of their pizzerias was making national news. There was a hostage crisis. Someone named Mr. Noid was holding hostage the customers and employees at one of their stores. Noid's demand was simple: Discontinue that advertising before it ruined his prospects for any enduring friendship with another human being. Mr. Noid didn't kill anyone in the hostage crisis, and I haven't seen the Noid on a Domino's commercial for several years. Things could have turned out far worse than they did.[5]

The example of Mr. Noid is one of my favorites because it is so unusual. And in fact this sort of case is not likely to happen often. A more common example of the principle that media effects cannot be inferred accurately from an analysis of content comes from research on attitudes toward AIDS. **Joy Berrenberg** and her colleagues wanted to know whether an educational film on AIDS prevention actually brought about positive effects in viewers. In a simple experiment, the researchers discovered that undergraduate students who watched the film expressed increased fear and dislike of a hypothetical person with AIDS. The film also increased viewers' perceptions that AIDS was a preventable disease. After studying their data, the researchers concluded that films that emphasize disease prevention may actually create a tendency for viewers to "blame the victim" when they confront others with the disease. In this case, an educational film with "positive" content may actually create some undesirable and unanticipated effects in many viewers.[6]

One lesson to be learned from these examples is that the human capacity to react in unanticipated ways to media messages must be carefully respected. For this reason, we have to be cautious about looking at any media content like violence and jumping to conclusions about how that content is affecting the viewers. The number of possible effects may be large. Of course, it is also possible that there are no significant effects at all. In order to find out whether violent content really affects viewers, carefully designed research studies are the most trustworthy sources.

THE CAUSAL LINK BETWEEN VIEWING
VIOLENCE AND BEHAVING AGGRESSIVELY

The Research of Albert Bandura

Since the late 1950s, researchers have attempted to answer the question about whether viewing media violence actually causes people to behave more aggressively. **Albert Bandura,** a Stanford psychologist, designed some of the earliest studies with children. He had a theory about how TV viewing could cause

people to act in particular ways. His theory (**social learning theory**) emphasized the importance of **rewards** and **punishments.**

According to Bandura, if a child watched a person on TV who seemed
very attractive and who received rewards for acting aggressively, then the child
would be more likely to imitate that character's behavior. On the other hand,
if a child saw a character who received punishment for acting aggressively, then
the child might refrain from acting out any aggressive impulses in real life.
Bandura's theory was not just about TV. It was a general theory about the way
people learn behaviors. The basic principles could explain how children learn
to help people as well as hurt them. Many of his experiments tested the theory
with TV and violence because the government was giving out grant money to
do research on that topic.

In a typical experiment that Bandura designed, he randomly assigned children to watch one of two different videos. In one version, one of the leading
characters acted aggressively and received rewards for his actions. In the other
version, the same aggressive behavior received punishment. When the video was
over, Bandura permitted the children to play freely in a room where his assis-
tants could carefully monitor what happened. They counted the number of times
each of the children imitated one of the acts of aggression that they had seen in
the video.

The results of these studies are consistent. Children who saw aggressive
behavior rewarded were more likely to imitate the aggression than the children
who saw it punished. Critics complained that some of Bandura's early studies
used videos that didn't come from actual TV shows. In addition, Bandura considered it "aggressive" when children smacked a large "bobo" doll that toymak-
ers specifically designed for that purpose. Bandura overcame these early problems with additional studies, and scholars around the world now accept the basic
principle of social learning.[7]

The results of Bandura's studies should come as no surprise to most parents.
When my own children were young, I can remember them tuning in reli-
giously to the popular animated series, *He-Man*. When the neighborhood children would come over to play afterwards, they often pretended to be the characters from the show. I watched many a heated argument over who was going
to take the role of the hero, He-Man, and who was reluctantly going to accept
the evil role of his arch rival, Skeletor. If I ever needed to intervene once the
play began, it was usually because the person playing He-Man was busy perform-
ing his heroic—yet very aggressive—actions. The person who was He-Man
had a license to be aggressive. He-Man was a good guy who received rewards
for his aggressive acts.

Bandura's studies helped researchers to understand a number of things about
TV violence and children. First, viewing TV violence could cause children to
behave more aggressively, particularly if the violent characters were attractive
and received rewards for their actions.

Second, in many of these studies, the effects emerged most strongly for boys
—not girls. Many researchers interpret this finding in the context of biological differences between the sexes. Throughout the animal kingdom, nature has

---

STUDY BOX 5-1　Prolonged Exposure to Media Violence

Dolf Zillmann and James Weaver reported an experiment with college students that was designed to test the impact of prolonged exposure to media violence. They recruited 93 students (53 males, 40 females) to participate in the study. These students were randomly assigned to one of two film-viewing groups. In the "innocuous film" condition, they watched *Little Man Tate, Driving Miss Daisy, Rich in Love,* and *Postcards from the Edge* on successive days. In the "violent film" condition, students watched *Universal Soldier, Under Siege, The Hitman,* and *Excessive Force.* The day after they watched the last movie, the participants were told that they were needed to help identify emotional expressions on the faces of people in photographs. After each participant completed this task, he or she was provided with either positive or negative feedback that was given randomly. Some of the participants were told that they had done a good job. Others were told that their ratings were terrible or awful. After this task, each participant was brought to a professor's office and given a form to complete about the experimenter who had given them the feedback. The form asked the participant to provide a rating of how deserving the experimenter would be to receive financial support as a research helper. It also asked the participant, "If you had to make a Yes or No decision [for financial support], what would it be?" These measures were taken by the researchers to be an opportunity for the participants to express hostility toward the assistant. The results indicated that both male and female participants who had watched the violent films earlier in the week were much more likely to express hostility in their ratings of the assistant. Of great interest to the researchers, this effect held regardless of the nature of the feedback the assistant had delivered in the ratings task. The researchers concluded that "the findings support the proposal that repeated, prolonged exposure to exceedingly violent drama is capable of facilitating hostile behavior for extended periods after exposure" (p. 159).

SOURCE: Zillmann, D., & Weaver, J. B., III. (1999). Effects of prolonged exposure to gratuitous media violence on provoked and unprovoked hostile behavior. *Journal of Applied Social Psychology, 29,* 145–156.

---

programmed the male of the species with a predisposition to behave more aggressively than the female. The researchers thought that perhaps this aggressive predisposition resulted in boys being more sensitive to the impact of media violence. As it turns out, some studies on media violence show that the effects extend to females as well as males. For a brief description of a recent study that found both sexes affected by media violence, see Study Box 5-1.

A third conclusion that can be drawn from Bandura's social learning effect is that the effect is quite general. It doesn't matter whether researchers make up the videos used in these experiments or borrow them from standard TV programs like old *Batman* and *Superman* cartoons. The principles remain the same. The presence of attractive TV characters who receive rewards for acting aggressively seems to promote more aggressive behavior in children.[8]

Finally, in studies of this type, it is important to understand that differences between the two experimental groups do not necessarily imply anything about a particular child. Not every child who saw the aggression being rewarded behaved aggressively after the video. Some of the children who saw the aggression punished acted aggressively just the same. In fact, as in most experiments of this type, *most* of the aggressive behavior that researchers observed after TV viewing was not the result of watching one of the two videos at all. There are many other factors that are important in determining aggressive behavior at any given instant. Probably one of the most crucial factors has to do with the years of modeling and teaching that children receive from parents and the other important adults in their lives. Still, although the effect of video violence observed in these experiments is statistically small, it is predictable and reliable.

While Bandura's studies offered initial insights into the effect of TV violence, many questions remained. One of the most important ones had to do with the type of aggression that researchers were measuring in these studies. Children were doing more hitting, kicking, biting, scratching, and so on in the context of playing with other children. What about more serious acts of aggression? When the government started funding Bandura's research, heavy interest was expressed in the possibility that media violence causes an actual increase in the crime rate. Could violence in the media really cause more beatings, robberies, assaults, and murders? This is a more difficult question to answer confidently. A number of researchers have tried to gather data that might help us to provide an answer. What about the possible relationship between media violence and more serious acts of aggression among adults?

The Long-Term Studies of
Leonard Eron and Rowell Huesmann

One of the most impressive lines of research in the area of media violence comes from two psychologists, **Leonard Eron** and **Rowell Huesmann.** Working together with other researchers (Lefkowitz and Walder) back in the 1960s, the team studied over 800 children under the age of 10. There were two things that were of particular interest. First, Eron and Huesmann wanted to know how much violence these children watched on TV. Second, they wanted to know how aggressive each child was in daily life activities. Through conversations and questionnaires given to parents, teachers, and the children themselves, they were able to assign a number to each child that indicated the quantity of violence in their daily diet of TV. Higher numbers indicated more violence. They were also able to assign another number to each child that indicated how aggressive the child was in day-to-day situations. After they gathered this information, they looked at the relationship between these two numbers across the entire group of children.

What did they find? Eron and Huesmann found that there was a tendency for those children who watched higher levels of TV violence to also have higher scores on the ratings of aggressive behavior. Researchers now recognize this finding as one that appears again and again in the literature. It might seem straightforward to conclude from this data that children are more aggressive because of their TV diet. Unfortunately, it isn't quite that easy. For one thing, since the researchers measured everything at the same time, there is no way to tell which came first—the TV viewing or the aggressive behavior.

Maybe children who behave aggressively like to watch more violent programs because they want to see people who act the way they do.

Even though the researchers found it intriguing that children who watched more violence were also more aggressive, they understood the need for more information. So, they waited. In fact, they waited until the children reached the age of 19. After collecting data on the 19-year-olds, they waited for another 11 years until the children were 30. At each of these two later ages, they gathered some new information about the criminal records that accumulated over the years. What kind of crimes and how many crimes did each person commit? How long were the prison sentences that the court assigned? After gathering these data, the researchers went back and examined how much violence these adults had watched on TV when they were children. The findings were interesting, to say the least. The children who had the higher numbers on TV violence also tended to be the adults who became involved in more serious crimes! Huesmann summarized the findings of the study when he wrote:

> Aggressive habits seem to be learned early in life, and once established, are resistant to change and predictive of serious adult antisocial behavior. If a child's observation of media violence promotes the learning of aggressive habits, it can have harmful lifelong consequences. Consistent with this theory, early television habits are in fact correlated with adult criminality. (pp. 129–130)[9]

Do these findings guarantee that if a child watches TV violence, a life of crime results? Not at all. First, it is important to understand that just as in the experiments done by Bandura, not every child who watched heavy amounts of TV violence ended up getting involved in crime. There was a tendency for this to be the case. Similar to Bandura's research, the tendency, even though it was definitely present, was small. Knowing the amount of TV violence children viewed only enabled the researchers to account for a small percentage of the crimes committed by the children as they matured over the 22-year period (less than 10%). Depending upon your perspective, we should view this small percentage as an alarming and important statistic, or we should view it as evidence that TV is not a very strong determiner of criminal behavior. One way to think about these two views is to consider a group of 10 children in your neighborhood. If these 10 children collectively committed 20 acts of aggression over some period of time, then the data indicate that perhaps two of these acts might be safely attributed to media violence. On one hand, this sounds like a small and insignificant effect. On the other hand, if this effect is multiplied for the total number of aggressive acts committed in society, it is easy to see reason for concern.

Second, even though the researchers could predict a certain number of crimes based on childhood viewing of TV violence, we can't be absolutely sure that the childhood viewing was a causal factor in the later crime that turned up in the lives of the adults. Perhaps there was something else about the families of the children that predisposed them to watch either violent or nonviolent programs. This same factor may have helped lead the children to either a life of crime or a life of civic responsibility. The researchers tried to measure as many of these other factors as possible. After using some sophisticated statistical analyses, they still concluded that the children's early TV viewing very likely contributed to criminal activity later in life.

Eron and Huesmann's research is important because it potentially links media violence with real-life violence. One of the criticisms made of many of the studies in this area is that we cannot extrapolate the results from laboratory studies to the real world. What other evidence might there be that television violence is a culprit in increasing real-life violence?

The Research of Brandon Centerwall

Dr. Brandon Centerwall graduated from Yale in 1975. He is a medical doctor and teaches at the University of Washington as a psychiatrist in the behavioral sciences. His analysis of crime statistics paints a very disturbing picture. In 1945, just before TV emerged on the scene in the United States, statistics show three homicides per 100,000 people. By 1974, that figure had doubled. Similar data emerged for Canada. One could argue that during these years, many changes occurred in addition to the introduction of TV. Centerwall agrees. However, in an exhaustive series of studies, Centerwall claims that the data really do point to TV as the major culprit in the rise of homicides.[10]

Centerwall selected other countries that were very similar to the United States in a number of ways. South Africa was one such country. When Centerwall examined the homicide rate in South Africa between 1945 and 1974, he discovered that the rate actually dropped by 7% during that time. Centerwall argues that one of the only major differences between South Africa and the United States during those years was the ban on TV imposed by the South African government. What happened in South Africa when the government lifted the ban in 1974? By 1983, the murder rate had increased by 56%. By 1990, the increase registered 130%—more than doubling in less than 20 years. The pattern of data strongly resembles the ones for the United States and Canada. In order to avoid a distorted picture of the data in South Africa due to racial tensions, Centerwall excluded all homicides against Blacks in his analysis of that country. Apparently when racial tension resulted in homicide in South Africa, Blacks were typically the victims.

While we can't be absolutely certain that Centerwall's analysis is correct, it is difficult to explain his findings without taking account of TV. Centerwall claims that roughly half of all homicides in the United States are a direct result of television. Even if we adopted a more conservative estimate, the numbers would still be serious.

The Catharsis Hypothesis

Even though the research considered so far has tended to indict media violence as a cause of aggression, some researchers were slow to accept this idea. **Seymour Feshbach** advanced one of the most popular alternative views very early in the violence controversy (1960s). Feshbach thought that viewing TV violence could actually be therapeutic for a person filled with anger or frustration. TV could help purge those pent-up emotions. He borrowed this idea from the ancient Greeks. The idea of **catharsis** (to cleanse or purge; to get rid of) goes back to the Greek culture, which thrived on good drama. The Greeks believed that a person could get rid of grief and misery by going to a play that featured other characters who were grieving.

Feshbach simply extended the idea of catharsis to media violence. He reasoned that a person could cleanse pent-up feelings of anger by watching other people act aggressively. According to him, media violence was actually a positive thing. It could tend to lower the amount of aggressive behavior that might occur if angry people couldn't release their frustrations by watching others act out violence on TV.

Feshbach reasoned that watching TV would tend to calm down angry people, making them less likely to react with intense anger. He also believed that watching violence would enable the angry people to engage in aggressive fantasies. If people could act out anger in their heads, then maybe they would have less need to act it out in real life. The network executives loved this theory. After all, if Feshbach was right about the effects of media violence, then the networks were actually providing an important public service by giving us a steady diet of TV violence. The crucial task for Feshbach was to actually prove that his idea had some merit.

The initial evidence that Feshbach offered in support of his theory looked convincing. He located a detention facility for boys and reasoned that the boys who lived in this place would be angry and frustrated about their situation. After gaining the cooperation of the authorities who ran the facility, Feshbach randomly assigned the boys to watch either a violent TV diet or a nonviolent TV diet for several weeks. Feshbach carefully monitored the behavior of each boy during the experiment. He relied on reports made by the houseparents of any incidents involving aggressive behavior. At the end of the study, the results were clear: The boys who had watched TV violence behaved *less* aggressively than the boys who had watched no violence. The results seemed to support the theory of catharsis.[11]

The lesson from Feshbach's research is that we should be slow about making definitive conclusions from any single study. Other researchers who examined what Feshbach had done were quick to criticize his conclusion. Imagine that you were a boy in this detention facility. Watching TV was one thing you could do to pass the time and entertain yourself. Like most of the boys of this age, your favorite programs were the ones packed with violence and suspense. One day, Feshbach's research team arrives and tells you that you can no longer watch your favorite programs because you are participating in a study. To make matters worse, you notice that the researchers permit some of the other boys to watch those shows for no apparent reason. How do you react? Perhaps you feel like hitting someone! If most of the other boys deprived of viewing violence felt like you did, it could easily explain why the boys who watched violence behaved less aggressively than the boys who watched nonviolence.[12]

Feshbach's findings demonstrated that people will act more violently if they can't watch their favorite TV programs than they will if they can watch them.

Most researchers now agree that this is the best interpretation of the results of Feshbach's study. The results do not support the catharsis idea.

A Priming Analysis of the Effect of Media Violence

Over the years, many studies show that viewing media violence does not calm people down. In fact, a series of experiments by **Leonard Berkowitz** and his associates at the University of Wisconsin–Madison shows that angry people and media violence make for an especially volatile mix. Quite the contrary to Feshbach's idea of catharsis, if angry people watch media violence, they are *more* likely to behave aggressively.

Recently, Berkowitz and his colleague, **Eunkyung Jo,** have offered an explanation for how this **facilitating effect** of media violence might operate.[13] The key word in their explanation is **priming.** Priming is a process that can be understood simply in terms of associations. If you read a news story about an airplane crash, the story might "prime" thoughts that you have in your mind associated with airplanes. You might start thinking about an upcoming trip that you have to take. The story might also prime thoughts about where you will choose to sit on the plane. You might remember that you haven't made your seat reservation yet, so you decide to make a phone call to your travel agent. In short, priming is a process where one thing that you think about reminds you of other things in your mind that you have associated with that thing. Berkowitz and his colleagues believe that the mass media are potent sources of images or ideas that can prime our thoughts and actions. According to these researchers, when

> . . . people witness, read, or hear of an event via the mass media, ideas having a similar meaning are activated in them for a short time afterwards, and . . . these thoughts in turn can activate other semantically related ideas and action tendencies. (p. 45)

According to this analysis, several things appear likely to happen when people view images of media violence. First, the violence can prime thoughts that are related to hostility. At least for a short period of time, such thoughts might affect the way we see other people and interpret their actions. I was reminded of this process recently when I was out jogging for my daily exercise. As I ran by a parked car, a woman sitting in the driver's seat let out a loud shriek. I had startled her as I ran by the car. As I circled back around toward the car to offer an apology, the woman explained that she was in the middle of reading a newspaper story about a serial killer. The thoughts and feelings that this story had evoked may have primed her to react in a very different way to my presence than she would have otherwise. Second, in addition to priming violence-related thoughts, media violence might prime thoughts that lead one to believe that aggressive behavior might be warranted in certain situations and might bring about certain benefits.

Finally, media violence might prime action tendencies that cause people to be more inclined to act violently. My brothers work in a state prison system and reported to me recently that the prison inmates are almost always more unruly and violent immediately after they have watched a violent movie. I expressed some astonishment that the prison administration actually supplied such films for weekend entertainment and was told that this practice is common in many prison systems.

Despite the many studies by Berkowitz and others that clearly show evidence for priming and a facilitative effect of media violence on aggressive behavior, catharsis theory became very popular. This probably had something to do with the networks, who had a lot to gain in the violence controversy if the theory was viable. Catharsis is an idea that has died hard. There are still many who espouse this idea in discussions about the effects of media violence. However, if the research over the last 30 years tells us anything conclusively, it tells us that we should allow the theory of catharsis to rest in peace.

DESENSITIZATION TO VIOLENCE

The research summarized above points to the reasons why there is such a strong consensus among scientists that media violence causes aggressive behavior. We shouldn't conclude our look at this area of research without discussing another powerful effect that seems to be emerging from current studies. Media violence may be **desensitizing** us to violence in real life. It may be making us numb to violence so that we don't react to it as we would if we had never seen it on the screen. What evidence is there for this effect?

The first type of evidence is anecdotal. Researchers who have taken the time to examine Hollywood movies have noted something very interesting about the ones that have sequels. Inevitably, when producers make a sequel to a violent movie, they pack it with more violence than they did the original film. If one looks only at the number of people killed by violent actions, the statistics are revealing. The first production of *RoboCop* featured 32 dead bodies. The second version featured 81. In *Deathwish,* the body count climbed from 9 in the first version to 52 in the second. *Rambo* killed off 62 people in the initial debut. By the time Rambo III rolled around, that number had soared to 111. George Gerbner, the researcher who took the time to chart these statistics, noted that the trend is even evident in the critically acclaimed *Godfather* movies. In the first film, 12 people were killed. The second film depicted 18 deaths, and the third installment featured 53![14]

One way to explain the increased violence in movie sequels is that Hollywood is attempting to satisfy the people who bought tickets to the first movie. Producers may intuitively realize that when they keep the same level of violence in the sequel, viewers won't get the same emotional charge as they did the first time around. So, they provide more blood and gore. If this intuition is correct, it points to the possibility that some of our entertainment is actually getting more violent over time. The desensitization idea suggests that there is no easy way to go backwards. The entire momentum is toward an ever-increasing level of violence.

Is there any research to suggest that exposure to media violence may actually desensitize people to violence in real life? In order to answer this question, two researchers, **Ronald Drabman** and **Margaret Thomas,** set up an interesting study.[15] They randomly assigned children to watch either a violent or nonviolent TV show. After each child finished watching the show, the experimenter drew attention to another TV monitor in the room. The experimenter told each child that the monitor was displaying pictures of two children who were interacting in an adjacent room. He also explained that he had to leave the room and would return shortly. Just prior to leaving, the experimenter instructed the child to watch the TV monitor in case any trouble broke out between the children in the other room. If trouble did break out, the experimenter instructed each child to leave the room and go around the corner to notify him. Actually, the monitor displayed a videotape in which the two children began fighting. The fighting grew more severe and, eventually, the screen went black. Drabman and Thomas wanted to know if watching a violent video just prior to these instructions would cause children to be less sensitive to the fighting that they witnessed. The answer they got was clear. Children who had watched the violent video were far less likely than the other children to actually make an attempt to notify the experimenter about the fight that they observed on the monitor. These results support the idea that watching media violence can desensitize one to violence in real life. In the next chapter, I will return to the topic of desensitization when I discuss research on the effects of sexually explicit media content. We will discover that there is even more evidence for the basic desensitization idea in that context.

WHY DO PEOPLE LIKE MEDIA VIOLENCE?

As you have made your way through this chapter, perhaps you have wondered about why people even watch media violence. There wouldn't be so much controversy about it if people weren't somehow attracted to it. What are they attracted to? This is not a very easy question to answer. Researchers who study media effects have devoted much more of their energies to understanding the impact of media violence than they have to the question of the appeal of this sort of entertainment. One thing that we do know is that the assumption that people generally enjoy media violence should not be taken for granted. In one essay, Joanne Cantor pointed out that anyone studying the Nielsen ratings will be struck with the unpopularity of televised violence. The ratings for 1995 showed that among children between the ages of 2 and 11, situation comedies were much more popular than violent cartoons that were broadcast on Saturday morning.[16] One researcher, **Jeffrey Goldstein,** devoted an entire book to the appeal of media violence. At one point, he observed: "It is worth remembering that violent entertainment is the preferred form of entertainment only for a minority of the general audience. Most viewers appear to prefer comedies and sitcoms to violent entertainment."[17] Still, the minority of the audience that does prefer violence is a sizable one. What can we say about why they are drawn to this form of entertainment?

Recently, my wife, Cheri Sparks, who has her doctorate in social psychology, and I tried to analyze the appeal of media violence.[18] We came up with three general reasons why people are attracted to this type of entertainment. First, it does seem that violent entertainment may hold inherent appeal for some individuals. There may be some who literally experience a kind of sensory delight when they view mayhem and destruction on the screen. These images may be novel, exciting, and attractive in their own right. Second, some people may experience postviewing gratifications from viewing events, characters, and themes that tend to appear in violent contexts—while not necessarily enjoying the violence itself. For example, one researcher, Dolf Zillmann, has suggested that viewers form alignments with the characters in a movie or program. That is, we decide very quickly whom we like and whom we dislike. When good things happen to the characters we like, we find it enjoyable. Similarly, when bad things happen to characters we dislike, we also experience pleasure. Since a good deal of violent entertainment encourages the viewer to form alignments with different characters, viewers will enjoy violent films to the extent that their favored characters have good outcomes and their disfavored characters have bad ones.[19] Finally, violent media may contain other themes that viewers tend to enjoy. Perhaps violent films tend to contain more sexuality or more suspense. Viewers may be attracted to this sort of media for these factors—rather than the violence. Although there is some research evidence to support all three of these explanations for the appeal of violent entertainment, researchers need to study these issues much more carefully in order to come to a better understanding of why violence is so attractive to some people.

CONCLUDING COMMENTS

The purpose of this chapter is to provide an overview of the research on media violence. This is a challenging task because there are many studies to consider in this literature. When all is said and done, what should you take out of all the research?

First, the researchers who do these studies agree strongly that viewing violence does cause an increase in aggressive behavior. But, it is also important to note that from a statistical point of view, the effect is not very large. People behave aggressively for many reasons. The contribution that media violence makes to aggressive behavior is only one small piece of the puzzle.

Second, even though the statistical contribution of media violence to aggressive behavior is small, this does not mean that the effect is unimportant. In today's media environment, millions of people may view the same violent program or movie. Even very small statistical effects will translate into large social problems when this many viewers are involved.

Third, the idea that viewing media violence can reduce aggressive behavior is no longer viable. Results from dozens of studies refute this idea. When network executives argue for symbolic catharsis or declare that media violence has no effect, we should believe them to the same extent that we believe the major tobacco companies when they tell us that smoking does not cause lung cancer. In short, we shouldn't believe them at all.

Finally, even though most of the research on media effects deals with violent content, there are many other important effects that scholars have studied. Our picture of media impact would be woefully incomplete if we did not consider these other areas as well.

SUMMARY

This chapter began by encouraging you to think about copycat crimes and the prevalence of violence in today's media content. In raising the question of the possible causal connection between media violence and aggressive behavior, the chapter reviewed some of the important surveys and experimental research relevant to this issue. It discussed some of the key theoretical concepts, such as priming and desensitization. Finally, you were encouraged to think about why people like media violence.

KEY TERMS AND CONCEPTS

"Copycat" phenomenon 72

Social learning theory 77

Rewards and punishments 77

The Catharsis Hypothesis 82

Facilitating effect of media violence 83

Priming 83

Desensitizing effect of media violence 84

KEY NAMES

George Gerbner 74

Newton Minow 74

Joy Berrenberg 76

Albert Bandura 76

Leonard Eron and Rowell Huesmann 79

Brandon Centerwall 81

Seymour Feshbach 81

Leonard Berkowitz and Eunkyung Jo 83

Ronald Drabman and Margaret Thomas 85

Jeffrey Goldstein 85

WEB LINKS

1. For information on media violence from the Center for Media & Literacy, try . . . http://www.medialit.org/Violence/indexviol.htm

2. For a statement about the health risks of media violence from the American Academy of Pediatrics, try . . . http://www.aap.org/policy/00830.html

3. For a Web site that provides multiple resources on media violence, try . . . http://www.ncmsalliance.org/mediaviolence.htm

To learn more about the topics in this chapter, enter the Key Terms and Concepts and Key Names found in this chapter as subject and keyword searches on your InfoTrac College Edition.

NOTES

1. Liebert, R. M., Neale, J. M., & Davidson, E. S. (1973). *The early window: Effects of television on children and youth*. New York: Pergamon Press.

2. Gerbner, G., Gross, L., Morgan, M., & Signorielli, N. (1994). Growing up with television: The cultivation perspective. In J. Bryant & D. Zillmann (Eds.), *Media effects: Advances in theory and research* (pp. 17–41). Hillsdale, NJ: Erlbaum.

3. Minow, N. (1996). *Abandoned in the wasteland: Children, television and the first amendment*. New York: Hill and Wang.

4. Smith, S. L., Wilson, B. J., Kunkel, D., Linz, D., Potter, W. J., Colvin, C. M., & Donnerstein, E. (1998). Violence in television programming overall: University of California, Santa Barbara Study. In Center for Communication and Social Policy, University of California, Santa Barbara (Ed.), *National television violence study (vol. 3)* (pp. 5–220). Thousand Oaks, CA: Sage.

5. I can't remember exactly where I first heard the story of Mr. Noid, and I have had difficulty verifying all of these details since I read the initial account of the incident. As a result of searching on the term "Noid" on a news Web site (http://www.wweek.com/), I have at least been able to verify that the incident happened. I am certain the way I first read the story in the press was along the lines that I have given in the text. If you, the reader, have any other documenting evidence about this event, I would appreciate learning about it.

6. Berrenberg, J. L., Rosnik, D., Kravcisin, N. J. (1990). Blaming the victim: When disease-prevention programs misfire. *Current Psychology: Research & Reviews, 9,* 415–420.

7. Bandura, A. (1994). Social cognitive theory of mass communication. In J. Bryant & D. Zillmann (Eds.), *Media effects: Advances in theory and research* (pp. 61–90). Hillsdale, NJ: Erlbaum.

8. Stein, A. H., & Friedrich, L. K. (1972). Television content and young children's behavior. In J. P. Murray, E. A. Rubinstein, & G. A. Comstock (Eds.), *Television and social behavior: Vol. 2. Television and social learning* (pp. 202–317). Washington, DC: U.S. Government Printing Office.

9. Huesmann, L. R. (1986). Psychological processes promoting the relation between exposure to media violence and aggressive behavior by the viewer. *Journal of Social Issues, 42,* 125–139.

10. Centerwall, B. S. (1989). Exposure to television as a cause of violence. In G. Comstock (Ed.), *Public Communication and Behavior* (Vol. 2, pp. 1–58). San Diego, CA: Academic Press.

11. Feshbach, S., & Singer, R. (1971). *Television and aggression*. San Francisco: Jossey-Bass.

12. Liebert, R. M., & Sprafkin, J. (1988). *The early window: Effects of television on children and youth*. New York: Pergamon Press.

13. Jo, E., & Berkowitz, L. (1994). A priming effect analysis of media influences: An update. In J. Bryant & D. Zillmann (Eds.), *Media effects: Advances in theory and research* (pp. 43–60). Hillsdale, NJ: Erlbaum.

14. Jhally, S. (1994). *The killing screens: Media and the culture of violence* [video]. Northampton, MA: Media Education Foundation.

15. Drabman, R. S., & Thomas, M. H. (1976). Does watching violence on television cause apathy? *Pediatrics, 57,* 329–331.

16. Cantor, J. (1998). Children's attraction to television programming. In J. H. Goldstein (Ed.), *Why we watch: The attractions of violent entertainment* (pp. 88–115). New York: Oxford University Press.

17. Goldstein, J. (1998). Why we watch. In J. H. Goldstein (Ed.), *Why we watch: The attractions of violent entertainment* (pp. 212–226). New York: Oxford University Press.

18. Sparks, G. G., & Sparks, C. (2000). Violence, mayhem, and horror. In D. Zillmann and P. Vorderer (Eds.), *Media entertainment: The psychology of its appeal* (pp. 73–91). Mahwah, NJ: Erlbaum.

19. Zillmann, D. (1998). The psychology of the appeal of portrayals of violence. In J. H. Goldstein (Ed.), *Why we watch: The attractions of violent entertainment* (pp. 179–211). New York: Oxford University Press.

6

■

Sexual Content in the Media

HUMAN SEXUALITY
BRINGS OUT PASSIONATE OPINION

Recall back in chapter 3 when you read about Edgar Dale's content analysis of movies in the late 1920s. About 75% of the film content he examined could be classified as either crime, love, or sex. This should tell us something at the very outset about sexual content in the media. It is not a recent phenomenon. In fact, if we wanted to go back centuries into human culture, we would find that media dealing with human sexuality in some way is never far from the cultural scene. This should hardly be surprising. The sexual appetite is basic to human existence and future survival. Therefore, it seems reasonable that human sexuality would show up constantly in art and entertainment.

When we consider sexual content in the media and the impact of that content, we enter a highly charged arena that is populated with a number of interest groups. First, more than any other area of media content, people with religious concerns have historically expressed their views with fervor. Back in 1977, when the sitcom *Soap* hit the airwaves, the National Council of Churches launched a vigorous campaign that resulted in many letters of complaint being filed with the ABC network and the advertisers who sponsored the program. Several advertisers withdrew their ads and several affiliate stations decided not to air the first program of the series. Other stations decided to run the program later in the evening in order to protect children who might have been in the audience during the earlier time slot.[1] This kind of pressure strikes many as an insidious kind of censorship, even though no laws prohibiting expression are involved. The passion that many bring to this topic from their religious convictions is matched by those who seek to protect free expression under the First Amendment at all cost. The resulting clash of values and voices between these two positions can make a hotbed (pun intended) of rhetoric. As you might imagine, the TV networks and Hollywood studios want no part of government censorship. They want to be free to produce the content that will make them the most profit—regardless of who might be offended on the grounds of an inappropriate or excessive sexual depiction. They also fear a government that can restrict the flow of any type of information by legal decree.

Despite the fears of Hollywood, U.S. law does permit the government to restrict the flow of certain messages. Complicating the rhetorical scenario is the fact that law enforcement officials tend to have strong opinions about sexually explicit media. **Obscenity** is not protected under the First Amendment. If media content is judged as fitting the legal definition of obscenity, it can theoretically be restricted from circulation. Fortunately or unfortunately, depending upon your viewpoint, the legal test for obscenity is very rigorous, and few judges or courts have been willing to declare many media messages to be obscene. Essentially, in order to win an obscenity case, a plaintiff must establish that the media message in question was designed primarily to stimulate or appeal to sexual or prurient interests, that it has no redeeming artistic value, and that it violates contemporary community standards. Because all three of these criteria must be met, the history of efforts to declare media legally obscene shows little consistent success. Because of the community standard criterion, it is theoretically possible to have a movie or magazine declared to be obscene in one community but not in another. Despite the legal nightmare involved in tests of obscenity, the legislative branch of government has always had some stake in the issues surrounding sexual content in the media.

A variety of political interests are at stake in the debates about sexual content in the media. Many feminists have been quite outspoken about the dangers for women of certain types of sexual depictions. Their early voices of concern have been joined by others. Sometimes, a case of strange bedfellows (pun intended again) can be formed in debates about sexual content. Feminists and members of the religious right often find themselves opposing the same sorts of sexual content in the media. This may be one of the few political issues that they agree on, and they typically find this agreement to be an uncomfortable state of affairs. Other groups have children's interests at the forefront of their campaigns. Believing that early exposure to explicit sexuality can induce various psychological harms in children, these groups fight against public displays of sexually explicit magazines at convenience stores and call for strict enforcement of the MPAA movie code that prevents children from being admitted to watch some movies without a parent or adult guardian.

Unwary scientific researchers often fail to realize that, in conducting research on the effects of media sex, they begin to enter into a volatile mix of religion, law, and political agendas. It is important to understand at the outset that regardless of what the findings might be from a given study, the researcher who studies sexual content in the media is probably more vulnerable to criticism than in any other area of media studies. There are simply too many passionate voices expressing too many passionate opinions. A few years ago, I had the chance to talk with one media researcher who had published some results that showed negative effects of being exposed to pornography. He was struggling with the fact that some people had interpreted his results as little more than a political statement from the religious right. They accused him of being a "Bible thumper." The researcher told me with a tone of frustration that his own theological leanings were toward agnosticism, and he certainly had no alignment with the religious right. He was simply trying to report the results of his study in an objective, scientific fashion. Some media researchers are unwilling to conduct studies on the effects of sexual content because of their fear of having to deal with the controversial political fallout that might arise from a study's findings. Fortunately, there is still an abundance of good research in this area that helps to inform us about the impact of sexual media content.

SORTING OUT DEFINITIONS AND TERMS

The area of sexual content is fraught with definitional ambiguities. Sexual content is a general label that can refer to something as innocuous as a kiss between two married adults or a brutal rape in a XXX pornographic video. Researchers have struggled with the use of terms to describe the content that they use in their investigations. Over time, the term **pornography** seems to have become associated with material that features explicit sexual behavior and nudity in a context frequently characterized by depictions of one character exerting physical or psychological dominance over another. Often, this type of material contains explicit violence that is shown at the same time as explicit sexuality. The term **erotic media** seems to be associated more with material that features explicit sexual content in the absence of violence and without the overt power dynamics that appear in pornography.

One way to think about media content is to think about classifying media messages according to the quantity and explicitness of both sex and violence. TV soap operas may contain lots of sexual content and low to moderate levels of violence. But on each of these dimensions, the content is not very explicit compared to what is offered in movies. Hard-core pornographic films typically contain heavy amounts of very explicit sexuality and violence. Erotic films are filled with explicit sexuality but little or no violence. Before we can gain an accurate picture of the effects of sexual content in the media, we need to understand what type of content we are talking about. Because the government has been very concerned with the effects of pornography, much of the research has concentrated on studying the impact of very explicit sexual material that also features images of dominance and/or violence. The research history of this material is tied closely to government-funded efforts. Let's turn attention to that history and to the research findings that have emerged over the last few decades.

THE COMMISSION ON
OBSCENITY AND PORNOGRAPHY

In 1967, the U.S. Congress established the **National Commission on Obscenity and Pornography.** Formed under the presidency of Lyndon B. Johnson, the commission was put in place because of growing concern about the role of pornography in crime and juvenile delinquency. Part of the charge of the commission was to study existing laws pertaining to pornography and to arrive at a better understanding of the distribution of this material. Media effects scholars were most interested in another aspect of the commission's charge—to study the effects of pornography on the public.[2] On the basis of what was found, specific recommendations for legislation were to be formulated. In order to meet this charge, the commission sponsored several research projects that examined the impact of sexually explicit materials. University researchers were commissioned to undertake new research designed to answer the question about impact. It is important to note here that the term pornography as it was used in 1967 did not carry the same connotations as it does today, particularly with respect to violent content. Much of the material studied by the commission was sexually explicit, but not violent. It is also important to note that much of the material was not nearly as explicit as some of the mainstream material available in today's neighborhood video stores. Nevertheless, the report that was issued in 1970 was the most comprehensive document on the topic up to that time. It did include study of a wide diversity of sexual content.

Major Finding

By the time the commission published its report in 1970, Lyndon B. Johnson was no longer president. Richard Nixon had assumed this position, and he was not prepared to hear the findings that were published. The following is a key passage from the report itself:

> The Commission believes that there is no warrant for continued governmental interference with the full freedom of adults to read, obtain or view whatever such material they wish. Extensive empirical investigation, both by the Commission and by others, provides no evidence that exposure to or use of explicit sexual materials play a significant role in the causation of social or individual harms such as crime, delinquency, sexual or nonsexual deviancy or severe emotional disturbances.[3]

Essentially the commission report stated that there were no known harms of pornography on any population studied. President Nixon didn't buy it. He rejected the commission's report—probably an act that was made easier by the fact that the commission had been formed under his Democratic predecessor. The important question today for scholars and students of media effects is "Does the conclusion of the Commission Report accurately reflect the state of affairs regarding the effects of pornography?" Clearly, Richard Nixon didn't think so, but what about the scholarly community?

A Reexamination of the Commission's Findings

Two theoretical notions that were widely discussed in the aftermath of the commission report were the **trigger hypothesis** and the **safety valve theory.** The trigger hypothesis essentially claims that exposure to sexually explicit materials will cause a response in some individuals that provokes them in such a way that it might lead them to commit a sex crime such as rape or indecent exposure. The safety valve theory, in contrast, claims that exposure to sexually explicit material will satisfy whatever urges might cause a person to commit a sex crime. If this idea has merit, then we might actually see a decrease in sex crimes in communities that have ready availability to these materials. Of course, in today's electronic environment, virtually anyone can have access to these materials via the computer, making the concept of availability a more difficult one to assess for any given community.

One aspect of the research findings that led the commission to conclude that pornography is not harmful had to do with the findings pertaining to the rate of sex crimes in Denmark following the relaxation of legal restraints on the flow of sexually explicit materials. This evidence could be interpreted as support for the safety valve theory. However, subsequent analysis of this data by one researcher, **Berl Kutchinsky,** reveals that the decrease in some of the sex crimes may be attributed to the fact that public attitudes became more lenient, resulting in fewer reports to the police. While this explanation for the decrease could not be applied to every sort of sex crime (it doesn't seem to account for a decrease in molestation of young women), it does seem to call into question the strength of the evidence in favor of the safety valve theory.[4] Following the publication of the commission report, another researcher, **J. H. Court,** collected data that shows inconsistent results across the world in the analysis of sex crimes. Sometimes these crimes seem to decrease with the spread of pornography, sometimes they increase, and sometimes they remain the same.[5] One thing that seems to be relatively stable across countries, however, is that rape does not decrease when pornography is permitted to flow freely. One recent study that analyzed data from Japan over a 23-year period found that availability of pornography was definitely correlated with increases in rape and sexual assault.[6] While the data on this issue remain somewhat inconclusive because of their correlational nature, there appears to be sufficient reason to take the possible link between pornography and sexual assault seriously.

As it turns out, the commission noted in its own summary of the data a number of qualifications that serve to caution the reader about accepting the overall conclusion too readily. First, the material used in the research was collected over a very limited time period and the findings might not generalize to other times and other types of material. Nearly 30 years after the commission report, this limitation seems potentially important. Much has happened in the interim in terms of the type of material generally available to the public and the easy access to that material. Second, for ethical reasons, the commission could not study the impact of sexually explicit material on children. Thus, while no evidence of harm was reported by the commission, it would make little sense to conclude that children are risk-free if exposed to this kind of media. I personally remembered this point several years ago when I visited a family who lived below me in a 2-flat housing unit in a large metropolitan area. Two of the young children in that household, both under the age of 10, were glued to the TV screen during my visit, watching nude women cavort across the screen in a presentation being broadcast on *The Playboy Channel.* This is one situation that the commission failed to study and probably couldn't study because of prohibitions by committees on ethical treatment of human subjects. I don't mean to suggest that nudity is necessarily harmful to young children. But even the programmers at *The Playboy Channel* would admit that its entertainment is created for adult viewers. We have little research that investigates the meanings and effects that such programs might create for children.

The final upshot of the Commission Report on Obscenity and Pornography was that the overall finding triggered controversy among politicians, parents, and researchers alike. As one might expect, the finding was readily embraced by media sources that had a stake in publishing sexually explicit materials. If you go back to the pages of *Playboy* magazine in the early 1970s, you will find frequent mention of the commission report and its overall finding that exposure to sexually explicit materials is harmless. I had the chance to witness firsthand the media industry's reliance upon the commission report during the 1980s. I was called upon to appear on a TV talk show in Cleveland along with Marilyn Chambers, a star who appeared in many sexually explicit films. At the end of the program, Ms. Chambers retrieved a faded scrap of newspaper from her purse and proceeded to read the final conclusion from the commission report about pornography's harmlessness. I only had 15 seconds to put this conclusion in a proper perspective with the research that followed the commission report. Ms. Chambers seemed uninterested and even annoyed with my response. As the controversy intensified in the 1970s, some researchers renewed their efforts to study the impact of exposure to sexually oriented media. The research that emerged out of this renewed effort served to question further the overall conclusion of the commission report. Let's take a brief look at some of the later research.

RESEARCH FOLLOWING
THE COMMISSION REPORT

The 1980s were years of rather intense scholarly study of the effects of sexually explicit materials. Many experiments were conducted that manipulated the quantity and type of exposure and studied their impact on a range of attitudes, including attitudes toward women, sexual violence, and family values. **James Weaver** summarized this evidence well in a recent essay.[7] His summary includes a characterization of the current content available and how that content affects the viewer's perceptions and behaviors.

Content Available

Weaver divides the available content into three categories. First, his analysis revealed that the bulk of material features standard nonviolent themes. The content of most films and videos in this category is preoccupied with sexual activity, usually from the masculine perspective. There is a heavy emphasis on heterosexual intercourse, lesbianism, group sex, anal intercourse, and oral-genital contact with visible ejaculation.[8] Weaver notes, "The predominant theme of standard-fare pornography, in other words, spotlights the sexual de-sires and prowess of men, whereas consistently and persistently portraying women as sexually promiscuous and obsequious."[9]

A second category of material that is much less prevalent involves coercive and/or violent themes. One of the predominant features in this type of mate-rial is the "rape myth" scenario. In this sequence of actions, a woman is taken by force against her will and raped. At some point in the sequence, the woman is shown enjoying the rape. There are many variations on this general theme but the central idea is that the woman enjoys being dominated or abused by violence during a sexual encounter. Finally, the third category outlined by Weaver is the idealized world of sexual fantasy, sometimes referred to as "erotic." This category is probably populated by the fewest number of films and videos.

Perceptual Consequences of Viewing

Contrary to the Commission Report on Obscenity and Pornography, the newer research on this topic has dramatically changed the way most researchers assess sexually explicit content and its effects on viewers. One line of studies, con-ducted by **Dolf Zillmann** and **Jennings Bryant,** is particularly instructive.[10] The general design of these studies was to expose volunteers to weekly 1-hour viewing sessions of mainstream pornography that had been carefully scruti-nized by the researchers to make sure that violence and coercion were absent. Following these sessions, the researchers asked the participants questions about relationships and perceptions of women under the guise of another study. Far from indicating the absence of any harmful effects, the findings of these stud-ies show rather conclusively that people who watch mainstream pornography are more likely to think that rape is not so severe a crime, that most sexual prac-tices are more prevalent than they really are, that their own sexual relationships are not particularly satisfying, and that trust in their own partners is misplaced.

Studies conducted by **Ed Donnerstein** and his colleagues tend to show that all of these perceptual effects are present after viewing sexual depictions that are accompanied by violence and coercion.[11] However, his research does not necessarily reveal these effects for nonviolent depictions. The resolution of the question about whether or not these effects are typically present after view-ing nonviolent material is a question that future studies will have to address more directly. At the present time, most of the evidence showing these effects as a result of nonviolent material comes from the research by Zillmann and his colleagues. Whatever the resolution of this issue turns out to be, both research

groups have agreed that depictions of the rape scenario and sexual violence promote attitudes of sexual callousness toward women and cause more lenient attitudes toward the perpetrators of rape. Donnerstein emphasizes that such images are not limited to films and videos that carry the X rating. He argues that
they frequently show up in R-rated films. While the images in these films may
be less explicit than ones in X-rated material, the pairing together of sex and
violence in the R-rated films is often very apparent and quite capable of bringing about the effects discussed above.

Behavioral Consequences of Viewing

Think about what would be required to establish a clear cause-and-effect relationship between exposure to sexually explicit materials and some antisocial behavior like rape. Researchers would need to carefully manipulate exposure to different media content and then provide an opportunity for aggressive behavior.
They would then record which participants actually behaved aggressively. Of
course, in the case of a behavior like rape, to set up such an experiment would
be unthinkable. Researchers run into these ethical issues whenever they think
about designing studies that would clearly indict pornography as a causal factor in the increase of sex crimes. For this reason, some scholars take the position that the evidence needed to make a claim for this causal proposition is simply not possible to gather. Other scholars agree but emphasize that there are
certainly strong hints available in the present data about the behavioral consequences of exposure to pornography.

While it isn't possible or desirable to set up a situation where real-life sexual aggression might occur, certain types of aggressive behavior can be studied
in the laboratory. Over the years in media effects studies, aggression has often
been studied in the context of some sort of scenario involving the administration or *perceived* administration of electric shock. The **electric shock paradigm** goes back to the famous experiments done by **Stanley Milgram** on
obedience to authority.[12] In these studies, the participants were ordered by the
experimenter to administer electric shocks to another person whenever that
person gave a wrong answer on a learning task that was part of the experiment.
Real shocks were never delivered, and the person who was supposedly receiving them was actually a member of the team of experimenters. But the participants still believed that they were, in fact, administering painful electric shocks
to another person. By taking note of how many shocks people were willing
to give and how long they held the shock button in the "on" position, the
researchers could tell which conditions would generally produce the highest
levels of "obedience" to authority.

When this electric shock paradigm is used in studies on the effects of sex-
ually explicit materials, the findings are quite revealing. In one classic study by
Kenneth Leonard and **Stuart Taylor,** 40 undergraduate males who were
in the presence of a female viewed slides that were either neutral or erotic.[13]
In this case, the female was actually a member of the team of experimenters.
When the erotic slides were shown, the female reacted according to one of

three different randomly assigned scripts. In the "no cues" script, she showed no reaction at all. In the **nonpermissive cues** script, she made a variety of disapproving comments about the slides (for example, "this is disgusting," or "oh, that's awful"). Finally, in the "**permissive cues**" script, she made a variety of positive comments (for example, "that looks like fun"). After the slide-viewing session, the males were told that they were going to take part in a competition with the female that involved reaction times. Each person was given the opportunity to administer a shock to the other. The experiment was rigged such that the males would discover that the female had decided to administer a very high level of shock. The experimenters were most interested in the level of shocks that the males would choose to deliver to the female once they discovered this information. Would their chosen shock levels vary as a function of their slide-viewing condition? The results of the study clearly revealed that the answer to this question was yes. Can you guess which group of males delivered the highest levels of shock to the females? Why?

The results of the study showed that the males who had watched the erotic slides in the presence of a female who displayed permissive cues were much more likely to deliver higher levels of shock. The authors reasoned that males in this condition concluded that the female would more easily tolerate inappropriate electric shocks because she had already tolerated the sexually explicit material in the slides. In short, the males adopted calloused perceptions of the females on the basis of their earlier tolerance.

What do we learn from this sort of experiment about the effects of sexually explicit media? It appears that males who perceive that females are tolerant of explicit sexuality will be more willing to aggress against them if there is provocation to do so. This finding could have implications for the way women are depicted in pornographic films. If male viewers have a steady diet of promiscuous females who are tolerant of and even eager to engage in unusual sexual behaviors, calloused attitudes toward women in general might result. Such attitudes could lead to more severe treatment of women under conditions of provocation. This finding appears consistent with the results of some other studies in the literature conducted by Donnerstein and Zillmann.

One of the big issues in interpreting experimental results such as the ones reported by Kenneth Leonard and Stuart Taylor is trying to figure out how the experiment might apply to behavior that takes place outside of the carefully controlled world of the experimental laboratory. This issue is referred to as one of **ecological validity** (sometimes called external validity). Some critics of this type of experiment would argue that it is very difficult to know for sure whether we can learn very much about the "real" world from these sorts of studies. After all, how many people have you seen carrying around portable electric-shock machines that they use whenever they are angry? According to these critics, if these sorts of details (sometimes referred to as the **mundane realism** of the experiment) don't match situations encountered outside the laboratory, then we know very little about how the results inform our understanding of real-world events. Experimenters answer this criticism by arguing that the details inside the laboratory might not match the details outside the laboratory, but the meaning that people assign to those details is similar to the meaning that people assign to events in the real world. This emphasis on the meaning that is attached to responses in an experiment is referred to as **experimental realism. Leonard Berkowitz** and Ed Donnerstein discuss this issue at length in one of their articles about the effects of media violence.[14]

THE MEESE COMMISSION
REPORT ON PORNOGRAPHY

The wave of research that followed the first Commission Report on Obscenity and Pornography convinced many in the government that a new report was needed on this topic. In July, 1986, the Attorney General of the United States, Ed Meese, released the *Attorney General's Commission on Pornography Final Report*. While the title of this report was similar to the first one, the two reports diverged widely in terms of their purpose, operating procedure, and final conclusion. Unlike the early commission, the **Meese Commission** did not become involved in the conduct of new scientific research on the topic. Instead, it relied on existing studies and anecdotal data gathered from interviews and examinations of the commercial market for pornography. The purpose of this report probably had more to do with an attempt on the part of the attorney general to put some teeth into existing obscenity statutes than it did with coming to an opinion about the harms of pornography based upon science. Several of the commissioners were outspoken opponents of pornography. For example, **James Dobson** of *Focus on the Family* was one of the members of the commission. Dobson has long been known in the Christian community as a leading spokesperson for family values and a staunch opponent of pornography. Given this type of constituency, it was inconceivable that the Meese Commission would arrive at any other conclusion except one that asserted the harms of pornography.

Major Conclusion

Not surprisingly, the Meese Commission came to a far different conclusion than the earlier commission about the effects of pornography. In some respects, the summary it offered about the relative harms of sexually violent material, mainstream pornography depicting various degrees of domination, and purely erotic depictions was very consistent with the available evidence summarized earlier in this chapter. But the report drew heavy criticism from the scientific community for a number of reasons. First, scientists objected to the weight that the commission seemed to attach to the interviews it conducted with people who were selected through a process that could hardly be called scientific. It appeared that part of the Meese Commission procedures involved providing an outlet for anyone who had a gripe about the pornography industry. Second, the commission seemed to be confused on how to interpret correlations. Consider this passage from the commission report:[15]

> We recognize, therefore, that a positive correlation between pornography and sex offenses does not itself establish a causal connection between

the two. It may be that some other factor, some sexual or emotional imbalance, for example, might produce both excess use of pornographic materials as well as a tendency to commit sex offenses.

This statement shows a proper understanding of how to interpret correlations, and the commission would have been wise to stop with this statement. But the report goes on:

> But the fact that correlational evidence cannot definitively establish causality does not mean that it may not be *some* [emphasis mine] evidence of causality, and we have treated it as such.

This statement is, at best, ambiguous. It is true that the presence of a correlation may be evidence of causality. But it may *not* be. When the commission members state that they "have treated it as such," it sounds as though they may have actually treated these correlations as some evidence of causality. If they did that, then they misinterpreted the evidence. In fact, the correlations may not be evidence of causality at all.

In the end, the academic community was not pleased with the Meese Commission Report because it went beyond the scientific evidence to formulate its conclusions. It also seemed to have a very strong bias against pornography from the outset. This turned out to be unfortunate because a strong scientific conclusion regarding the new evidence about sexually explicit materials was desperately needed. Because academic researchers could not fully embrace the Meese Commission Report, much of their rhetoric was directed to revealing the scientific shortcomings of the report. Researchers found it extremely difficult to discredit the report while simultaneously emphasizing that many of the studies summarized in it were important and credible. Some of the scientists who had published findings about the harms of sexually explicit materials were seen in the news media criticizing the Meese Commission. Consequently, many of the important studies and their conclusions about the harms of sexually explicit materials got lost in a sea of controversy about the report itself.

SEX ON PRIME-TIME TV

To this point, the bulk of the chapter has been about the effects of pornography or highly explicit depictions of sexuality. While these sorts of depictions are certainly quite prevalent in movies, videos, and Internet sites, the research on these depictions says little about the more common sexual depictions that appear on prime-time television. The fact that these images are less explicit is not a good reason to ignore their potential influence. Before you finish with this chapter, you should have a clear understanding of the research in this area as well.

One general effect of sexual material that shouldn't be overlooked is its capacity to induce elevated levels of **physiological arousal** and **sexual arousal.** Physiological arousal includes general responses like elevations in heart rate, blood pressure, and skin conductance (for example, sweaty palms). Sexual arousal may include some of these general responses but is much more specific to the sex organs. In addition to measuring such arousal with self-report instruments, some researchers have actually measured sexual arousal in males with instruments designed to detect increased blood flow to the penis.[16] Measures designed to detect symptoms of arousal in the vaginal area have also been used for females.[17] As you might imagine, the procedures followed in studies that use these measures are scrutinized very carefully by university human-subjects committees. Typically, the instruments are self-attached in private and computer readings verify that the instruments are functioning properly. The research shows that sexual content is arousing. There are a number of questions that researchers would like to have more data on because the current understanding is quite limited. Are males and females aroused by different stimuli? Does arousal vary directly as a function of the level of sexual explicitness? Some scholars have noted that the most arousing material is not necessarily the most explicit.[18] However, there does not appear to be an abundance of research data on this topic. To the extent that low levels of explicitness can induce high levels of arousal, then TV soap operas and other prime-time offerings that feature verbal and visual depictions of sex are potentially very arousing. What are the implications of this possibility?

The Dynamics of Excitation Transfer

According to Dolf Zillmann's **theory of excitation transfer** (which you will encounter again in the next chapter), general arousal from any source can intensify an emotional experience and make it much more prominent than it would be ordinarily without the arousal.[19] The implication of this theory is that if people become aroused from watching sex on television, whatever emotions they experience immediately after viewing may be much more intense than they would be ordinarily. For example, if a person became angry right after viewing a sexually provocative show, their anger would be more intense. On the other hand, if a person experienced feelings of warmth and affection toward their viewing partner, those feelings would also be intensified.

The theory of excitation transfer is incredibly flexible. Arousal can intensify both positive and negative emotions. In addition, the source of the arousal can be almost anything. Yes, watching sexual content on television can be arousing, but so can jogging (at least in terms of the general symptoms of increased heart rate, and so on). Whenever arousal is present in the system, the possibility of intensified emotions exists. A former student of mine apparently learned this lesson well and decided to share her experience with me several weeks after the course she took from me was over. She greeted me one day by saying that the theory of excitation transfer had saved her engagement. I was more than a little curious to hear the details. Apparently, every time she wanted to discuss wedding plans with her partner, they got into an argument. Following a lecture on excitation transfer, the student had a lightbulb experience. She already knew that her partner was not particularly fond of talking about the details of the wedding. But as she thought back over their discussions, she realized that she was inevitably trying to hold these discussions immediately after her partner's daily jogging. The theory predicted that his negative reaction to discussions of wedding plans would be intensified by arousal left over from the jog. Once she realized this, she changed her behavior. She made it a point to make sure that she only discussed pleasant topics after exercise. She saved the wedding plans for more serene moments. According to her report, this single change had made a tremendous difference. I don't know how the newlyweds are faring today, but at least in this instance, the theory of excitation transfer turned out to have a very practical edge.

Content Analyses

As it turns out, there have been many more studies about the sexual content of TV than about the effects of that content. One researcher, **Bradley Greenberg,** has studied the content of afternoon soap operas for many years. In one recent study, he reported that over the last decade, the number of sexual incidents per hour had increased.[20] Most of the sex centered around incidents of sexual intercourse between unmarried partners or partners who were not attached. Increases were observed in both visual and verbal depictions of sexuality. Greenberg noted that while depictions of sex on the soaps were increasing, many of the incidents of sex outside of marriage were not sanctioned by characters in the program and were portrayed as objectionable. In order to explain this paradox, Greenberg tends to favor the view that the TV networks are attempting to appease multiple audiences. Some people like sexual content. Others will not watch the shows if the attitude toward the sexuality seems to favor promiscuity. By depicting sex and then expressing moral objection, the networks can spike their ratings by appealing to both groups.

Sex on TV is hardly limited to soap operas. One of the reasons sexual content is so controversial is because of its potential impact on children and adolescents and the ready availability of TV content to those younger viewers.

In another content analysis of the most popular prime-time shows viewed by children and adolescents, **Monique Ward** found that nearly 30% of all the interactions that took place on an average episode contained verbal references to sexual issues.[21] On some episodes, that statistic soared to 50%. A great proportion of the messages related to sexuality emphasized the competitive nature of sexual relations and featured many comments by males about the physical appearance of females. A more recent study directed by **Dale Kunkel** for the Kaiser Foundation emphasized the "sobering" finding that only 10% of the programs in their study that depicted sexual intercourse included any mention of sexual risk or responsibility. The report concluded:

> In the future debate about sex on television, it may well be more important to consider *how* sex is shown rather than simply *how much* it is shown. This study confirms that sexual messages are a frequent part of the television landscape, but it also makes clear that such messages follow a pattern that poses cause for some concern. When television presents sexual content, there is scant attention devoted to sexual health issues that are essential considerations in weighing one's options for sexual activity today. By providing more balance in addressing these concerns, television could be help-

---

STUDY BOX 6-1 The 2000 Report on Sexual Content on TV

In February 2001, the Kaiser Family Foundation released its second major content analysis of sexual content on TV. The report was based upon more than 1,100 randomly selected programs from the 1999–2000 TV season. What did the report find? Over two thirds of all the programs that were included in the analysis contained sexual content of some sort (68%). A similar analysis done 2 years earlier showed that only 56% of the programs contained sexual content. Apparently, sex on TV is on the rise. If the analysis is confined to only the shows that aired on the major networks during prime time, then 75% of all the shows included sexual content—also an increase over the figures from 2 years before (67%).

One change that the newest study detected in sexual depictions was in the percentage of teens who were involved in sexual intercourse. In the analysis of the 1997–1998 season, only 3% of characters involved in intercourse were teens. That figure increased to 9% in the analysis of 1999–2000 programming. While sexual depictions of intercourse among teens seem to be increasing on TV, it also seems that messages about "safe sex" are more likely. In the 1999–2000 season, 25% of all the shows that depicted sexual intercourse made some reference to sexual health issues. Two years earlier, only 10% of these depictions contained similar references.

What might be the reasons for the rise of sexuality on TV? One possibility is that as the networks have come under increasing fire for programming violence, they have turned to sex to appease audiences who might be hungry for arousing content. But there might be another principle at work that could help to explain the increase. Recall from the last chapter that the principle of desensitization predicts that once a certain level of explicitness has been crossed, it becomes extremely difficult to go back in the reverse direction. Over time, content that initially triggers an intense emotional reaction becomes commonplace. Producers may sense that in order to keep ratings high, the line needs to be constantly pushed. If this principle holds true, future content analyses of sexual content on TV will find that even more sex is turning up on TV and that the sex is more explicit. If this trend continues, the challenge for researchers of media effects will be to investigate how these changes might make a difference in terms of influencing the beliefs, attitudes, and behaviors of the TV audience.

Source: The Kaiser Family Foundation at http://www.kff.org/content/2001/3087

---

ing young people make more informed—perhaps even life-saving—decisions about sex in their own lives.[22]

The conclusion of Kunkel's report sounds all too familiar. A decade ago, a team of researchers concluded on the basis of their content analysis that adolescents were unlikely to learn very much about contraceptives or the risk of sexually transmitted disease from watching TV depictions of sexuality.[23] Historically, the research findings of scholars have tended to have little impact on the practices of the entertainment industry. The report by Kunkel and his colleagues quoted above was published in 1999. However, the research program has recently been updated with a report for the year 2000. One encouraging theme in the 2000 report is that while sex on TV is increasing, so too may be the depictions of safe-sex practices. You can read more about the highlights from the 2000 report in Study Box 6-1.

Sexual Behavior and Viewing

Most of the studies on the impact of sex in the media have taken place on older populations and have dealt with content that is more explicit than that which is typically seen on prime-time TV. This state of affairs is certainly easy to understand. From an ethical standpoint, it is certainly more problematic to study younger viewers in the context of a research design that requires exposure to sexual media content. From the standpoint of theory about media impact, it makes sense to study the more explicit depictions of media sexuality since these would be the materials that one might suspect would have the most effects on viewers. Despite the fact that not much research attention has been devoted to the effects of TV sexuality, there are at least two studies that deserve mention here.

One study that was supported by ABC-TV studied how well adolescents (ages 12–16) understood sexual innuendos on prime-time TV. The findings revealed that even the youngest of these viewers understood the innuendos well and felt comfortable talking about them.[24] In a second study that used a correlational research design, pregnant and nonpregnant girls and women between the ages of 13 and 29 were studied. The results of the study revealed that the pregnant girls were more likely to have greater media exposure to those programs and movies that depicted sexual content. They also tended to be more likely to watch these programs and movies in the company of their boyfriends than did the members of the nonpregnant sample. Of course, you know from reading chapter 2 that there are various pitfalls involved in concluding from this correlation that watching the sex in the media caused a greater likelihood of becoming pregnant. In this case, the researchers were not even able to establish the time sequence of the relationship (the measure of pregnancy came before the measure of media exposure), much less rule out possible third variables that may have been related to both media exposure and pregnancy status.

While the actual amount of research evidence on the impact of TV sex upon behavior is minimal, the knowledge that researchers have gained from studying other areas of media impact would certainly suggest that there is reason to be concerned about the way sex is depicted in prime time. One thing that we can be certain about on this topic is that it will remain controversial. More than any other area of media effects, the number of angles on sexual content in the media (religious, political, scholarly, legal) will continue to make for a "hotbed" of dispute.

CONTROL OVER MEDIA CONTENT

Sex and the Internet

In the last 5 years, the number of sites in cyberspace has mushroomed tremendously—into the hundreds of millions. At no time in human history has sexually explicit media been so readily available as it is today. We owe that fact—good or bad—to the Internet. The significant aspect to this easy availability is that children are part of the consuming audience in a way that they have never been before. Controversies have hit public libraries and schools about whether or not to load blocking software onto their computers to prevent children from surfing to objectionable sites. Sometimes the blocking software doesn't work properly and screens out material that isn't sexual in nature. Researchers have little to say about the effects of sexually explicit media on children because few committees on the protection of human subjects would ever approve research of this sort. The widespread assumption, of course, is that Internet pornography is harmful to children. For that reason, solutions to the problem are not typically sought in research. Advocates seeking **strategies to control the flow of sexually explicit materials** turn instead to **legal, social/economic, and education** solutions. From the looks of things, this struggle to control the material is an uphill battle.

Legal Control

One of the reasons for the heated controversy about media sex is that obscenity does not enjoy protection under the First Amendment. Obscene speech is illegal. Consequently, the government has often attempted to restrict the flow of sexual media that might be judged as obscene. As mentioned earlier, the legal battles against obscenity have not been very successful. Obscenity is a difficult thing to define. Moreover, Americans may object to sex in the media but they simultaneously tend to defend the right of the media to produce it. The quest for censorship is almost always one that fails to enjoy popular support.

Another legal avenue that has occasionally been tried by opponents of pornography is to claim that certain sexual depictions serve to deprive some members of society (usually women) of their civil rights. These claims have usually met with failure in the courts and state legislatures around the country. One reason for the failure of these efforts is concern about the implications that such rulings would have for other kinds of media content. Do people really want to live in a world where a given group of individuals can lay waste to the media industry by claiming that certain kinds of content injure their civil rights? For now, at least, the courts have answered that question in the negative.

Social or Economic Control

Instead of passing and enforcing laws against sexual content, some groups pursue a strategy that is based on social norms and economic impact. Religious groups will often launch boycotts of advertisers who try to sell their goods on objectionable programs. Sometimes, groups will boycott particular business establishments that sell sexually oriented material. When I lived in Cleveland, one of the convenience store chains became the target of such a boycott. The stores responded by announcing an open chance for customers to vote on whether they should continue to carry sexually oriented magazines like *Playboy* and *Penthouse*. Customers had to come into the store to cast their ballots. Since participation in the boycott meant avoiding the stores, it was no surprise when the company announced that the public had overwhelmingly voted to support their policy of continuing the sale of the magazines. As a public relations ploy, the strategy worked brilliantly. The stores looked good in the public eye for having an open election. But because the boycott was going on at the same time, the results were virtually guaranteed to support the continued sale of the material—a result that the stores undoubtedly wanted. Eventually, the boycott ended and things returned to normal. Boycotts and economic pressure sometimes work in isolated cases over the short term. But history shows them to be relatively ineffective over the long haul.

Control through Education

In a free society that protects freedom of speech and expression, the preferred form of control over media content is probably education. If people learn about media impact, they can take steps to deal with it and manage it in their daily lives. As evidence for this fact, Ed Donnerstein has shown that participating in his experiments can actually be beneficial—despite the fact that male college students who go through his experiments are exposed to violent pornography.[25] Compared to males who don't have the chance to participate in the studies, the ones who do actually become more sensitive to issues involving rape myths after they have gone through the instructional debriefing required by human-subjects committees. Research by **Neil Malamuth** shows similar findings.[26] Education in this case turns out to be effective. When you finish this course on media effects, you will be in a far better place to think through the issues of media impact in your own life. You are then in a better position to make informed choices about your own media diet and, in the future, the media diets of your children.

SUMMARY

Few topics stir such passionate opinion as sexual content in the media. Researchers have tended to distinguish between pornography, violent sexuality, and eroticism as they have studied media impact in this domain. Early evidence from the Report of the Commission on Obscenity and Pornography led to the conclusion that this material was relatively harmless. Subsequent reanalysis of some of the data in the report, combined with a new wave of research that followed its publication, modified this conclusion. The Meese Commission Report reversed the conclusion of the first commission report, but for a variety of reasons, it was widely criticized by social scientists. Nevertheless, the broad consensus of the scientific community is that exposure to sexually explicit material is associated with a host of negative perceptual and attitudinal consequences. Some research also suggests that negative behaviors might also be more likely following exposure. Research on sexual content on TV has concentrated mainly on content analyses rather than studies of impact. The main concern is with *how* sex is depicted rather than with *how much* is depicted. More research needs to be done on the impact of less explicit media sex such as the depictions on soap operas and prime-time TV.

KEY TERMS AND CONCEPTS

Obscenity 91

Pornography 92

Erotic media 92

National Commission on Obscenity and Pornography 93

trigger hypothesis 94

safety valve theory 94

Electric shock paradigm 97

Permissive cues versus nonpermissive cues 98

Ecological validity 98

Mundane realism 98

Experimental realism 99

Meese Commission 99

Physiological arousal 100

Sexual arousal 100

Theory of excitation transfer 101

Control strategies 105

legal 105

social/economic 105

education 105

KEY NAMES

Berl Kutchinsky 94

J. H. Court 94

James Weaver 95

Dolf Zillmann and Jennings Bryant 96

Ed Donnerstein 96

Stanley Milgram 97

Kenneth Leonard and Stuart Taylor 97

Leonard Berkowitz 99

James Dobson 99

Bradley Greenberg 102

Monique Ward 102

Dale Kunkel 102

Neil Malamuth 106

WEB LINKS

1. For information on a content analysis of Internet pornography, try . . . http://www.sociology.org/content/vol003.001/boeringer.html

2. For information on sexual content from The Media Education Site, try . . . http://www.mediaed.org

3. For information on the 2000 report on sex on TV from the Kaiser Family Foundation, try . . . http://www.kff.org/content/2001/3087/

To learn more about the topics in this chapter, enter the Key Terms and Concepts and Key Names found in this chapter as subject and keyword searches on your InfoTrac College Edition.

NOTES

1. Liebert, R. M., Sprafkin, J. N., & Davidson, E. S. (1982). *The early window: Effects of television on children and youth*. New York: Pergamon Press.

2. Liebert, R. M., Sprafkin, J. N., & Davidson, E. S. (1982). *The early window: Effects of television on children and youth*. New York: Pergamon Press.

3. Commission on Obscenity and Pornography. (1970). *Report of the Commission on Obscenity and Pornography*. New York: Bantam Books.

4. Kutchinsky, B. (1973). The effect of easy availability of pornography on the incidence of sex crimes: The Danish experience. *Journal of Social Issues, 29*, 163–181.

5. Court, J. H. (1977). Pornography and sex crimes. *International Journal of Criminology and Penology, 5,* 129–157.

6. Diamond, M., & Uchiyama, A. (1999). Pornography, rape, and sex crimes in Japan. *International Journal of Law & Psychiatry, 22,* 1–22.

7. Weaver, J. B. (1994). Pornography and sexual callousness: Perceptual and behavioral consequences of exposure to pornography. In D. Zillmann, J. Bryant, & A. C. Huston (Eds.), *Media, children and the family: Social scientific, psychodynamic, and clinical perspectives* (pp. 215–228). Hillsdale, NJ: Erlbaum.

8. Hebditch, D., & Anning, N. (1988). *Porn gold: Inside the pornography business.* London: Faber & Faber.

9. Brosius, H., Weaver, J., & Staab, J. (1993). Exploring the social and sexual "reality" of contemporary pornography. *The Journal of Sex Research, 30,* 161–172.

10. Zillmann, D., & Bryant, J. (1988). Effects of prolonged consumption of pornography on family values. *Journal of Family Issues, 9,* 518–544.

11. Donnerstein, E. (1984). Pornography: Its effect on violence against women. In N. M. Malamuth & E. Donnerstein (Eds.), *Pornography and sexual aggression* (pp. 53–81). Orlando, FL: Academic Press.

12. Milgram, S. (1963). Behavioral study of obedience. *Journal of Abnormal and Social Psychology, 67,* 371–378.

13. Leonard, K. E., & Taylor, S. P. (1983). Exposure to pornography, permissive and nonpermissive cues, and male aggression toward females. *Motivation & Emotion, 7,* 291–299.

14. Berkowitz, L., & Donnerstein, E. (1982). External validity is more than skin deep: Some answers to criticisms of laboratory experiments. *American Psychologist, 37,* 245–257.

15. U.S. Department of Justice. (1986). *Attorney General's Commission on Pornography: Final report,* (Vol. 1). Washington, DC: U.S. Department of Justice.

16. Eccles, A., Marshall, W. L, & Barbaree, H. E. (1988). The vulnerability of erectile measures to repeated assessments. *Behavior Research and Therapy, 26,* 179–183.

17. Sintchak, G., & Geer, J. (1975). A vaginal plethysmograph system. *Psychophysiology, 12,* 113–115.

18. Harris, R. J. (1999). *A cognitive psychology of mass communication.* Mahwah, NJ: Erlbaum.

19. Zillmann, D. (1983). Transfer of excitation in emotional behavior. In J. T. Cacioppo & R. E. Petty (Eds.), *Social psychophysiology* (pp. 215–240). New York: Guilford Press.

20. Greenberg, B. S., & Busselle, R. W. (1996). Soap operas and sexual activity: A decade later. *Journal of Communication, 46,* 153–160.

21. Ward, M. L. (1995). Talking about sex: Common themes about sexuality in the prime-time television programs children and adolescents view most. *Journal of Youth & Adolescence, 24,* 595–615.

22. Kunkel, D., Cope, K. M., Farinola, W. J. M., Biely, E., Rollin, E., & Donnerstein, E. (1999). *Sex on TV.* The Henry J. Kaiser Family Foundation [online]. Available: http://www.kff.org/content/archive/1457/

23. Brown, J. D., Childers, K. W., & Waszak, C. S. (1990). Television and adolescent sexuality. *Journal of Adolescent Health Care, 11,* 62–70.

24. Liebert, R. M., Sprafkin, J. N., & Davidson, E. S. (1982). *The early window: Effects of television on children and youth.* New York: Pergamon Press.

25. Donnerstein, E., & Berkowitz, L. (1981). Victim reactions in aggressive erotic films as a factor in violence against women. *Journal of Personality and Social Psychology, 41,* 710–724.

26. Malamuth, N. M., & Check, J. V. P. (1980). Sexual arousal to rape and consenting depictions: The importance of the woman's arousal. *Journal of Abnormal Psychology, 89,* 763–766.

7

■

Frightening Media

I will never forget the night from my childhood when my parents made a fateful decision that they could never have known would affect me for the rest of my life. It was a Friday evening, and my older brothers had gathered around the TV set in keen anticipation of their favorite weekly program, *The Twilight Zone*. Up to this point in time, my parents had insisted that I could not watch the show because it came on after my bedtime. But on this particular evening, for whatever reason, my parents relented and allowed me to join my brothers in front of the set. I was 6 years old. By the end of the program, I was certain that I would never be able to walk into a department store again. I was quite literally terrified! (After writing these words, I went to the Internet and found the details of the particular episode that frightened me. My memory was very accurate. The episode, "The After Hours," was broadcast on Friday, June 10, 1960. It was the first season of the program. Perhaps I was allowed to watch it because the school year was ending and my parents were less concerned about bedtime.)

Despite the fact that numerous cable stations run old episodes of *The Twilight Zone,* I have never cared to rewatch the particular episode that scared me that night. When I have described the episode to my students, many of them shake their heads in that knowing way. Some have even tried to fill me in on some of the plot details that have become fuzzy in my mind over the years. I don't really care to know. What I do know is that when I watched that program as a child, my mind could not have dreamed that a TV show could depict such a spooky and terrifying scenario. *The Twilight Zone* might be one of the oldest classic examples of how **paranormal TV media content** can terrify people.[1]

As I recall it, the episode depicted a woman who worked in a department store as one of the salespeople. At the end of the day, when she went to leave the store, the elevator took her to the ninth floor of a building that only had eight floors listed on the elevator panel. Over the course of the episode, the woman discovered that she was actually a mannequin. The mannequins took turns becoming real people who worked in the store. But after a while, they had to return to their mannequin identity. This particular woman had forgotten that she was really a mannequin. The other mannequins had to beckon her back by not permitting her to leave the store at the end of the day. Her elevator trips took her to a floor that only existed in the "twilight zone." It was on that floor that the other mannequins met her and reminded her of who she really was. I know that *Twilight Zone* fanatics would have much more to add to this brief plot description. But because of the fact that I have never cared to see this episode again, my sketchy recollection will have to do for the present purpose.

There were three features of this episode that I remember as particularly terrifying. First, the mannequins talked. I found this to be most unbearable. If mannequins could talk, then maybe anything could talk. What about the faces on my baseball cards? My GI Joe figures? This could mean big trouble. Second, the mannequins turned into real people. If I couldn't tell who was going to turn from a mannequin into a person or from a person into a mannequin, then I was in a real dilemma. Maybe my parents were sometimes mannequins. How could I be sure? Finally, the idea of getting into an elevator and being carried to a floor that didn't really exist was imponderable. Or let's just say that I didn't want to ponder it.

My parents could never have guessed that this program was going to affect me for such a long time. Indeed, I could never have imagined how this single program would embed itself so deeply into my psyche. Of course, I suffered all of the typical immediate effects of seeing a scary show. I wanted my brothers to turn the set off, but I was afraid that I would look like a wimp. So I continued to endure in silence. After the show was over, I didn't want to go to bed unless my brothers were coming upstairs with me. I wanted to sleep with the light on. I *never* wanted to watch *The Twilight Zone* again. In addition to these immediate effects, I find that I continue to suffer some long-term residue from this program even to the present day. There is something about elevators that I just don't like. I feel an irrational anxiety every time the elevator door closes and begins to transport me. At work, I take the stairs. I justify this by saying that it keeps me in good physical condition. But it really has more to do with the fact that elevators remind me of the mannequin who found herself transported to the nonexistent floor. I also feel uneasy around store mannequins—especially at closing time. I don't like to be in department stores when they are about to close. I consciously reflect on the fact that the mannequins in *The Twilight Zone* turned into people after the store closed its doors.

For reasons that are difficult for me to grasp, I have passed this fear down to my children. When my kids were around 5 years old, if we found ourselves passing by a mannequin in a local department store, I would draw my child's attention to the mannequin. In a game that amused me, but not my children, I would try my hand at ventriloquism. Pretending that I was the mannequin, I would say, "Hello there, little girl, what's your name?" It is little wonder that my kids are not very fond of mannequins, either. I believe that my behavior goes back to my own emotional trauma suffered at the hands of Rod Serling and his roving *Twilight Zone* mannequins. Perhaps, by casting myself as the mannequin's voice, I somehow hoped to gain control over these "people" who had terrified me so much during my childhood.

If all of these consequences of viewing that episode sound like negative ones, it is important to add at least one positive note. I have devoted a large portion of my research career to studying the effects of frightening media on children. This has been very rewarding. Perhaps, if I had not suffered such intense fear myself, I wouldn't have felt so drawn toward this topic. The research on frightening media really didn't get started in earnest until the late 1970s. At that time, a researcher at the University of Wisconsin–Madison, **Joanne Cantor,** received a major grant from the National Institute of Mental Health to study the emotional impact of frightening movies and TV programs on children. I was fortunate enough to work with Professor Cantor on this research. Cantor and I, along with a few other researchers (**Barb Wilson** and **Cindy Hoffner**), continue to study frightening media to the present day. What have we found? In the remainder of this chapter, I attempt to provide a brief summary of the research findings in this area. One thing emerges from this research very clearly: Paranormal themes are often the most terrifying for both children and adults. After years of research, we think we know why.

FRIGHT REACTIONS TO
MEDIA ARE PREVALENT

In considering the effects of media violence on aggressive behavior, the most frequently researched media effect in the literature, it is important to note that the statistical effect definitely exists, but the size of the effect is small (see chapter 5). Not many people become more aggressive because of something they see in a movie or TV show. In contrast, the emotional effects of frightening media are far more prevalent, even though they tend to receive less attention in the research literature.

Anecdotes of copycat crimes clearly support the notion that media violence sometimes affects aggressive behavior. Similarly, there are many anecdotes about the emotional impact of frightening films. When the film *Jaws* made its debut, tourism in ocean resort towns plummeted. People expressed terror at the prospect of becoming the victim of a "great white" attack. On the paranormal front, an issue of *The Journal of Nervous and Mental Disease* in 1975 carried reports of clinical psychiatric patients who had to seek hospitalization and months of treatment after viewing the movie *The Exorcist.*[2] Apparently, images of demon possession haunted these patients to the point of social and emotional malfunction. In the case of the film *Silence of the Lambs,* one graduate student in my department reported to me that she had been unable to eat meat for many weeks after viewing the film. And a remarkable number of adults report that they suffered trauma as a child from stories of the Winged Monkeys and the Wicked

Witch of the West in that all-time classic *The Wizard of Oz.* Anecdotes of intense fright reactions to media are common. I am almost certain that if you are reading this book, you can pause and think of at least one instance in your media experience where you found yourself frightened, anxious, spooked, or otherwise disturbed by some media image. The chances are also good that this image was part of a movie or TV show that depicted something from the realm of the paranormal. You are not alone in your experience.

As early as 1933, a researcher named **Herbert Blumer** found that 93% of the children in his sample reported having experienced fright from a movie.[3] In a classic study of the effects of television published in 1958, another researcher named **Hilde Himmelweit** found that one third of the children in her study reported having been frightened by something seen on television.[4] The most recent data from the last few years reveals that about 75% of elementary school children report fright from something seen in a movie or TV program.[5] In interviews about TV and children, parents often express concern about children's fright reactions. They often report that their children suffer nightmares as a result of watching frightening programs. Interviews with children confirm that this topic is an important one. In one study conducted in 1983 by researchers Palmer, Hockett, and Dean, over one third of the children interviewed reported that there were specific scenes or programs that they were sorry they had ever seen.[6] Fortunately, the research goes beyond the documentation of the prevalence of these responses and offers some explanation and understanding about what is happening. One of the most important findings to emerge from this research is that the media content that frightens children is different, depending on the age of the child.[7]

WHAT SCARES ONE CHILD
MAY NOT SCARE ANOTHER

Research on children's fright reactions made a breakthrough with the insight of Joanne Cantor. Cantor noticed that the developmental psychology of **Jean Piaget** helped her sort out reports of fright that she recorded from children and their parents. According to Piaget's theory, children pass through a series of stages in their cognitive development. The way they process, interpret, and think about the world around them depends upon where they are in this sequence of stages. Children in the general age range of 2–7 years old think **perceptually.** The **concrete, visual appearance** of things tends to dominate the child's interpretation and reaction to the world. In contrast, children older than 7 years begin to make a shift toward more **conceptual or abstract thought.**[8]

After studying these distinctions in Piaget's theory, Cantor realized that they might help explain her data on fright responses. Children in the younger age group tended to show fright in response to scenes and characters that looked grotesque and menacing (e.g., the wicked queen in *Snow White,* the Wicked Witch in *The Wizard of Oz,* or the Incredible Hulk). The fact that many of these characters appear in cartoon form and could never occur in the real world didn't seem to make any difference. The young child was not able to focus on this more conceptual or abstract observation.

In contrast to the younger children, older kids tended to report fright from movies and TV shows that featured events and characters that *could* actually occur in the real world. Their fears tended to involve scenes depicting violence or bodily harm to a character. They also included depictions of natural and technological disasters like floods, fires, storms, earthquakes, or nuclear holocaust. Cantor reasoned that because of the older child's focus on the conceptual or abstract instead of the visual, the really scary media to them was that which depicted threatening things that might actually happen. Complicating the situation for these older children is the fact that they don't understand the low probability of many of the "real" events that they see in the media. They have a hard time telling themselves that these things won't really happen to them. They also haven't lived long enough to develop a sophisticated set of coping skills that enable them to deal with the harsh realities they see in the media.

Upon viewing a scene from a movie about a child kidnapping, children at 8 or 9 years of age may understand that kidnappings are real and could actually happen. They may also fail to comprehend that the probability of a kidnapping in their neighborhood is very low. And they may realize all too well that kidnappings are serious business and potentially life threatening. This combination of ingredients makes it particularly likely that older children will react with emotional distress to this sort of media depiction. This kind of depiction has much more fright potential for an older child than the wicked queen from *Snow White*. The older child simply writes off the queen as pretend or impossible. Young children, who tend to operate at the perceptual level, may find the wicked queen to be far more disturbing than the kidnapping movie. To them, the real possibility of a kidnapping is simply beyond their comprehension. And if the movie never actually showed physical injury, the young children would probably not react strongly to the content.

EXPERIMENTING WITH
THE INCREDIBLE HULK

When I worked with Cantor on this research, I decided to do my doctoral dissertation on children's reactions to *The Incredible Hulk*. While this may sound like a very unusual topic for scholarly study, the experiment I conducted was logistically quite complex, and the findings were very important in supporting Cantor's extensions of Piaget's theory. After screening nearly every episode in the series, we elected to show children of both older and younger ages a brief segment that depicted a hospital employee becoming injured in an explosion. David Banner, played by the late Bill Bixby, witnessed the explosion and ran into a burning storage room to rescue the worker. While Banner was dragging the worker to safety, a subsequent explosion hurled him up against a wall, making him very angry. When David Banner becomes angry, he undergoes his strange metamorphosis into the huge, monstrous Hulk. While the Hulk's transformation might not be called paranormal, it certainly falls into the more general category of "weird" or "strange." After showing the transformation (which included his eyes turning green, his shirt tearing, and his shoes ripping), the segment concluded by showing the Hulk gently lifting the worker to safety. In the closing scene, the camera followed the Hulk down a hallway and showed him jumping out of a window and growling ferociously.

Why did we show this segment to children and what did we learn as a result? Following Cantor's logic, we reasoned that older children would show more fright than younger children during the first part of the segment. The prospect of an explosion and fire were events that could really happen. Because of the appreciation for the distinction between fantasy and reality, older children would be able to understand the dangers confronted by the characters in this crisis. However, once David Banner began to transform into the Hulk, we thought that the pattern of fright reactions would change. Older children would recognize that the Hulk, despite his monstrous appearance, was really a "good" guy who would probably save the day. These children could discount the ugly visual appearance and focus on the more abstract reality that the Hulk was the answer to the problem. We reasoned that younger children would view the situation very differently. When the Hulk appeared, we thought that these children would be unable to think about very much except the fact that the Hulk's appearance was scary. We expected that the younger children would show more fright at this point in the program. We also expected that this would last until the end of the segment because the Hulk was present right up until the closing shot.

When children watched this segment, we had them come to a room in their school building that teachers had set aside for our research. Each child came separately, and we were able to monitor their heart rate and other physiological reactions as they watched. These reactions helped us interpret what the child felt during the show. The results were just as we had expected. The older children showed more fright during the explosion and fire and calmed down as the Hulk appeared. Younger children showed just the opposite tendency. They were calmer at the beginning of the show and got much more upset at the appearance of the Hulk.[9]

Perhaps you are thinking that researchers should not be going around scaring little kids. We couldn't agree more. We deliberately chose a program that most children were familiar with before the experiment. None of the emotional reactions we observed were very extreme. We also made sure that parents and children agreed to participate in the procedure and that the Human Subjects Committee at the University of Wisconsin–Madison approved of everything in the experiment. Finally, we talked with each child afterwards and made sure that no harmful emotional reactions had occurred. Actually, children seemed to enjoy these procedures. In Study Box 7-1, I detail a little more about the exact procedures that we went through to make sure that children suffered no harm from participating in the experiment that showed clips from *The Incredible Hulk*.

What have we learned from experiments like this one? First, Cantor's ideas about the kinds of media that frighten children at different ages are confirmed.

STUDY BOX 7-1   Research Procedures for Protecting Children

As you might imagine, studies of children's fright reactions must be undertaken with great care. This care is taken from the very beginning of the planning of a study. In getting ready to run the study that called for preschool and elementary school children to view a clip from *The Incredible Hulk,* the choice of the video material was where cautious planning started. Below, I detail the various steps and considerations that went into the planning of this experiment. As you can see, minimizing the risk to children was paramount throughout the procedure.

1. At the outset, we looked for a program that was sufficient to induce a detectable level of fear—but not a program that was so intense that it would terrorize children. It was important to select a program that children were familiar with so that they wouldn't feel too frightened by some completely unknown scenario. In the case of *The Incredible Hulk,* the program was being broadcast on weekday afternoons in Madison, Wisconsin, during the time of the study. We reasoned that there was a good chance that many children had seen an episode once or twice and that they would have some familiarity with the general plot.

2. After selecting the program, we had to secure the permission of a local nursery school and an elementary school to cooperate with us in conducting the study. This meant making sure that each school facility had a room that could be dedicated to the data collection during the day. More importantly, it meant securing the approval of the school administrators to show the children the video material. The school administrators had to watch the video and give their official approval before we could move ahead.

3. In the case of the elementary school, the local school system had its own review board for all research conducted in the district. We had to submit a full proposal to this board and give the board members the opportunity to view all of the video material before we could proceed with our plans.

4. In addition to the approvals required from the participating schools, the University Human Subjects Committee had to give its own approval to our procedures and materials. Once all of these approvals were in place, we could proceed with the mechanics of the procedure. But at each step of the process, the children's welfare was paramount.

5. First, parents of all the schoolchildren received a letter describing the research project. A permission slip was enclosed for their signature if they agreed to permit their child to participate. Parents who knew that their children might be particularly sensitive to programs like the *Hulk* simply didn't sign the permission slip, and their children were never considered for participation in the study.

6. After the permission letters were sent to parents, we set up times for parents to come to the school and preview the video material and meet the experimenters. Parents who viewed the material and thought that it might be too intense for their children could simply refrain from turning back the permission forms.

7. Once the permission forms were submitted, the research team visited the school classroom and gave a general demonstration of the experimental procedure. We watched a few programs together with the class while one of the children wore the physiological electrodes we used in the procedure. These electrodes were attached to the fingers of one hand. We showed the class how a computer monitored their heart rate during the

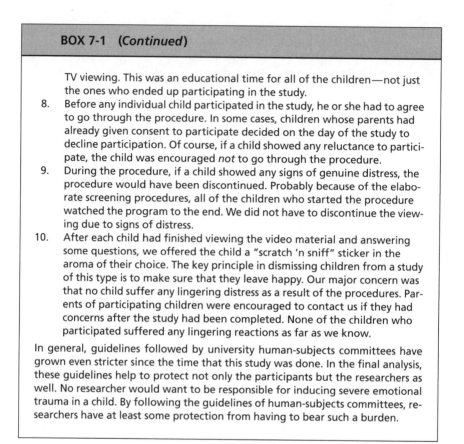

BOX 7-1   (Continued)

TV viewing. This was an educational time for all of the children—not just the ones who ended up participating in the study.

8. Before any individual child participated in the study, he or she had to agree to go through the procedure. In some cases, children whose parents had already given consent to participate decided on the day of the study to decline participation. Of course, if a child showed any reluctance to participate, the child was encouraged *not* to go through the procedure.

9. During the procedure, if a child showed any signs of genuine distress, the procedure would have been discontinued. Probably because of the elaborate screening procedures, all of the children who started the procedure watched the program to the end. We did not have to discontinue the viewing due to signs of distress.

10. After each child had finished viewing the video material and answering some questions, we offered the child a "scratch 'n sniff" sticker in the aroma of their choice. The key principle in dismissing children from a study of this type is to make sure that they leave happy. Our major concern was that no child suffer any lingering distress as a result of the procedures. Parents of participating children were encouraged to contact us if they had concerns after the study had been completed. None of the children who participated suffered any lingering reactions as far as we know.

In general, guidelines followed by university human-subjects committees have grown even stricter since the time that this study was done. In the final analysis, these guidelines help to protect not only the participants but the researchers as well. No researcher would want to be responsible for inducing severe emotional trauma in a child. By following the guidelines of human-subjects committees, researchers have at least some protection from having to bear such a burden.

For younger kids under age 7, if it looks scary it probably will be scary. For older kids, if the depiction could really happen and the consequences are physically threatening, it probably will generate some fear. While most fear reactions tend to be short-lived, in some cases children can suffer media fear that lasts long beyond the program. Coping with these fears can be a real challenge for the parent.[10]

WHY IS THE PARANORMAL SO SCARY?

Ironically, the seeds of understanding why paranormal media depictions are so often experienced as frightening and upsetting are contained in my early experience with *The Twilight Zone*. At the age of 6 I had come to understand the difference between reality and fantasy. At precisely the point in my life where I thought I had this distinction sorted out, along comes Rod Serling to toy with my mind. The transformation of people into mannequins looked as if it could actually happen in real department stores. I was just uncertain enough about this possibility that I found it to be terrifying.

Some of the most frightening movies that deal with paranormal themes are those that deftly juxtapose reality with the paranormal world. In a survey of college students that I did some 20 years after *The Exorcist* was first released, this film was still the most frequently mentioned as a movie that had induced enduring fright.[11] In follow-up interviews, I discovered that students often expressed the idea that the film had made them feel as if demon possession was real. And if it was real, many felt vulnerable and unprepared to deal with it. This is the nature of the paranormal world, almost by definition. If it does exist, most of us would confess to understanding it very poorly. And how can we control or protect ourselves against something we don't understand? We can't, and that's one of the things that makes us afraid. It is no wonder, then, that many a director intent on scaring the audience has turned to the paranormal for the horror film's basic ingredient. If the film can convince the viewer that it might just be possible in real life, then the rest of the task is easy. The mystery and uncontrollability inherent in the paranormal takes over from there and finishes the job of terrorizing the viewer. Not only is this a particularly deadly combination for young children who have just begun to sort out the difference between fantasy and reality, but it is also extremely potent for adults, many of whom carry a fair amount of uncertainty about the existence of paranormal phenomena.[12]

When I look back over the films that are mentioned again and again by college students as the ones that terrified them and caused them to experience lingering anxiety and fear, many of them depict paranormal phenomena in a context that strongly suggests the events could actually happen. There is no better way to do justice to the nature of these fear responses than to report them verbatim as they were originally reported in my research. The following descriptions are the recollections of college students from film experiences that they had in their childhood—usually around the ages of 9–11.

Poltergeist

[A family experiences the horror of discovering that their house is built on a burial ground. Ghosts arrive through the fuzziness of the TV screen and proceed to haunt the family in various ways.]

Respondent #1 *"This movie made me so scared that I felt like my heart froze, like I sort of went into shock. I totally remember this feeling of almost having a heart attack because I still get it now when I'm scared. I hate that feeling. I feel so uneasy. I'm like a basket case. Till this day that movie stayed with me. There are little things from the movie I can identify with when I see them now, and I'll get flashback feelings of how scared I felt. For example: clowns, closets, a fuzzy TV, and that little girl's voice all give me the willies. I really feel that that movie has scarred me for life."*

Respondent #2 *"I was 10 years old, and, of course, my imagination went wild. At the end of the film, I went to my room quietly . . . and being a pretty spoiled kid, I had my own black-and-white TV in my room. Well, needless to say, it was unplugged and hauled into my closet with blankets piled on top of it. To this day, I still unplug the TV* *every night before I go to bed . . . the idea of static in the reception magically appearing on the screen still frightens me."*

Respondent #3 *"I still get chills when I remember the part where the little girl in the movie looks at the snowy TV set and says, 'They're here!' I think the greatest effect of this experience is the fact that no one ever reassured me that events in this movie weren't real. This is probably the most important factor that shaped my belief that supernatural beings probably do exist."*

Respondent #4 *"The lingering effects of the fear I experienced that night are numerous. Because the haunting situation, in my mind, is not entirely impossible, I still find myself worrying about it at times. I feel the same fear emotions and reactions, like increased heart beat and paranoia, when I am confronted with some of the film's major symbols. Seeing a snowy TV screen at night, worrying that the tree outside my brother's window will attack him whenever it storms, thinking our house might have been built over a graveyard, clowns, and closets are all residual effects of my frightening media experience."*

The *Nightmare on Elm Street* Series

[Freddy Krueger returns from the grave to kill young children. He is only able to get them while they are sleeping. He comes to them in their dreams with sharp knives in place of fingers.]

Respondent #1 *"When the movie was over, I went home petrified to death. For about the next month and a half, I was terrified of going to sleep. I was afraid that if I went to sleep Freddy Krueger was going to kill me in my dreams. The first night I didn't sleep a wink. The next night I had trouble falling asleep and staying asleep once I got there."*

Respondent #2 *"There were many times during the movie that I thought about things such as whether or not the door was locked, or if these things could really happen. My aunt had a basement door that I continually kept an eye on to see if Freddy would come out of it. During the movie I convinced myself that I could not ever fall asleep again, because Freddy would get me. I remember this movie as being the most scary thing I have ever experienced, even to this day. To this day I seem to be afraid of dark unfurnished basements, and I do not think I will ever get over that."*

Respondent #3 *"I knew the part about the dreams was purely fiction, yet I could not make myself fall asleep that evening or for several evenings following that one. To this day, I am still especially disturbed when I hear about kids being abducted or killed."*

Respondent #4 *"This movie has a scene in it that I will never forget. It is the one where Freddy's arms stretch out to an arm span of some 30 feet and then slash someone to pieces. The reason why this scene scared me so bad is still unclear to me, but I think it might have something to do with Freddy having the superhuman ability to stretch out* *his arms and catch me no matter how far away I get and that it looked pretty creepy. For many nights after that I could not sleep without having a dream about Freddy reaching out and slashing me. Even now, I could do without alleys, because I am afraid if I look back I might see Freddy waiting for me with open arms, so to speak."*

The Exorcist

[A young girl is possessed by a demon and a local priest must perform an exorcism as the only remedy.]

Respondent #1 *"As I viewed this movie, I was filled with fear and terror. I had never been so frightened by a movie before. I thought that I was going to be possessed. I prayed throughout the entire movie that this would not happen to me. I tried to go to sleep, but I was too worked up to relax. By the time it was over, I was very exhausted. I finally fell asleep. That night, I had nightmares that I was possessed. When I went home the next day, I forgot all about the movie. Until I went to bed, that is. That night, I was paranoid. Every noise I heard was what I thought was the devil in my house. Every once in a while I have a nightmare still, or become a bit frightened by an unfamiliar noise. Still, to this day, I will not watch* The Exorcist.*"*

Respondent #2 *"Never in my life had I been so afraid to go to sleep. This insomnia lasted for about a week before I finally got a good night's sleep, with the assistance of a trip to church. I have yet to watch a movie that has even remotely compared to the fear I felt when I watched* The Exorcist. *To this day, I have still never seen the last 10 minutes of that movie, simply because I don't ever want to see it again. I also refuse to watch the second and third parts of this movie as well. I must also have a Bible or a crucifix in the room that I sleep in before I go to bed. I will never play with or purchase a Ouija board or even be in the same room with someone who is. All this results from my most traumatic experience in my life, watching* The Exorcist.*"*

Respondent #3 *"After seeing* The Exorcist, *I was literally afraid that if I didn't go to church every week, and do only right, this could actually happen to me."*

Respondent #4 *"The music played a tremendous part in building the evil tone of the movie. For years, whenever "Tubular Bells" would be played over the radio I would quickly switch stations or shut off the radio completely. In Indianapolis, on I-65, there was a business that had its name printed in large letters on the side of its building. Whenever we were traveling and went past this spot, I looked the other way. I knew exactly where this building was located and knew when to avert my gaze to the opposite side of the road. I went so far as to turn my whole body away from the building. The name of the business was "Tubular Sales." Close enough for me!"*

Clearly, based on these descriptions, one area that has been overlooked in all the controversy about paranormal media is the fact that the images and plots contained in these movies and TV shows are often very scary—particularly for children.[13]

WHAT'S A PARENT TO DO?

Cantor's research team has also addressed the issue of what parents should do to help their children through frightening experiences that come during or after media exposure. One thing she discovered was that parents inevitably resort to what seems like a logical approach for dealing with children's fright reactions to TV and movies. They tell their children, regardless of age, that what they are seeing is "not real" or "just pretend." Actually, the research shows that this strategy can be effective with older children who have come to distinguish between **reality and fantasy.**[14] The problem is that parents also tend to use the strategy with younger children (under age 7) who often are not capable of comprehending why this should cause them to be less afraid.[15] If something *looks scary,* the fact that Mom or Dad is saying "it isn't real" doesn't seem to matter much. Younger children may come to understand that their **parents believe that labeling something "not real" should make it less threatening.** And they do acquire some superficial knowledge about the difference between reality and fantasy. But usually, this knowledge is not sufficient to make much difference in processing media images.

To illustrate the young child's difficulty with the concept of reality, I often relate a family incident that occurred when my daughter Erin was 4 years old. My wife, Cheri, wanted to demonstrate that Erin understood the difference between reality and fantasy. As we drove around the neighborhood at Christmastime, Cheri spotted a large plastic statue of Rudolph the Red-Nosed Reindeer. She called the statue to Erin's attention and asked, "Is that Rudolph *real?*" Erin answered promptly, "Of course not, Mom." It certainly appeared as if Cheri had made her point. But, just to make sure, I asked one more question: "Erin, did that Rudolph eat breakfast this morning like you did?" Erin's response was just as prompt as her first one: "Of course, Dad!" Erin's understanding of the plastic Rudolph is typical of how young children understand their parents upon hearing that certain TV characters are not real. Children may be able to correctly label the character as pretend, but this label does not mean quite the same thing that it does to an adult. For Erin, Rudolph wasn't real, but he still ate breakfast. In the case of the Wicked Witch, young children may say that she's not real, but this doesn't tend to reduce fright reactions because the witch **looks so scary.**

The research on helping children to cope yields a number of practical conclusions. For older children, it may be very helpful to talk about the fact that media productions contain staged scenes for entertainment purposes and that the characters are not real. When the older child shows fright from viewing events that could actually happen, some attempt to work through the low probability of these events in the child's life may be helpful. Researchers refer to this approach as employing cognitive strategies. **Cognitive strategies** encourage the child to think about the things they already know and relate those things to the aspects of the movie that are scary. A few years ago, a professor of chemistry at my university phoned me to seek my advice on how to handle the fears of his 10-year-old son. Apparently, his son had seen some doomsday preaching on a religious channel and had become terrified of the fact that the world would end very soon. This kind of fear—fear that something seen on TV might actually happen—is very typical for a child of this age. My advice was to tell the child two things simultaneously. First, I advised that whenever the child vocalized his fear, the parent should tell him matter-of-factly that the world was not going to end soon. And second, I advised that the child be reminded of how many days had passed by since the last conversation without the world ending. Gradually, I predicted that the fear would diminish as the boy came to understand through his own experience that the world was unlikely to end very soon. That's exactly what happened. It isn't clear from the excerpts included earlier in this chapter, but most of the students who reported being scared by a paranormal depiction also noted that their fears diminished over time.

For younger children, the best strategy in coping with media-induced fear is to prevent them in the first place. In order to do this, parents need to heed the research findings. Hollywood is of little help here. In fact, movie advertising can be very misleading when it comes to children's fright reactions. Many of the films that carry a "G" rating and promise "family entertainment" are also films that feature characters who look very scary. Unfortunately, unwitting parents who strive to treat their young child to a movie often find that the only thing they have succeeded in doing is scaring the child. My own daughter expressed fear of the Jabberwocky in *Alice in Wonderland*—one of *Showtime*'s special Fairy Tale productions that targeted an audience of children. The research data reveals hundreds of reports from parents about scenes and characters from "family"-oriented films that scared their children. Many of these scenes are from animated classics produced by none other than the Disney studios. The key thing for parents to think about in avoiding this kind of entertainment for their young child (especially in the age range of 2–5) is ***how the characters look.*** Even slight variations in normal appearances (e.g., long fingernails, beady eyes, or sharp teeth) can be enough to trigger a fear reaction. Of course parents also need to know their own children. Some kids are much more sensitive to these visual features than others. There is no substitute for spending time with a child during viewing in order to become more familiar with how emotional reactions are likely to vary.

If a young child does become scared of something seen on TV or in a movie, parents should not hesitate to turn the set off at the first sign of trouble. As logical as this advice is, some parents become convinced that their children need to continue to watch the program in order to "conquer" their fear. But there is no research evidence to support such behavior. And it is probably better to avoid extensive discussions with a very young child about the frightening show. It is better to cuddle the child and distract him or her from the program by reading a book or playing a game. Consistent with the young child's tendency to process things perceptually, there may be some truth to the maxim "out of sight—out of mind." Researchers summarize this type of strategy with the young child as a noncognitive strategy. **Noncognitive strategies** refrain from trying to encourage the child to think about the source of their fear. They work instead to distract the child or avoid the object of fear altogether.

IS IT FUN TO BE SCARED?

While the research reveals that many people regret having seen certain scenes in TV shows or movies and suffer long-term fright reactions, this is hardly the complete picture. In nearly every study conducted in which people are asked if they like to watch this type of media, the distribution of responses is similar. Roughly one third of the people report that they do not enjoy this kind of entertainment and will avoid it at any cost. Another one third of the people report that they enjoy this kind of entertainment and actively seek it out. The last group of people report that "it depends" on the content. There are certain themes that they find enjoyable and other themes that they can't take very well.[16]

Frightening Films and Roller-Coaster Rides

Researchers found the findings on enjoyment of frightening films to be intriguing. **Fear is a negative emotion.** A person who feels scared is a person who is experiencing a negative feeling. Fear, by definition, is unpleasant. How could it be that people experience frightening films as enjoyable? Actually, there are several possible answers to this question. One answer comes from **Dolf Zillmann's "theory of excitation transfer"**[17] that you encountered in the last chapter. Zillmann's idea is that when people become scared at a movie, their entire arousal system kicks into high gear. Heart rate and blood pressure increase, as do muscle tension and other physiological indicators. During the movie, the arousal helps to intensify the negative emotion of fear. But what about after the movie is over? Physiological arousal does not normally return to baseline levels very quickly. The arousal lingers on for a while. But the fear that people experience while viewing is usually replaced with feelings of relief and even joy. The threatening scenes are over and the film's protagonist may have emerged victorious. So a person may leave the film feeling a positive emotion. Because physiological arousal intensifies any emotion that a person feels, this positive emotion at the end of the film can be very intense. There is usually a high level of arousal left over from the fright. The end result is that even a mild feeling of relief that the film is over can be experienced as a kind of euphoria. A person may leave the frightening film feeling high—even though during the film, the only feeling was terror. Over the long run, instead of remembering the terror, a person tends to remember the last feeling experienced—euphoria.

The dynamics of excitation transfer that may take place in a scary movie are similar to what may happen during a roller-coaster ride. A person may not actually enjoy the feeling that results from thinking about the possibility that the coaster will fall from the track and plunge everyone to their deaths. But after the ride is over, the arousal generated during the terror transfers to feelings of relief and creates a kind of euphoria. There is solid evidence for the process of excitation transfer while people are viewing films.[18] And so, it may be that people don't really like feeling scared, but they like the feeling of euphoria that follows. Just as in the case of roller coasters, not everyone experiences scary movies the same way. For some, the terror of the ride outweighs any feelings of relief that follow. But for others, the transfer of arousal to a feeling of relief provides an experience that outweighs the terror. Of great interest to researchers is the fact that there is a relationship between the enjoyment of scary movies and the tendency to enjoy roller coasters. People who enjoy one also tend to report that they enjoy the other.

The Sexual Dynamic in Viewing Frightening Films

One research finding that emerges over and over again is that males enjoy scary movies much more than females. Why might this be so? According to Zillmann, it might have something to do with the ancient tribal practice of male initiation rites. For thousands of years, society has socialized males to conquer threatening stimuli and act as the protector. Modern society has discontinued this practice, but strong remnants remain. Fraternity hazing on college campuses is a constant problem. Viewed from the perspective of the tribal-initiation rite, it is no wonder that colleges have been unable to eliminate this practice. College administrators are attempting to buck several thousand years of male socialization. Zillmann believes that scary movies may also serve as an informal replacement of the ancient initiation right. Males can test their masculinity by exposing themselves to the most horrible images that Stephen King can dream up. If they are able to emerge from the theater victorious, they have proved their masculinity once and for all. According to Zillmann, females also participate in this rite. By withholding affection to the males who are not able to conquer the film's threatening images, females help to contribute to the ongoing socialization pattern. Females also participate in the rite by displaying the appropriate signs of discomfort and their need for protection during a scary film. This idea is sometimes referred to as **gender role socialization.**

In order to test his idea, Zillmann and his colleagues carried out a fascinating experiment. Females who participated in the study believed that their viewing partner was just a random male participant in the study. Actually, the male participant was one of the experimenters. During the movie, the male engaged in certain behaviors that the experimenters described as either "conquering" or "escapist." For half of the female participants, the male exhibited only "conquering" behaviors. He commented on how silly the film was and how it wouldn't scare anyone. For the other half of the female participants, the male exhibited "escapist" behaviors. He placed his hands over his eyes at the scary parts of the film. He commented on how he wished the film would end soon. At the end of the experiment, the females rated their male viewing partner on attractiveness. Can you guess what happened? Females rated the male as being very attractive when he expressed conquering behaviors. But they rated him as unattractive when he expressed escapist behaviors.

The researchers repeated this same experiment on male participants using a female experimenter. The results in this case were completely opposite of the ones for the females. Males found the female more attractive when she displayed the classic fear response indicating that she wanted to escape. Males rated the female very unattractive when she showed conquering behaviors. There was one very interesting limitation to the experimental results. The pattern of findings only emerged for people who were ordinary in physical attractiveness. Opposite-sex viewing partners still found those rare males and females who were judged to be gorgeous by their peers to be attractive, regardless of how they responded to the frightening film. The results of this study show that enjoyment of frightening films may reflect deeply ingrained socialized sex roles.

SUMMARY

In this chapter, you have seen some facets of the research on frightening media. One thing that emerges clearly is that paranormal themes are often front and center when fear reactions do occur. While the emotional effects of this type of media are not nearly as sensational as the effects of media violence, the effects may be far more common. For children, the research shows that there is a wide range of material capable of inducing emotional upset at various points in the child's development. For young children 2–5 years old, animated features hold the potential to terrify. For older children and even for adults, fictional violence represented in a realistic fashion or themes of the paranormal may be emotionally disturbing. News reports of war, famine, and other disasters may be distressing as well. By focusing on the research in this area, you should be a little better prepared to manage these emotional reactions in children entrusted to your care.

It would be too simplistic, though, to dismiss frightening films by focusing only on their capacity to induce negative emotions. As Zillmann's research shows, these films may be popular for good reason. They help to reinforce important patterns of socialization. It is also possible that, in some cases, a person experiences a frightening film therapeutically. The viewer is able to compare real-life circumstances favorably with the dread and horror in the lives of the film characters. While there is less research to substantiate this point, this possibility certainly seems reasonable.

In concluding thoughts on frightening media, I would call attention to the fact that the MPAA movie ratings and the new system for TV ratings are terribly vague when it comes to warning parents about frightening content. The wise consumer realizes that a movie like *Scream* is going to be potentially frightening to children. But fewer people may realize that Walt Disney's *101 Dalmatians* may also be upsetting to preschoolers. One reason to call attention to the research studies on children is to let Hollywood know that it is time for the industry to create program and movie labeling that draws directly from the academic research. The vast majority of parents want a more specific labeling system that gives information about the specific content. Researchers agree that this seems like the best approach. Now the message has to get through to those people in Hollywood who can do something about it.

KEY TERMS AND CONCEPTS

Paranormal media content 109

Perceptual thought versus conceptual or abstract thought 112

"Fantasy" media content versus "reality" content 120

The meaning of the word "real" from the perspective of a child 120

Cognitive and non-cognitive strategies 121–122

The emotional experience of "fear" 122

Excitation transfer theory 122

Gender role socialization 123

KEY NAMES

Joanne Cantor 111

Barb Wilson and Cindy Hoffner 111

Herbert Blumer 112

Hilde Himmelweit 112

Jean Piaget 112

Dolf Zillmann 122

WEB LINKS

1. For a news report describing people's fears from media, try . . . http://www.umich.edu/~urecord/9899/Mar29_99/9.htm

2. For survey results that reveal seven of the scariest films ever, try . . . http://news.uns.purdue.edu/UNS/html4ever/981016.Sparks.films.html

3. For a good overview on frightening media by Joanne Cantor, written for the National Parent Information Network, try . . . http://npin.org/pnews/1999/pnew599/int599e.html

To learn more about the topics in this chapter, enter the Key Terms and Concepts and Key Names found in this chapter as subject and keyword searches on your InfoTrac College Edition.

NOTES

1. The term *paranormal* has been defined in many ways in the scholarly literature. I use it here to refer to events that clearly violate the known laws of nature. Such events might include ESP, astrological forecasts, prophetic dreams, psychic detectives, space aliens, UFOs from outer space, palm reading, astral projection, psychokinesis (moving objects just by thinking about them), and so forth.

2. Bozzuto, J. C. (1975). Cinematic neurosis following "The Exorcist." *Journal of Nervous and Mental Disease, 161,* 43–48.

3. Blumer, H. (1933). *Movies and conduct.* New York: Macmillan.

4. Himmelweit, H. T., Oppenheim, A. N., & Vince, P. (1958). *Television and the child.* London: Oxford University Press.

5. Cantor, J. (1994). Fright reactions to mass media. In J. Bryant & D. Zillmann (Eds.), *Media effects: Advances in theory and research* (pp. 213–245). Hillsdale, NJ: Erlbaum.

6. Palmer, E. L., Hockett, A. B., & Dean, W. W. (1983). The television family and

children's fright reactions. *Journal of Family Issues, 4,* 279–292.

7. Cantor, J., & Sparks, G. G. (1984). Children's fear responses to mass media: Testing some Piagetian predictions. *Journal of Communication, 34*(2), 90–103.

8. Flavell, J. (1963). *The developmental psychology of Jean Piaget.* New York: Van Nostrand.

9. Sparks, G. G., & Cantor, J. (1986). Developmental differences in fright responses to a television program depicting a character transformation. *Journal of Broadcasting and Electronic Media, 30,* 309–323.

10. Cantor, J. (1998). *"Mommy, I'm scared": How TV and movies frighten children and what we can do to protect them.* San Diego, CA: Harcourt Brace & Company.

11. Sparks, G. G. (1997). Unpublished raw data.

12. Sparks, G. G., Nelson, C. L., & Campbell, R. G. (1997). The relationship between exposure to televised messages about paranormal phenomena and paranormal beliefs. *Journal of Broadcasting & Electronic Media, 41,* 345–359.

13. For years, the Committee for the Scientific Investigation of Claims of the Paranormal (CSICOP) has published *Skeptical Inquirer,* a journal devoted to scientific skepticism of paranormal claims. CSICOP often takes the media to task for exploiting paranormal themes in order to make a profit. Rarely, however, has the committee considered the fright potential of paranormal depictions.

14. Cantor, J., & Wilson, B. J. (1984). Modifying fear responses to mass media in preschool and elementary school children. *Journal of Broadcasting, 28,* 431–443.

15. Wilson, B. J., & Cantor, J. (1987). Reducing children's fear reactions to mass media: Effects of visual exposure and verbal explanation. In M. L. McLaughlin (Ed.), *Communication yearbook 10* (pp. 553–573). Newbury Park, CA: Sage.

16. Sparks, G. G. (1986). Developmental differences in children's reports of fear induced by the mass media. *Child Study Journal, 16,* 55–66.

17. Zillmann, D. (1980). Anatomy of suspense. In P. H. Tannenbaum (Ed.), *The entertainment functions of television* (pp. 133–163). Hillsdale, NJ: Erlbaum.

18. Sparks, G. G. (1991). The relationship between distress and delight in males' and females' reactions to frightening films. *Human Communication Research, 17,* 625–637.

8

■

Persuasive Effects of
the Media

WHAT IS PERSUASION?

What does it mean to say that the media have persuasive power? Scholars have identified at least three dimensions of **persuasion** that help to answer this question. First, when you are persuaded, there is a change in your **attitude.** You feel differently about something as a result of being exposed to some message. I can remember a conversation with my older brother several years ago in which he told me that he had changed his attitude about smoking cigarettes. He no longer felt very good about his smoking habit and had resolved to change it. A few months later when I checked back with him, I discovered that he was still expressing this new attitude. Unfortunately, he was still smoking just as much as he did before he adopted his new attitude. This helps to illustrate the fact that a change in attitude is only part of what is involved in persuasion.

In addition to attitude change, significant persuasion also results in changes of **behavior.** It wasn't until my brother actually started to alter his smoking behavior that I became convinced that he had been persuaded by antismoking messages. A few weeks after he started smoking less, he found the new behavior to be very difficult to maintain. Nicotine has addictive properties, and as almost any smoker will testify, the habit is not easily broken. After battling the urge to smoke for months, my brother finally kicked the habit. He hasn't smoked in over a decade. Truly significant persuasion results in behavior that **persists over time.** Together, these three features (attitude change, behavior change, and change that persists) help to define what we mean by persuasion.

As you read in chapter 3, the history of media effects research revolves around the idea that media messages exert persuasive influence on people. In this chapter, we will explore the basis for this assumption in more detail. Are the media really persuasive?

SUBLIMINAL PERSUASION:
THE MAGIC KEY?

Shortly after I earned my master's degree in communication (1976), I took a part-time teaching job that required me to teach a course on persuasion. One of the questions that arose in the class at the very outset was about the effectiveness of something called **subliminal persuasion.** I knew a little about the topic from my graduate studies but not enough to feel competent teaching a class of curious undergraduates who wanted the truth about this persuasive technique. My students' curiosity was being fueled by two books published in the 1970s by **Wilson Bryan Key.**[1] Key argued that media advertising contained hidden or subliminal appeals that penetrated into the unconscious mind of the consumer. Because these messages presumably bypassed the conventional process of rational scrutiny that people typically give to persuasive messages, they were supposedly particularly effective in motivating human behavior. According to Key, advertisers were so committed to the technique that occasionally, they even put subliminal messages on the product itself.

After reading about the contention that a popular brand of cracker had the word "sex" hidden on the surface of the product, I became suspicious. I purchased a box of the crackers and proceeded to spread them out over the kitchen table at the home of my mother-in-law. With a magnifying glass in hand, I examined each cracker carefully to see if I could find evidence of the subliminal technique. As I was deeply engaged in my search, my mother-in-law came into the room and asked me what I was doing. Without batting an eye, I replied, "I'm looking for sex." Only after I uttered these words did I realize that I had a lot of explaining to do. At that point in my study, I was prepared to explain much more than I had been ready to explain to my persuasion class. As it turns out, the academic study of subliminal persuasion is a fascinating one. Let's take a brief look at some of the highlights.

Early History

Subliminal messages are messages that presumably enter the unconscious mind without being detected. The primary example of such a message was outlined in 1957 by an advertising expert, **James Vicary.** Mr. Vicary claimed that in extensive tests he designed for movie audiences watching the film *Picnic,* he had clearly established that subliminal messages were persuasive. He claimed that by splicing into the film the phrases "Eat Popcorn" and "Drink Coke," he dramatically increased the sales of these products at the concession counter. Even though the phrases were on the screen for only one third of one millisecond (too brief to be perceived consciously), they registered in the brain and stirred the urge to eat and drink. According to Vicary, after people were exposed to the subliminal messages, Coke sales increased 18% and popcorn sales increased 58%.[2] As you might imagine, this revelation caused quite a controversy. Articles appeared in popular magazines that scorned this technique as highly unethical. In one article that appeared in the *Saturday Review,* Norman Cousins wrote that subliminal persuasion was so insidious that we should "take this invention and everything connected to it and attach it to the center of the next nuclear explosive scheduled for testing."[3]

Even before any supporting data could be examined on the effect that Vicary announced, the Federal Communications Commission threatened that any use of the technique by broadcasters would result in loss of their broadcasting license. The National Association of Broadcasters also prohibited the practice of subliminal persuasion for any of its members, which included nearly every broadcast facility in the United States. The advertising community wanted to see the supporting data from Vicary's study before it rendered a final opinion about subliminal persuasion. The little-known truth about the history of this topic is that James Vicary confessed in 1962 that the study reported in 1957 was, in fact, a fabricated account that was intended to increase the number of customers for his marketing business.[4] But the confession appeared in an advertising trade journal and the word never seemed to circulate very widely. The notion of subliminal persuasion now had a life of its own. Despite Vicary's confession, the idea was so intriguing that it just wouldn't go away.

The Presumed Mechanism

How is subliminal persuasion supposed to work? When Key popularized the notion of subliminal persuasion in the 1970s, he argued that many of the subliminal messages in advertising revolved around two themes: sex and death. Any casual reader of **Sigmund Freud** would recognize these two themes instantly. According to Freud, the death wish and thoughts about the sexual appetite are repressed in the unconscious mind because there are few socially acceptable outlets for their expression. Subliminal messages, which directly enter the unconscious mind, unlock these repressed urges and motivate a person to purchase the particular product that the unconscious has linked with those urges. It is no accident that many of the supporters of the notion of subliminal influence in the psychological community are those who take a **psychoanalytic** or **Freudian perspective** in their general outlook toward human behavior.

Two Important Questions

There are two important questions that need to be answered regarding subliminal persuasion. First, to what extent are subliminal messages actually present in today's mass media? Second, if they are present, are they persuasive? The first question is difficult to answer. The advertising community is not particularly interested in confessing to the use of subliminal messages, and there appears to be no good source to document their prevalence. Back in the 1980s, I asked an advertising executive at Wyse Advertising if he had any insights on the use of subliminal messages in advertising. His answer was only an estimate, but it was more concrete than anything I had encountered up to that point or have encountered since. He estimated that about 10% of all ads use some form of subliminal technique. Of course, there are also various audiotapes and videotapes marketed to the public that supposedly encourage weight loss, relaxation, avoidance of tobacco use, and similar behaviors. So, even though we can't be certain about the exact prevalence of subliminal messages, we can be confident that at least some messages attempt to employ the subliminal strategy.

Are subliminal messages effective? In order to answer this question, two psychologists, **Anthony Pratkanis** and **Anthony Greenwald,** decided to run an experiment that tested the power of subliminal tapes marketed to the public to increase self-esteem and memory.[5] The tapes that they used contained classical music that was clearly audible or **supraliminal.** The manufacturer had altered the tapes to include subliminal audio that could not be perceived consciously. Some of the tapes contained messages designed to enhance the listener's self-esteem (e.g., "I have high self-worth and high self-esteem"); others contained messages designed to improve memory (e.g., "My ability to remember and recall is increasing daily"). After testing volunteers on measures of self-esteem and memory, the experimenters randomly assigned them to listen to the tapes daily for 5 weeks. There were four experimental conditions. Each of the four groups received tapes that contained labels indicating the type of subliminal content that they would hear. For two of the groups, the labels were correct and indicated either the memory or self-esteem message. For the other two groups, the labels were incorrect. For one group, the tapes labeled "self-esteem" actually had subliminal messages about memory. Likewise, for the final group, the tapes labeled "memory" actually had subliminal messages about self-esteem.

The results of the study were very clear. First, the authors found absolutely no evidence that the subliminal messages were effective in changing self-esteem or memory. Second, the study revealed what the authors dubbed as an **illusory placebo effect.** The volunteers who listened to the tapes labeled as self-esteem tapes thought that the tapes had increased their levels of self-esteem. The volunteers who listened to the memory tapes thought that the tapes had increased their memory ability. This happened regardless of the actual subliminal content of the tapes. Thus, the effect that emerged here was a placebo effect because the volunteers expressed opinions that were based on the labels on the tape. The effect was illusory because, in fact, actual levels of self-esteem and memory were unaffected by any of the tapes.

The study by Pratkanis and Greenwald is typical of many that scholars have published over the last 40 years. While psychologists have documented the fact that some subliminal messages can affect human behavior, these effects do not last for more than just a few seconds after the message is perceived. Moreover, there is virtually no evidence that subliminal messages are capable of influencing the kinds of large changes in attitude and behavior that marketers of products attempt to bring about in consumers. As Pratkanis concluded in a recent article on this topic, "Perhaps now is the time to lay the myth of subliminal sorcery to rest and direct our attention to other, more scientifically documented ways of understanding the causes of human behavior and improving our condition."[6] It is worth noting that there are still some cognitive psychologists who believe that subliminal persuasion is a possibility that may be documented in future research.[7] Until more confirming data appear in the literature, however, the consensus of scholars is probably best summarized in the statement by Pratkanis. From the perspective of a consumer who might wonder about whether to buy a subliminal tape to facilitate weight loss, relaxation, or some other desirable result, it is important to realize the inherent inconsistency in such marketing strategies. The effectiveness of subliminal messages is predicated on the notion that the messages enter the mind undetected. When a consumer buys a tape that promises to deliver subliminal messages of a certain type, then the process is no longer under cover. Once the nature of the subliminal message is known, the entire presumption of the message's effectiveness is undone. It is no longer subliminal. Any positive benefits that listening to such tapes might produce cannot be attributed to the subliminal nature of the messages. Following the study by Pratkanis, these effects are more plausibly due to the power of prior expectations or to the placebo effect.

A final warning about claims for the effectiveness of subliminal persuasion is in order. As I have taught classes in persuasion over the years, I occasionally have heard or read about fantastic claims that seem to support the notion that subliminal appeals are effective. For example, a TV program on the PBS network reported that some department stores incorporate subliminal messages about honesty into their music systems as a way of reducing shoplifting. One store supposedly reported that the move had saved them hundreds of thousands of dollars. The problem with such claims is that the data do not come from carefully controlled laboratory experiments. We have no way of knowing whether the department stores in question took other security measures at the same time that they implemented subliminal messages. Perhaps the reduction in shoplifting was due to changes in the economy or the time of year. In the end, these kinds of anecdotal reports simply fail to meet the strict rigors of scientific testing. For that reason, you should be very careful about attaching too much significance to them.

HOW MEDIA MESSAGES PERSUADE
WITHOUT EVEN TRYING

While there is little evidence in favor of subliminal persuasion in the media, this does not mean that the media have little persuasive power. In fact, numerous examples seem to show that people are often persuaded by media messages that weren't even designed explicitly to change attitudes or behavior. A high proportion of media messages are designed to entertain. Over the years, scholars have learned that these entertainment messages can exert a powerful influence on attitude and behavior. Let's take a brief look at some of these examples.

One well-documented example of media influence that was purely unintended occurred when "the Fonz" applied for a library card in an episode of the popular sitcom *Happy Days*. In the weeks following this episode, libraries around the country reported a 500% increase in library card applications.[8] Apparently, children and young adolescents who admired the Fonz were motivated to copy his behavior and get a library card for themselves. There was no persuasive ploy featured in the *Happy Days* episode; the producers of the program had no idea that this scene would trigger a surge in library card applications.

Another example of unintended media influence involved the infamous 1983 broadcast by the ABC-TV network, *The Day After.* This movie depicted the aftermath of a nuclear war in the United States. Once again, the movie was primarily designed for entertainment purposes, not persuasion. But two researchers discovered that exposure to the movie was sufficient to change attitudes about the seriousness of nuclear war. People who watched the movie were especially likely to change their attitudes and express the view that nuclear war was a critical concern. They also expressed their intent to take some action to help prevent nuclear war.[9]

The persuasive impact of *Happy Days* and *The Day After* was not very controversial. Few people could get upset about children wanting library cards or people wanting to do something to curb the risk of nuclear war. Occasionally, however, the impact of entertainment media is not so positive. Consider the well-known case of the CBS movie *Cry Rape.* As social psychologist Elliot Aronson describes the situation, this movie depicted a rape victim who discovered that pressing charges against her rapist could result in an ugly ordeal that only prolonged a rape victim's suffering.[10] In the weeks following the broadcast of the movie, actual rape reports to law enforcement authorities decreased significantly. Apparently, viewers were persuaded by the nature of the rape victim's experience in the film and learned the lesson of the high cost of pressing charges.

What can we learn from these examples of persuasion that occurred in the context of entertainment programs? Think about the last time you went to a movie or watched your favorite TV program. The chances are good that, as you sat back in your seat to relax, you were not preparing to process a persuasive message. As psychologists have studied the persuasion process, they have discovered that ordinarily people approach a persuasive situation with their defenses up. **Richard Petty** and **John Cacioppo** describe this situation in their **elaboration likelihood model** of persuasion. According to them, there are two main routes by which people might be persuaded. One of these is called the **central route to persuasion.** The central route is a highly rational or cognitive route to persuasion. People scrutinize the message carefully and tend to think up many counterarguments that the persuader must defeat in order to be successful.[11] This route to persuasion is especially likely if people know that the message they will hear is **counter–attitudinal** (i.e., different from the position they hold themselves). Persuasion through the central route is more difficult for the would-be persuader to achieve. Whenever a salesperson calls me on the telephone, I find that I am ready to resist the message no matter how good it sounds. I am motivated to think up one counterargument after another. If the salesperson is persistent, I may just decide to say goodbye and hang up the phone. But when I sit down to watch a movie or TV show, I am not planning on having to do a careful analysis of a persuasive message. In the entertainment context, all sorts of messages can get through my normally strong defense system and exert their influence. Persuasion that takes place with less careful scrutiny of the message is referred to by Petty and Cacioppo as **peripheral–route persuasion.** In persuasion by the peripheral route, certain cues in the message lead people to accept the persuasive proposition with little cognitive thought or scrutiny. When people are persuaded while watching movies and programs that are designed to entertain, any influence that occurs is likely to be peripheral-route influence. From the perspective of advertisers who attempt to use the media to sell their products, the biggest obstacle to success is the fact that people recognize a TV commercial or a magazine ad as an attempt to influence attitude or behavior. This recognition can trigger central-route processing, which is a more difficult path to influence. This may be one reason that many advertisers use creative ways to entertain their audience rather than using a strong persuasive appeal. If people process an ad as another entertaining bit of media, they might be more willing to change their attitudes or behaviors with little thought or scrutiny instead of weighing carefully the relative advantages of a particular product. Perhaps this helps to explain why advertisers were willing to pay over $75,000 per second for an ad in the 2001 Super Bowl game. Over the years, people have become accustomed to processing the ads during this game as entertainment instead of persuasion. Advertisers may realize that this state of affairs is very favorable for their purposes—which, ultimately, are persuasive.

The Theory of Media Cultivation

The idea that consumption of entertainment media can change people's attitudes is an idea that has been formalized in one of the major theoretical perspectives of mass communication. **George Gerbner**'s theory of **media cultivation** does not use the term "persuade" to describe the impact of media, but his perspective fits very well into the present discussion. According to Gerbner, the world of media entertainment presents a particular view of **social reality.** For example, content analyses of prime-time TV programs reveal that about 12% of the male characters who hold jobs work in law enforcement. This proportion is a rather gross exaggeration of what actually exists in the real world. In reality, only about 1% of employed males hold jobs in the general area of law enforcement.[12] What happens to the person who makes a steady habit of watching prime-time TV? According to Gerbner, this person gradually becomes "cultivated" into the television view of social reality. Even though there is no particular intent on the part of the creators of the media messages to change attitudes or beliefs, over time, the heavy viewer will begin to believe that the real world resembles the world presented in the media. According to Gerbner, the heavy TV viewer tends to believe that the world is a more violent place than it really is. Accordingly, heavy TV viewers are more likely to express **fear of criminal victimization** and to overestimate their own chances of being involved in violence. While the theory of media cultivation emphasizes gradual changes in beliefs and attitudes, some of Gerbner's studies show behavior changes as well. According to some of the results, heavy TV viewers are more likely to purchase home security devices because of their beliefs in the high probability of criminal victimization. Gerbner summarizes his view in the following way:

> The repetitive "lessons" we learn from television, beginning with infancy, are likely to become the basis for a broader world view, making television a significant source of general values, ideologies, and perspectives as well as specific assumptions, beliefs, and images . . . One example of this is what we have called the "mean world" syndrome . . . [W]e have found that long-term exposure to television, in which frequent violence is virtually inescapable, tends to cultivate the image of a relatively mean and dangerous world. Responses of heavier compared to matching groups of lighter viewers suggest the conception of reality in which greater protection is needed, most people "cannot be trusted," and most people are "just looking out for themselves." [13]

Gerbner and his colleagues believe that they have uncovered evidence in several studies for two processes that show evidence of media cultivation. The first process, **mainstreaming,** refers to what happens when people of different groups are exposed to the same media. Over time, Gerbner believes that the differences that might be expected on the basis of group membership become less pronounced because everyone is being similarly cultivated by media messages. The second process, **resonance,** refers to what happens when a person's real-life environment strongly resembles the environment depicted in the media. For such a person, a "double dose" of the same message is received, making the impact of media cultivation particularly likely. For example, a person who lives in a high-crime neighborhood might naturally fear criminal victimization. If that person also consumes heavy doses of the violent world of TV, the cultivating effect of the media would be particularly powerful because the message is already consistent with the person's real-world experience.

Gerbner's theory of cultivation has certainly had its critics over the years. One of the major constraints that causes reservation among media scholars is that the theory describes processes that seem to defy conclusive testing. Gerbner maintains that the process of media cultivation occurs gradually over time. Consequently, laboratory experiments, which by their very nature observe changes over short time intervals, are not able to shed any insight on the process. Unfortunately, this leaves the survey method as the only major methodological tool for testing the theory. As you know from chapter 2, the survey method is limited in its ability to document causal relationships with certainty. Typically, evidence for media cultivation is presented with positive correlation coefficients between TV exposure and some particular belief about the world. As you will see in the following example, such correlations are difficult to interpret unequivocally as evidence of a causal process.

In an effort to explore the evidence in favor of media cultivation, two researchers, **Anthony Doob** and **Glenn Macdonald,** conducted a survey in the city of Toronto.[14] When they examined their data, they found the same basic relationship between TV exposure and fear of criminal victimization that Gerbner had found in many of his studies. The relationship was positive and statistically significant, showing that heavy TV viewers were more likely to fear being the victim of a crime. While Gerbner tends to interpret such a relationship as evidence for media cultivation (viewing TV causes fear of victimization), Doob and Macdonald wondered whether the relationship wasn't due to a variable that Gerbner had ignored in previous studies: level of crime in a person's neighborhood. They reasoned that people who live in high-crime neighborhoods might naturally fear criminal victimization because crime is indeed a high risk. Moreover, they thought that such people might also tend to stay inside their homes more than people who live in safer places. As a result, the people in high-crime neighborhoods might naturally tend to watch more TV. According to this scenario, the correlation observed by Gerbner between TV viewing and fear of victimization might not result because of a cultivation effect. Instead, it might result because both of these variables are simultaneously affected by the level of crime in one's neighborhood. When Doob and Macdonald divided the city of Toronto into four areas (high- versus low-crime areas in both the city and suburbs), they found that the relationship between TV viewing and fear of victimization was no longer present in three of the four areas. They interpreted this result as evidence in favor of the role of the neighborhood variable and against the media cultivation hypothesis. Gerbner might interpret the same result as evidence for the resonance hypothesis. As it turned out, in the high-crime area of the city, there was still a significant relationship between TV viewing and fear of victimization. This is exactly where Gerbner would expect there to be the strongest relationship between the two variables, due to the double dose of the message received by residents of this type of neighborhood. In the final analysis, Gerbner and his colleagues have produced enough data over the last few decades to keep the theory of media cultivation alive and well. Most researchers do give some credence to the idea that media messages unintentionally exert an influence on the attitudes and beliefs that people hold about the real world.

Do Media Messages About the Paranormal
Influence Paranormal Beliefs?

In the last chapter, you read about the research on frightening mass media and the intense emotional reactions that scary films have on children and adults. I was personally involved in conducting many of these studies. After a number of years, I started paying more attention to the actual content of the movies that people reported as scary. One of the themes noted in the chapter 7 discussion was that many scary movies have paranormal content. Depictions of the paranormal might include ghosts, witches, devils, psychics, ESP (extrasensory perception), UFOs and space aliens, and people who claim they can talk to the dead. One question that I became interested in was whether or not these depictions, quite apart from their capacity to scare people, could change people's beliefs. Are you more inclined to believe in the existence of space aliens after watching a movie like *Close Encounters of the Third Kind?* Just as Gerbner was concerned about the possibility that media messages might cultivate beliefs about the level of crime in the real world, I became concerned about the possibility that media depictions of the paranormal might cultivate beliefs about the existence of a paranormal world.

In order to study this possibility, I began with a very simple experiment.[15] College students were randomly assigned to watch a 30-minute episode of the program *Beyond Reality.* This episode depicted people who could "astral-project" themselves to different locations. What is astral projection? According to those who practice it, it is the ability to leave one's body through deep meditation or a drug-induced state and transport one's spiritual essence to some other location in the universe. The city of Indianapolis has an institute where one can pay hundreds of dollars to learn how to master this incredible skill. (My personal advice would be to save your money.) I was interested in whether or not seeing such behavior depicted in a fictional, entertainment-type program would affect what people believe about the reality of astral projection.

When the USA network aired this episode, they started it off with an announcer's voice and a brief tag that said, "The following incidents are based on actual reports." In my experiment, I decided to assign the students to watch the program in one of four conditions. In the first condition, or the "reality" condition, I included a tag that emphasized the fact that the actors and actresses in the show were fictitious, but the events shown were based on actual reports and were real. In the second condition, or the "fiction" condition, the preliminary tag emphasized that the events were completely fictitious. In the third condition, or the "impossible" condition, the tag emphasized that the events were completely fictitious and also impossible from a scientific perspective. It included a statement that events like this had never actually happened and that if they had happened, it would violate the known laws of nature. In a fourth condition, the "no tag" condition, the students watched the program without any tag at all. Finally, in a control group condition, some students watched an episode of the situation comedy *Perfect Strangers,* which had no references to any paranormal phenomenon. A few weeks before the students watched the program, I measured the extent to which they believed in astral projection and other paranormal activities. After the program was over, I once again measured these beliefs to see if there was any change. Of course, in order to be careful about tipping the students off to what I was studying, I took steps to draw their attention to the fact that I was not very interested in their reactions to the program. Instead, students were led to believe that I was really interested in what they thought about the commercials in the program. At the very end of the study, I asked the students what they thought the study was about. The nearly unanimous verdict was that the study was concerned with reactions to advertising. Most students expressed surprise to learn later about the true purpose of the experiment.

What did the results of the study reveal? The major results concerned the students who watched the program with no tag at all and the students who watched the program with either the fiction tag or the impossible tag. The students who saw no tag *increased* their beliefs in astral projection over their pre-viewing levels; the students in both of the other two conditions *decreased* their beliefs in astral projection. The difference between the groups was statistically significant ($p < .05$; see chapter 2 for a review of this concept). You might ex-pect that the students who were told that the program was real would have in-creased their beliefs the most. That's not what happened. In fact, there was a slight decrease in belief in astral projection among these students, although the decrease was not statistically significant. It could be that telling these students that the events were real caused them to wonder about why they had been told this fact. As they thought about it, they ended up doubting the veracity of the events more than if they had been told nothing at all. This experiment dem-onstrated that, depending upon the information included in a program, view-ers' beliefs about a paranormal phenomenon could be affected. I have now completed several studies that investigate the relationship between media de-pictions of the paranormal and paranormal beliefs.[16] Taken together, these studies show that media messages do exert an influence on what people believe. Depending on the message, people may be persuaded to change their beliefs.

INTENTIONAL PERSUASION IN THE MEDIA

So far in this chapter, we have seen how subliminal persuasion may be practiced in the media even though the evidence for its effectiveness is slim to none. We have also seen how persuasion might occur as a result of media exposure to en-tertainment messages that are not particularly designed to change attitudes and behaviors. One implication of the fact that entertainment messages can per-suade unintentionally is that media practitioners could study these instances and learn to master the principles of persuasion so that they could be applied in an intentional way. Clearly, many messages appear in the media that are designed explicitly with persuasion in mind. How well do these messages work? If they do work, what are the theoretical principles behind their success? The rest of this chapter will focus on these two questions.

The Great American Values Test

One of the major weaknesses of academic research on media effects is that too many of the studies are conducted in the carefully controlled confines of the laboratory. While much is learned from this approach about whether certain message features can cause specific effects, there is the inevitable limitation in generalizing the effects to what happens in a more natural environment (see chapter 2). For this reason, three researchers, **Sandra Ball-Rokeach, Milton Rokeach,** and **Joel Grube,** decided to break away from the confines of the lab-oratory to test the persuasive impact of TV in the real-world setting. The find-ings of their study, the "great American values test," are among some of the most important findings on the persuasive impact of the media.[17] Let's look briefly at what these researchers managed to do.

Back in 1979, the research team was able to produce a 30-minute program designed solely for the purpose of their experiment. The program was co-hosted by Ed Asner of the old *Lou Grant Show* and Sandy Hill of ABC's *Good Morning America*. The program was structured such that the cohosts presented viewers with national survey results showing that Americans ranked "freedom" very high as a value priority but ranked "equality" quite a bit lower. The first part of the program was designed to encourage viewers to think about both of these values and to consider renewing their commitment to each one. The second part of the program was designed to convince viewers to likewise place high value on the importance of the environment and living in a "world of beauty."

The real master stroke that the researchers were able to pull off in this study came with the broadcast of the program. It aired on the evening of February 27, 1979, at 7:30 P.M. Somehow, the researchers were able to get all three commercial channels in Richland, Pasco, and Kennewick (the Tri-Cities area in eastern Washington) to air the program at the same time. This essentially guaranteed that if anyone in those cities watched TV during the 7:30–8:00 P.M. time slot, they would be exposed to the persuasive message. At the same time that the program was on in the Tri-Cities, the authors managed to arrange for the show to be totally blacked out in the city of Yakima, a comparable city about 80 miles away. In advance of the program's broadcast, they were also able to promote the show in *TV Guide* and commercial spots that appeared on the stations.

Through a combination of phone calls to randomly selected households in the four cities, follow-up opinion surveys, and mail solicitations from organizations that promoted the values of freedom, equality, and a world of beauty, the researchers were able to determine whether their program had any persuasive impact. The results were nothing short of impressive. On the mail solicitations that were mailed out to random recipients in the four cities, significantly more people from the Tri-Cities area donated to the causes than did the people from Yakima, the city where the program was not shown. Of particular interest in the study was a comparison between those people who reported that they watched the program without interruption versus those who never saw the program or those who were interrupted during the program by things like phone calls or an unexpected visitor. The uninterrupted viewers responded to the mail solicitations with anywhere from four to six times the amount of money contributed by the nonviewers. They gave about nine times the amount of money that the interrupted viewers gave. In general, the uninterrupted viewers also changed their value structure so that freedom, equality, and a world of beauty were all elevated as a result of exposure to the program.

Just as laboratory experiments have limitations in terms of generalizing results beyond the experimenter's carefully controlled research situation, natural experiments such as the one conducted by Ball-Rokeach, Rokeach, and Grube are also limited in terms of reaching conclusions about the exact reasons for the results. Perhaps the differences in the amount of money given by the various groups had little to do with the fact that some people were interrupted during the program and others were not. Maybe there was something different about the people who reported interruptions in viewing (for example, living in a busier household) that made it less likely that they would give money to *any* solicitation. Nevertheless, despite the study's limitations, it is clear that the broadcast did exert a powerful influence on the audience. Advertisers were probably not surprised by the results.

How Does an Advertiser Determine Success?

As we attempt to address the question of persuasive effectiveness of the media, it is important to keep in mind that effectiveness is a relative term. If you were an advertiser who paid for a 30-second ad on TV, how would you decide if the ad was worth the cost? One criterion that advertisers use is the cost-per-person statistic. Because national TV ads reach millions of people, the cost per person for the ad is often extremely low (just pennies per person), even though the total cost of the ad might be over $1 million. Of course, even if the cost per person is extremely low, the investment would not be worthwhile if no one responded to the ad by purchasing the product. How many purchases need to result from one ad to make the advertising venture worthwhile? When millions of people are in the audience, a very small response rate might still make the ad cost effective. The point here is that from the advertising perspective, a relatively small effect can transfer into profits. An ad is often deemed to be an effective example of persuasion when 99% of the audience fails to respond. The 1% who do respond are more than enough to offset the cost of the ad.

Some Evidence for the Effectiveness of Advertising

Having recognized the important point that advertising effectiveness may not always be impressive in terms of the percentage of people who respond to the message, it is still instructive to contemplate some of the impressive results that have been achieved with persuasive campaigns in the media. The same ad executive from Wyse Advertising who told me that 10% of advertising contains some subliminal technique told me that a single-page ad in a large metropolitan newspaper is expected to yield a minimum revenue that equals 10 times the cost of the ad. Thus, if the ad costs $15,000, the department store that runs the ad expects revenues to increase $150,000 over the amount that would have been received if the ad had not appeared. If you're in the advertising business, these figures translate into the realization that newspaper advertising is a powerful persuasive technique.

Many other companies have also realized that media advertising is a powerful choice. A few years ago, the executives of the Northwest Mutual Life Insurance Company discovered that their company had very poor name recognition. In fact, people tended to recognize 33 other insurance company names better than theirs. But after 2 weeks of advertising on TV, they improved their name recognition so that only two company names were recognized ahead of theirs. It cost the company $1 million to accomplish this feat, but the effort was considered to be cost efficient.[18]

Advertisers discovered the power of television to increase sales back in the 1950s. That's when the Mattel toy company decided to pour money into a TV ad campaign. The results of that campaign are now legendary. The company increased their value by a factor of about 25![19]

The effectiveness of campaigns like Mattel's raised a number of issues related to children. For the most part, Mattel was advertising to the children in the TV audience. A number of studies by **Charles Atkin** reveal that children who are heavy viewers of TV ads are more likely to consume the products in those ads and more likely to ask their parents to buy the products that they see advertised.[20] A political action organization, Action for Children's Television (ACT), actively lobbied Congress for years to prohibit advertising directed to children. Even though the data point clearly to the conclusion that children are heavily influenced by advertising, lawmakers found the proposals from ACT to be unworkable. The Saturday-morning time slot is still an advertising bonanza directed to children. The fact that advertisers continue to pay huge sums of money for their messages should be instructive. Advertising works. It is persuasive.

The Third-Person Effect

Suppose someone asked you if you thought that the mass media persuaded people to change their attitudes and behavior. What would you say? Suppose someone asked you if you thought that the mass media persuaded YOU to change your attitudes and behavior. If you are like many people, you will agree that the media influence others. However, when the question turns in a personal direction, you will resist admitting that you are personally affected. This tendency to think that media influence is stronger for other people than it is for one's self is a phenomenon that media researchers have documented in several studies.[21] Years ago, a psychologist named **Phillip Zimbardo** noticed the same tendency when he studied persuasion in the context of cult groups that employ brainwashing. He referred to this tendency as the **"illusion of personal invulnerability."** He discovered that students of persuasion tended to think of themselves as people who would never succumb to the pressures of brainwashing. At the same time, they found it easy to assume that the same brainwashing techniques would work on others. Zimbardo noted that this attitude was not particularly healthy. In order to maximize resistance to persuasion, it is best to have a proper understanding of one's own vulnerability.[22]

SOME KEY PRINCIPLES OF
MEDIA PERSUASION

If media messages are persuasive, what are the key ingredients that contribute to their power? Psychologists have studied the persuasion process scientifically for over 50 years. As a result of their study, much has been learned about the dynamics of persuasion. Study Box 8-1 details some of the common principles

STUDY BOX 8-1   Weapons of Influence

In his analysis of persuasion, Robert Cialdini has identified at least six principles that he claims are ubiquitous in daily life. By learning to recognize these principles, you may be able to guard against the persuasive attempts that you are bombarded with from the mass media. After you read about the principles, see if you can identify how they are used in the media. The principles are as follows:

1. **Reciprocity:** If someone does something for you, you usually feel like you need to reciprocate and do something in return. This principle can be used to persuade you. When some charity group sends you free address labels with its logo and slogan to place on your mailing envelopes, you may be more vulnerable to the charity's persuasive pitch. Since the group gave you something, your automatic response may be that you need to give it something. The danger, of course, is that you end up giving much more than you received.

2. **Commitment and Consistency:** People strive for consistency in their behavior. Sometimes, your determination to appear consistent can be used against you. Suppose you resist the reciprocity rule and decide to use your address labels without sending any money to the charity. You might not be off the hook just yet. As you continue to attach the address labels on your envelopes, you realize that every piece of mail you send out is an expression of support for the charity. A few months later, when the charity solicits you for a donation, you may feel more inclined to give in order to maintain consistency with your prior commitment.

3. **Social Proof:** When we are not sure how to behave, we look to others around us for guidance. Producers of TV sitcoms know that their programs will be perceived as funnier if they include laugh tracks. Apparently, people are persuaded that the content of the show is more humorous if they hear other people laughing at the one-liners.

4. **Liking:** If we like someone, we are more susceptible to being influenced by that person. One car salesman attributes his great success to the cards he sends his customers that simply say "I like you." The power of this strategy may reside in the fact that few people want to believe that such an expression of affection could be disingenuous. After all, you are a very likeable person, aren't you?

5. **Authority:** We tend to respond more readily to messages delivered by people whom we regard as authority figures. Who would you tend to believe more about the virtues of spending money to travel to Mars—the author of this textbook, or Leonard Nimoy, who played Spock in the *Star Trek* episodes? You may have found yourself instantly wanting to go with Leonard Nimoy. But does playing a part in a TV show really make one an authority? Persuasive practitioners often try to capitalize on our urge to go with an authority figure by presenting us with messages from people who only appear to be authorities. Appearances can often be deceiving.

6. **Scarcity:** We tend to go after things that appear to be in high demand. If everyone wants it, it must be good. How many advertisers use the scarcity appeal by telling us that their offers are good "only while supplies last." This phrase gives the impression that people are going to be beating down the door to obtain the product. If the product is in such high demand and will soon be gone, it must be worth whatever price is being charged. Right? Well, maybe. The danger of relying exclusively on the scarcity of a product to determine its worth is that you might soon discover that the true merits of the product weren't worth the price you paid.

SOURCE: Cialdini, R. (1985). *Influence: Science and practice.* Glenview, IL.: Scott Foresman.

of persuasion identified by **Robert Cialdini** in his classic text on the subject. Let's take a brief look at what the research has discovered about how people change their attitudes and behavior.

The Power of the Source

Back in the 1950s, **Carl Hovland** and **Walter Weiss** reported a ground-breaking experiment that is now famous in the annals of persuasion research.[23] In a simple experiment, they exposed people to a persuasive message that argued that atomic-powered submarines were perfectly feasible for future development. At the time they ran the experiment, such submarines were non-existent and little more than a fanciful dream. It might be similar to arguing today for the feasibility of establishing a city on Mars or for the feasibility of traveling back in time. Hovland and Weiss set up the experiment so that some of the participants received the message from the official newspaper of the Communist Party, *Pravda*. The rest of the participants received the message from J. Robert Oppenheimer, a well-known and well-respected atomic physicist. Prior to the experiment, the participants indicated their opinions on this topic. After they read the message, they indicated their opinions once again. You can probably guess which group of participants was more persuaded about the feasibility of atomic-powered subs. The participants who heard the message from Oppenheimer were much more likely to change their view. Why? As it turns out, the key reason has to do with the **credibility** of the source. Oppenheimer was a much more credible source than *Pravda*.

What makes a source more or less credible? Two of the chief components of source credibility are **expertise** and **trustworthiness.** Expertise has to do with the extent to which people perceive that the source of the message is a real expert on the topic that he or she is speaking about. Trustworthiness has to do with the extent to which people find the source of the message to be reliable or truthful. If advertisers can find sources who have both of these ingredients, they stand a good chance of putting together a persuasive ad. One practitioner of persuasion, **Tony Schwartz,** was able to design a brief antismoking commercial for the Foundation for a Smoke-Free Indoor Environment. The brief spot simply featured a single man talking to the camera. The spot worked because the man was not just any man. He was a source who had maximum expertise and trustworthiness. Below, I have included the text of this ad so you can see a vivid example of source credibility in action:

> My name is Patrick Reynolds. My grandfather, R. J. Reynolds, founded the tobacco company which now manufactures Camels, Winstons, and Salems. We've all heard the tobacco industry say that there are no ill effects caused by smoking. Well, we have plenty of cigarette-caused disease and death right here in the R. J. Reynolds family itself. My grandfather, R. J. Reynolds Jr., smoked heavily and died of emphysema. My mother smoked and had emphysema and heart disease. And two of my aunts, also heavy smokers, died of emphysema and cancer. Three of my older broth-

ers who smoke have emphysema. I smoked for 10 years and have small airways lung disease. Now tell me, do you think the cigarette companies are truthful when they tell you that smoking isn't harmful? What do you think?[24]

This brief spot managed to combine expertise and trustworthiness in a single source. Who would be perceived as more of an expert on the effects of smoking than a member of a family who owned a tobacco company? As for trustworthiness, by appearing to speak against the financial interests of his own family, the message delivered by Patrick Reynolds seemed particularly reliable. When the audience perceives that the source of the message has little to gain by delivering a particular message, then the source is likely to be perceived as particularly trustworthy.

Message Features: Simplicity and Repetition

Bill Moyers, an award-winning journalist who has made a series of videos for the Public Broadcasting Company, conducted an interview in one of his documentaries with **Fritz Hippler,** the mastermind of most of the German propaganda films made during Adolph Hitler's reign of terror.[25] When asked what made propaganda so effective, Hippler didn't hesitate. The two principles he identified were **simplicity** and **repetition.** These were essentially the same principles noted in another interview that Bill Moyers did with **Rosser Reeves,** the advertising man who developed campaigns for Dwight Eisenhower, M&M candies, Bic pens, and Anacin pain reliever, to mention just a few. Reeves stated that too many advertising people "get tangled up in their own underwear" instead of communicating messages that are simple and to the point.[26] Both Hippler and Reeves had discovered something that researchers have documented in laboratory experiments. John Cacioppo and Richard Petty showed that a repeated message was more persuasive than one that was heard only once. But repetition does have its limits. After about three exposures, Cacioppo and Petty found that people started to become bored by the same message, and persuasive impact started to decrease.[27] Commercial advertisers who use radio and TV often fail to appreciate how quickly a commercial message "burns out" with the audience. The research suggests that campaigns need infusions of new life with some regularity in order to prevent consumer boredom.

More Message Features: Fear, Guilt, and Humor

If you think about some of the commercials that you have seen or heard over the years, you will probably have little trouble identifying messages that used one of the three appeals listed above: fear, guilt, or humor. Let's look briefly at each one of these message features from the perspective of persuasion research. How effective are they?

Fear appeals have been a standard part of the persuader's arsenal for as long as persuasion has been practiced. Just last night, I saw a commercial for a children's fever-reducing remedy. The commercial seemed designed to induce some mild level of fear about what might happen if my child's fever went too high. Of course, use of the advertised pain reliever was presented as the remedy. Do such appeals work? In their exhaustive review of the theory and research results pertaining to fear appeals in persuasion, psychologists **Alice Eagly** and **Shelly Chaiken** answer the question:

> What is the effect of fear or threat on persuasion? . . . For the applied health professional, then, the most important question about public health communications is whether scare tactics enhance or inhibit their efficacy. On this bottom line issue, the research findings are fairly clear: The vast majority of experiments have found that higher levels of threat lead to greater persuasion than lower levels.[28]

Fear appeals do tend to increase persuasion. While this research conclusion seems simple enough, the theory and research behind the conclusion are anything but simple. Over the years, researchers have had to wade through many studies appearing to contain inconsistent findings. The theories in the area are quite diverse, yet no particular theory seems to enjoy clear support. One example of the complexity involved in predicting the success of fear appeals is the **protection motivation theory.**[29] According to this view, to the extent that fear appeals convince an audience of the severity of a threat, their vulnerability to the threat, and their ability to respond effectively to the threat, they will be persuasive. On the other hand, to the extent that the audience perceives that yielding to the persuasive message will be costly in some way, even high fear appeals might not be effective.

Sometimes, media messages bypass the strategy of inducing fear in favor of trying to make you feel *guilty* for not responding to a persuasive appeal. One reason for the prevalence of guilt appeals is that it is relatively easy to make people feel guilty. Parents who have their children's welfare at heart are easy prey for the persuader who wants to induce guilt. As a parent, how can I live with myself if I don't have the very best tires on my car to keep my child as safe as possible? Or how about the very best computer for my child's pursuit of education? Advertisers are well aware that it is relatively easy to play on feelings of guilt. Does it work? According to communication researcher, **Em Griffin,** guilt appeals are certainly persuasive—at least in the context of interpersonal communication.[30] If you feel guilty and I am standing in your face asking you to comply with a request, the chances are good that you will comply. People can be motivated to do many things because they feel guilty. But Griffin warns about some side effects of the guilt appeal that persuaders would do well to consider carefully. He maintains that most people tend to avoid and devalue the ones who make us feel guilty. This would seem to hold important implications for using guilt in a mass media campaign. Because there is no individual person who has to be confronted directly, media campaigns that are based on guilt may tend to backfire. Indeed, there is evidence that consumers respond with anger when a media advertisement makes them feel guilty.[31]

The final message ingredient examined briefly in this chapter is humor. If you've ever had the chance the see the annual Clio Awards given for outstanding achievement in advertising, then you know that many of the award winners are commercials that feature some type of humorous appeal. Practitioners of persuasion have long believed that being funny makes them more persuasive. The idea is based on the notion that humor tends to attract attention to the message, creates a more favorable attitude toward the source of the message and the product, and may produce a general orientation toward the message that is less critical. In other words, if people are laughing, they can't be thinking too hard about the arguments against your message. Perhaps the really funny thing in all of this is that researchers have had a difficult time documenting the superiority of humorous messages in persuasive campaigns. There may be good reason for the difficulty. While humor may attract attention, it may attract attention to itself instead of to the persuasive message. People may remember the joke—but not what product they're supposed to buy. It may also be the case that humor tends to discourage the consumer from taking the product very seriously. It may be true that people who are laughing are not thinking up reasons why they shouldn't buy the product. On the other hand, they may not be thinking seriously about buying the product at all. They are simply too busy laughing. Still, advertisers continue to use humor in campaign after campaign. Why? One reason may be because humor is tolerated much easier on repetition. It wears well. Another reason may be because advertisers are convinced that people feel positive sentiment toward the source that makes them laugh. In today's competitive media market, positive sentiment is a precious commodity. Regardless of the research findings, it is a relative certainty that advertisers will continue to pack their ads with humorous appeals.

The Health Campaign

It is one thing to use the media to persuade people to buy products. It is another thing to use the media to persuade them to adopt healthy behaviors. In fact, these two uses of the media often conflict. For years, TV and radio saturated the culture with commercial messages designed to encourage smoking behavior. More recently, the airwaves have been used to deliver a very different message about smoking (see Web Links at the end of the chapter). At the same time that the government wants to invest in persuasive messages to reduce drug use, the commercial messages during sporting events sell young people on the virtues of alcohol consumption. Is there any evidence that media messages can be used to change public health behavior for the good? As it turns out, persuasive principles are persuasive principles. The same principles that persuade people to engage in unhealthy behavior can also be used to persuade them to engage in healthy behavior.

Some of the most impressive data-sets that argue in favor of using the media to address public health problems come from other countries. Working in Bolivia, researchers **Thomas Valente** and **Walter Saba** reported the results of two surveys taken a year apart and involving over 3,000 respondents. The goal of these surveys was to evaluate the effectiveness of a major campaign to encourage reproductive health practices (the use of safe contraception, etc.). The campaign included 11 different TV and radio spots, and the researchers measured how the campaign affected both information and behavior. The results indicated that people who were exposed to the mass media campaign were more likely to adopt contraception into their sexual practices. There was also some evidence that the media campaign was likeliest to have an effect on those who did not have a rich interpersonal network. It is worth noting here that the effect of exposure to the campaign was not particularly large in statistical terms, but it was statistically significant (see chapter 2 for a review of these concepts).[32]

Similar to the findings in Bolivia, another survey of over 1,200 mothers in the Philippines found evidence that exposure to a media campaign about preventing the measles had a significant impact on increasing specific knowledge about the disease. Once again, the media—and not interpersonal networks—seemed to be the source of the information gains.[33] A study of nearly 1,700 smokers and ex-smokers by researchers working on the Finnish North Karelia Project also found that for the men in the study, weekly exposure to mass media health messages was significantly correlated with attempts to stop smoking. Unlike the studies in Bolivia and the Philippines, interpersonal communication also had an impact on efforts to quit. The respondents who received both media and interpersonal communication were the most resistant to the temptation to begin smoking.[34]

Health communication is an emerging area of study. To this point, much of the research has been correlational. You know from the preceding chapters that we must be careful about assuming that the media exert a causal force if we don't have the data needed to make that conclusion. Still, the evidence does seem to be mounting that persuasive health campaigns using the mass media can have an effect on individual behavior. Researchers at the University of Kentucky have done a number of investigations that look at how individuals differ in their response to media health messages. They have found that sensation seekers are more likely to use drugs and are more likely to respond well to media messages that are high in novelty and action.[35] Another researcher, **Richard Perloff,** has recently summarized research on media campaigns designed to convince people to have safer sex.[36] The implication that this research holds for addressing the AIDS crisis and other sexually transmitted disease is obvious. We shouldn't be surprised to find that research on media health campaigns is turning up evidence that persuasive tactics work. If the media are able to persuade people to buy products, laugh, adopt attitudes of fear toward their environment, and even take their own lives, they should be able to influence people to change their health habits.

In concluding this chapter, it is important to note that persuasion in the media is a topic that goes well beyond a single chapter in a text like this one. About all we can do here is touch some of the highlights. The next chapter explores some other dimensions of this topic when it takes up research on politics in the media. In politics, persuasion is the name of the game, and we will take a closer look at how that game is played.

SUMMARY

Significant persuasion involves attitude and behavior changes that persist over time. In the 1950s, James Vicary made claims about the effectiveness of subliminal advertising in the media. Although such advertising is practiced today, research studies have generally failed to find evidence that it works effectively. There is no doubt that media messages persuade, however. Much of this persuasion is unintentional. Gerbner's theory of media cultivation claims that media messages cultivate particular views of social reality. The theory is somewhat controversial but does enjoy some empirical support. Of course, the media is full of persuasive messages that are deliberately designed to influence. Researchers have studied the influence process and have identified many important variables and developed theoretical ideas to explain how persuasion works. Much of the research has concentrated on understanding how the source of a message affects persuasion and how particular message factors contribute to the process. Recent research in the field of health communication shows promise for documenting how media messages are capable of improving people's health habits.

KEY TERMS AND CONCEPTS

Persuasion 127

   attitude 127

   behavior 127

   persistence 127

Subliminal persuasion 128

Psychoanalytic or Freudian perspective 129

Supraliminal 130

Illusory placebo effect 130

Elaboration likelihood model 132

central versus peripheral route to persuasion 132, 133

Counter-attitudinal message 132

Theory of media cultivation 133

Social reality 133

   fear of criminal victimization 133

   mainstreaming 134

   resonance 134

The third-person effect 140

Illusion of personal invulnerability 140

Credibility 142

   expertise 142

   trustworthiness 142

Simplicity 143

Repetition 143

Protection motivation theory 144

KEY NAMES

Wilson Bryan Key 128

James Vicary 128

Sigmund Freud 129

Anthony Pratkanis and Anthony Greenwald 130

Richard Petty and John Cacioppo 132

George Gerbner 133

Anthony Doob and Glenn Macdonald 134

Sandra Ball-Rokeach, Milton Rokeach, and Joel Grube 137

Charles Atkin 140

Phillip Zimbardo 140

Robert Cialdini 142

Carl Hovland and Walter
   Weiss 142

Tony Schwartz 142

Fritz Hippler 143

Rosser Reeves 143

Alice Eagly and Shelly
   Chaiken 144

Em Griffin 144

Thomas Valente and
   Walter Saba 145

Richard Perloff 146

WEB LINKS

1. For information on a successful media campaign that reduced teen smoking, try . . .
   http://www2.cancer.org/zine/index.cfm?fn=001_05031999_0

2. For information on an antismoking campaign launched during the Super Bowl, try . . .
   http://www2.cancer.org/zine/index.cfm?fn=004_02122001_0

3. For a good all-around site that deals with persuasion in everyday settings, try . . . http://
   www.influenceatwork.com/index.html

To learn more about the topics in this chapter, enter the Key Terms and Concepts and Key Names found in this chapter as subject and keyword searches on your InfoTrac College Edition.

NOTES

1. Key, W. B. (1973). *Subliminal seduction.* Englewood Cliffs, NJ: Signet. Key, W. B. (1976). *Media Sexploitation.* Englewood Cliffs, NJ: Signet.

2. Pratkanis, A. R. (1992). The cargo-cult science of subliminal persuasion. *Skeptical Inquirer, 16,* 260–272.

3. Cousins, N. (1957, October 5). Smudging the subconscious. *Saturday Review.*

4. Danzig, F. (1962, September 17). Subliminal advertising—Today it's just historic flashback for researcher Vicary. *Advertising Age.*

5. Pratkanis, A. R., & Greenwald, A. G. (1988). Recent perspectives on unconscious processing: Still no marketing applications. *Psychology & Marketing, 5,* 339–355.

6. Pratkanis, A. R. (1992). The cargo-cult science of subliminal persuasion. *Skeptical Inquirer, 16,* 260–272.

7. Epley, N., Savitsky, K., & Kachelski, R. A. (1999). What every skeptic should know about subliminal persuasion. *Skeptical Inquirer, 23,* 40–45.

8. Public Broadcasting System. (1984). *On Television: The Violence Factor.*

9. Schofield, J. W., & Pavelchak, M. A. (1989). Fallout from "The Day After": The impact of a TV film on attitudes related to nuclear war. *Journal of Applied Social Psychology, 19,* 433–448.

10. Aronson, E. (1995). *The social animal.* New York: W. H. Freeman.

11. Petty, R. E., & Cacioppo, J. T. (1986). The elaboration likelihood model of persuasion. In L. Berkowitz (Ed.), *Advances in Experimental Social Psychology* (pp. 123–205). Hillsdale, NJ: Erlbaum.

12. Dominick, J. R. (1999). *The dynamics of mass communication.* Boston, MA: McGraw-Hill.

13. Gerbner, G., Gross, L., Morgan, M., & Signorielli, N. (1994). Growing up with television: The cultivation perspective. In J. Bryant & D. Zillmann (Eds.), *Media effects: Advances in theory and research* (pp. 17–41). Hillsdale, NJ: Erlbaum.

14. Doob, A. N., & Macdonald, G. E. (1979). Television viewing and fear of victimization: Is the relationship causal? *Journal of Personality & Social Psychology, 37,* 170–179.

15. Sparks, G. G., Hansen, T., & Shah, R. (1994). Do televised depictions of para-

normal events influence viewers' paranormal beliefs? *Skeptical Inquirer, 18,* 386–395.

16. Sparks, G. G., Nelson, C. L., & Campbell, R. G. (1997). The relationship between exposure to televised messages about paranormal phenomena and paranormal beliefs. *Journal of Broadcasting & Electronic Media, 41,* 345–359. Sparks, G. G., & Pellechia, M. (1997). The effect of news stories about UFOs on readers' UFO beliefs: The role of confirming or disconfirming testimony from a scientist. *Communication Reports, 10,* 165–172. Sparks, G. G., Pellechia, M., & Irvine, C. (1998). Does television news about UFOs affect viewers' UFO beliefs?: An experimental investigation. *Communication Quarterly, 46,* 284–294. Sparks, G. G., Sparks, C. W., & Gray, K. (1995). Media impact on fright reactions and belief in UFOs: The potential role of mental imagery. *Communication Research, 22,* 3–23. Sparks, G. G., & Miller, W. (2001). Investigating the relationship between exposure to television programs that depict paranormal phenomena and beliefs in the paranormal. *Communication Monographs, 68,* 98–113.

17. Ball-Rokeach, S. J., Rokeach, M., & Grube, J. W. (1984, November). The great American values test: Can television alter basic beliefs? *Psychology Today,* 34–41.

18. Aronson, E. (1995). *The social animal.* New York: W. H. Freeman.

19. Liebert, R. M., & Sprafkin, J. (1988). *The early window: Effects of television on children and youth.* New York: Pergamon Press.

20. Atkin, C. K. (1978). Observation of parent-child interaction in supermarket decision making. *Journal of Marketing, 42,* 41–45.

21. Shah, D. V., Faber, R. J., & Youn, S. (1999). Susceptibility and severity: Perceptual dimensions underlying the third-person effect. *Communication Research, 26,* 240–267.

22. Zimbardo, P. G., Ebbesen, E. B., & Maslach, C. (1977). *Influencing attitudes and changing behavior.* Reading, MA: Addison-Wesley.

23. Hovland, C., & Weiss, W. (1951). The influence of source credibility on communication effectiveness. *Public Opinion Quarterly, 15,* 635–650.

24. Hoffman, D., & Duggan, W. (Producers). (1989). *Guerilla media: A citizen's guide to using electronic media for social change. The inside story from Tony Schwartz* [Video recording]. Princeton, NJ: Films for the Humanities.

25. Moyers, B. D. (Producer). (1988). *World War II: The propaganda battle* [Video recording]. Washington, DC: PBS Films.

26. CEL. (1984). The 30-second president. In *A walk through the twentieth century with Bill Moyers.* Washington, D.C.: Public Broadcasting Service.

27. Cacioppo, J. T., & Petty, R. E. (1979). Effects of message repetition and position on cognitive response, recall, and persuasion. *Journal of Personality and Social Psychology, 37,* 97–109.

28. Eagly, A. H., & Chaiken, S. (1993). *The psychology of attitudes.* Fort Worth, TX: Harcourt Brace Jovanovich.

29. Rogers, R. W. (1975). A protection motivation theory of fear appeals and attitude change. *Journal of Psychology, 91,* 93–114.

30. Griffin, E. (1976). *The mindchangers: The art of Christian persuasion.* Wheaton, IL: Tyndale.

31. Pinto, M. B., & Priest, S. (1991). Guilt appeals in advertising: An exploratory study. *Psychological Reports, 69,* 375–385.

32. Valente, T. W., & Saba, W. P. (1998). Mass media and interpersonal influence in a reproductive health communication campaign in Bolivia. *Communication Research, 25*(1), 96–124.

33. McDivitt, J., Zimicki, S., & Hornick, R. C. (1997). Explaining the impact of a communication campaign to change vaccination knowledge and coverage in the Philippines. *Health Communication, 9*(2), 95–118.

34. Korhonen, T., Uutela, A., Korhonen, H. J., & Puska, P. (1998). Impact of mass media and interpersonal health communication on smoking cessation attempts: A study in North Karelia, 1989–1996. *Journal of Health Communication, 3*(2), 105–118.

35. Donohew, L., Palmgreen, P., & Lorch, E. P. (1994). Attention, need for sensation, and health communication campaigns. *American Behavioral Scientist, 38*(2), 310–322.

36. Perloff, R. M. (2001). *Persuading people to have safer sex: Applications of social science to the AIDS crisis.* Mahwah, NJ: Erlbaum.

9

■

The Effects of News and Political Content

DO CERTAIN NEWS REPORTS CAUSE MORE PEOPLE TO DIE?

Several years ago, soon after I had left a job at Cleveland State University for my current position at Purdue, I received a phone call from a news reporter who worked for the Cleveland *Plain Dealer*. Usually, phone calls from reporters mean that someone has read a press release from my university that gives details on one of my studies. In this case, however, the reporter was not interested in my research. Instead, he was interested in knowing my opinion about whether an article that he was about to submit for publication in the newspaper would bring about more death in the city of Cleveland. He believed that he was in an ethical dilemma. He wanted to report the news, but he also didn't want to bring about unnecessary harm to the city that he loved. This reporter's concern was not typical. I had never before received a phone call quite like his and I have not received one since. Why did this reporter think that his article might cause an increase in deaths in the city of Cleveland? Was there any basis for his concern? As it turns out, there certainly was! The article he planned to submit was a news report that told about the death of a well-known city official who had committed suicide.

Imitative Suicides and the News

About 20 years ago, a sociologist, **David Phillips,** published an article that presented a provocative set of findings. Phillips took note of the dates on which suicide stories appeared in newspapers. Then he went to the statistical archives for the area served by the newspapers and discovered that a few days following these stories, automobile fatalities in the area increased.[1] Phillips also noticed that the more publicity the suicide story received (front page versus succeeding pages), the greater the increase in automobile fatalities. Could it be that the publication of a suicide story in the newspaper actually served as a trigger for other people to commit suicide themselves? As incredible as it might seem, the more data that Phillips examined, the more convincing the case became. Phillips reasoned that if people were really using their cars to commit suicide, there should be more of an increase in single-car accidents than other types of accidents after the suicide stories appeared. This is exactly what he found.

The increase in fatalities following newspaper suicide stories may not be limited to automobiles. In another study, Phillips discovered the same kind of effect for fatal crashes involving private, business, and corporate-executive airplane crashes.[2] Again, the more publicity given to the suicide, the greater the number of plane crashes that occurred. The increase in crashes was limited to the states in which the suicide story was most heavily publicized. A prominent social psychologist, **Robert Cialdini,** is convinced that Phillips has unveiled an important media effect. He summarized his views in his own popular book on the subject of influence:

> The influence of suicide stories on car and plane crashes, then, is fantastically specific. Stories of pure suicides, in which only one person dies, generate wrecks in which only one person dies; stories of suicide-murder combinations, in which there are multiple deaths, generate wrecks in which there are multiple deaths. . . . I am left wholly convinced and, simultaneously, wholly amazed by it . . . Phillips' findings illustrate a distressing tendency for suicide publicity to motivate certain people who are similar to the victim to kill themselves—because they now find the idea of suicide more legitimate.[3]

Phillips reasoned that if the statistics he examined really indicated that news stories about suicide were causing an increase in suicides, the same effect might be observed with other types of media messages. He turned to the world of soap operas and found the same effect. Documented suicides and automobile accidents both increased immediately after soap opera story lines included plots that involved a suicide.[4] This sort of media effect that Phillips's data seem to support has turned up before in the context of books. When Johann von Goethe published his book *The Sorrows of Young Werther,* suicides increased in Europe to such a degree that the book was banned in several countries. The major character in the book takes his own life. Apparently, some empathetic readers decided to imitate the fictional character. The experience that Europe had with this novel is sometimes commemorated by media effects scholars by dubbing the imitative-suicide effect documented by Phillips and others as the **Werther effect.**

If you still are having a little trouble believing that news reports of suicides can trigger an increase in the suicide rate, consider the recent evidence documented by **Elmar Etzersdorfer** and **Gernot Sonneck** on the Vienna experience. In the late 1970s, it apparently became quite common for people to use the new subway system in Vienna as a way to commit suicide. The news media organizations adopted the practice of reporting on these suicides in a very dramatic way. Consistent with Phillips's data, suicide rates spiraled upward. In order to address this situation, the Austrian Association for Suicide Prevention developed guidelines for media reporting of suicides that discouraged such dramatic reporting. The suicide rate promptly dropped more than 80% and has remained low ever since. A good portion of this drop was probably the result of a media campaign aimed to discourage suicide, but some of the decrease was probably also related to the news media's change in reporting suicide stories with such sensation.

One important question that arises about the Werther effect is whether the effect is just a **repositioning** or **rescheduling effect** as opposed to an **additive effect.** That is, think about the situation where suicides increase after a well-publicized suicide story. Would the people who committed suicide after the news story decide to commit suicide anyway at some later point in time? If so, then over the long haul, we would expect to see some decrease in the normal rate of suicide such that the overall rate remained predictably stable. The media story in this case would simply cause a rescheduling of suicides. But when Phillips examined his data, he discovered that this was not what tended to happen. Instead, it appears that the sudden increases in suicide following a media story about a suicide result in a genuine addition to the number of suicides that would have occurred had the story never been published.

Given the research findings, you might be wondering what I told the conscientious reporter from the Cleveland *Plain Dealer.* I told him about Phillips's research and gave him some of the original study citations. Then I cautioned him about placing the story on the front page of the newspaper. Phillips's work definitely suggests that the imitative suicide effect decreases if the stories do not receive wide publicity by appearing on page one. I never received a copy of the story that the reporter wrote, but he told me that he would recommend to his editor that it appear somewhere other than the front page.

THINKING ABOUT THE NEWS

Phillips's studies on the impact of news stories about suicide do have a few important limitations in terms of documenting clear evidence for media effects. First, it isn't possible to know for sure that any of the people involved in the automobile or plane fatalities actually were exposed to the media suicide story. The only data Phillips presents are raw statistics. Some sociologists also note that the theoretical process behind this effect is not particularly clear. Why do some people commit suicide and not others? How can we understand the factors that bring about this effect? While there is a need to develop in more detail the theory behind Phillips's data, one of the first processes to take place after people process news reports is a relatively simple one: thought or rumination. It seems clear that if a person reads a news story about suicide or hears a brief account on TV, the story may or may not trigger additional thoughts or ruminations. Some people may shake their heads and forget the story in an instant. Others may be struck about some feature of the story and begin to ruminate in a way that connects the story with their own personal experiences. What determines the amount of thought a person devotes to a news story?

Need for Cognition

John Cacioppo and **Richard Petty** developed a concept in their research on attitude change that has proved helpful in some studies on media effects. These researchers introduced the idea that certain people have a high **need for cognition** compared to other people who have a low need for cognition.[5] That is, some people are simply motivated to think a lot. If there is an opportunity to think about a topic, people with a high need for cognition will be inclined to take it. One media scholar, **Elizabeth Perse,** thought that Cacioppo and Petty's concept might be useful for predicting who pays attention to local television news. In a survey of over 300 people, she found a statistically significant correlation between need for cognition and attention paid to government news.[6] This general finding was replicated in 1992 by **Mollie Condra,** who found that people with a higher need for cognition were more likely to be interested in media dealing with politics.[7] Most recently, in a study of Flemish television viewers, more evidence emerged for the notion that people with a high need for cognition prefer public television and news programming.[8]

The need for cognition concept suggests that some people may be more likely to think about a news report and ruminate on it after exposure. Of course, this variable alone would not be sufficient to explain why some people see news stories about suicide and imitate the suicide behavior. There are many different ways that one could ruminate on a news story about suicide that would not lead to imitative behavior. But in contrast to a person with low need for cognition who might put little thought into a given news story, the person with high need for cognition might, at the least, be more likely to continue thinking about the reported events.

Political Sophistication

Another concept that seems related to the need for cognition was introduced recently into the communication literature by **June Rhee** and **Joseph Cappella.**[9] These authors were interested in trying to explain why some news viewers come away from a story having learned very little information while other viewers learned quite a bit. Working in the realm of politics, these authors developed the concept of **political sophistication.** One's level of political sophistication is a function of knowledge and political ideology. If one knows very little and doesn't have a well-developed political ideology, sophistication is low. On the other hand, if one knows a great deal and has definite political views, then one's sophistication is high. Rhee and Cappella found that after exposure to news stories about health care reform and a mayoral election campaign, those viewers who were politically sophisticated had learned more and had higher quality arguments about the issues when they were given a chance to write about their own views.

Phillips's data on imitative suicides certainly suggest that exposure to news reports can trigger a certain kind of thinking among some consumers. Similarly, the studies that link need for cognition with a preference for viewing news seem to suggest that the news media may naturally tend to appeal to those with a disposition to think about ideas, concepts, or implications. The research on political sophistication seems to suggest the same kind of news effect on certain individuals. But is there any hard evidence that exposure to news in the media has a definite impact on what people are actually thinking? For the answer to that question, we need to look no farther than the theory and research associated with the notion of agenda setting that was introduced years ago by two journalism professors, **Maxwell McCombs** and **Donald Shaw.**[10]

Agenda-Setting Theory: A Theory About Thinking

For years, the **agenda-setting theory** of the press has been summarized succinctly in a single quotation from Bernard Cohen, a political scientist: "The press may not be successful much of the time in telling people *what to think,* but it is stunningly successful in telling its readers *what to think about.*"[11] The idea here is that the news media set the public agenda. Their coverage of issues helps to define for the public what they should be thinking about on a given day. As you read these words, the chances are very good that you haven't heard or used the words "impeachment" or "Monica Lewinsky" in the last few weeks. But if you think back to December 1998, the chances are much better that these words were often on your lips in your interactions with friends and family. The news media hardly stopped in their coverage and analysis of President Clinton's impeachment hearings. For weeks, the country was immersed in nothing else. During that time, the theory of agenda setting would have predicted that if a survey had been taken of public opinion, the crisis of the presidency would have been the number-one public concern. That is, according to the theory, public opinion about what should be on the public agenda is heavily influenced by the topics and issues that appear in the news. The coverage may not determine exactly what position people take on a given issue, but it helps to guarantee that the issue is considered to be an important one. Is there any evidence to suggest that this might be true?

The theory of agenda setting has by now spawned many individual research studies that support the basic idea of media influence. McCombs and Shaw first sought to test the theory in the context of the 1968 presidential campaign (Richard Nixon versus Hubert Humphrey). Their study included an exhaustive analysis of the media agenda that included four newspapers from North Carolina, *Time* and *Newsweek,* CBS and NBC television news, and the *New York Times*.[12] According to the results, the five issues given the most prominent coverage by the press were foreign policy, law and order, fiscal policy, public welfare, and civil rights. When McCombs and Shaw asked voters to identify the key issue of the campaign, quite apart from their perceptions of what the candidates had been saying, there was a remarkable convergence with the issues that emerged from the media analysis. Indeed, just as the theory predicted, the media agenda and the public agenda tended to correspond.

Of course, the mere fact that the media's agenda corresponded with the public's does not really provide the most powerful evidence in favor of agenda-setting theory. Recall from chapter 2 that in order to establish a causal relationship between two variables, it isn't sufficient to simply establish a relationship between them. It is also important to establish that the causal variable precedes the other in time. Researchers who study agenda setting are most interested in documenting that the media agenda actually precedes the public agenda. Is there any evidence that it does?

In one of the few experimental tests of the theory, **Shanto Iyengar** and **Donald Kinder** studied this question by exposing people to one of three different presentations of the news over a 4-day period.[13] The presentations differed according to the topic of one of the stories placed in the newscast on each day. For one group, the topic focused on pollution. For the second group, it focused on national defense. For the third group, the story dealt with inflation. After the 4 days of exposure, the researchers found that the experimental groups expressed greater concern about the issue that had been featured in their respective newscast.

The research by Iyengar and Kinder should remind you of some of the research covered in chapter 8. Recall the "great American values test" in which the researchers used a TV program to heighten the awareness of viewers of certain values. Not only did the program succeed in changing the priority that viewers assigned to those values, it also triggered a number of behavioral changes. While the show wasn't a news program in the strict sense and clearly had a persuasive edge, you might wonder if a continued focus on particular issues in the news could do more than just set the agenda about what topics people think about. Couldn't the news also have an impact on what people actually think about those topics?

In a revision of the agenda-setting theory, McCombs and Shaw believe that the answer to this question is a distinct yes. How do the media do this if they are not intentionally trying to persuade consumers? The answer is to be found in a concept known as **framing.** As **James Tankard** defines this term, framing is "the central organizing idea for news content that supplies a context and suggests what the issue is through the use of *selection, emphasis, exclusion,* and *elaboration*."[14]

One of my favorite parts of the local newspaper in the wintertime is the coverage of the aftermath of a big snowstorm. Consider how the media might frame such news coverage. In the wake of a huge snowfall, the news could concentrate on winter recreation and the fun that children in the area have playing with snowballs and sledding down steep hills. On the other hand, the media could focus on how slowly snow removal is progressing and attempt to track down local government officials to comment on the problem. Depending upon which way the story of the snowstorm was framed, consumers could have very different thoughts as a result of reading the news. Traditionally, this effect might be described in the standard agenda-setting terminology: "The media don't tell us what to think, they tell us what to think about." But a closer inspection of what goes on here suggests that there is more to it. By framing the story in terms of poor snow removal instead of recreational activities, the media are doing more than just telling us what to think about. In a very real way, they are telling us what to think by focusing attention on one particular angle of the story instead of another one. I can remember years ago when I lived in the Chicago area, the city changed mayors because of what many perceived as the failure of the administration to set up adequate snow removal. The press helped to frame the poor snow removal as a major failure in planning, and the public apparently accepted the frame. As **Em Griffin** concludes in his discussion of these theoretical concepts:

> McCombs and Shaw have established a plausible case that some people look to print and broadcast news for guidance on which issues are really important. Agenda-setting theory also provides a needed reminder that news stories are just that—stories. The message always requires interpretation.[15]

In the end, the way a story is framed by the media can have great impact on the interpretations that people carry away from the message.

The Spiral of Silence

One media theorist, **Elisabeth Noelle-Neumann,** believes that the media's impact on the interpretations that people carry away from a story can have a dramatic impact on the entire course of public opinion in the culture.[16] Her **spiral of silence** theory is based on the idea that most of us don't feel very comfortable speaking out about our views if we perceive that we are in the minority. If we think that our view is really the minority view, we would rather keep quiet than risk being isolated or rejected by those to whom we wish to feel attached. This process can eventually gather steam and spiral into a relative silence when it comes to certain minority views. That is, the more often that people who feel like they are in the minority decide not to speak their views, the less we hear those views and the more we tend to believe that most people agree with the majority viewpoint. According to Neumann, this process can lead to views that eventually die out and exert little influence even though they are actually held by substantial numbers of people. Once those large numbers of people get the impression that their views are not widely shared, they stop talking. And this simply reinforces the notion that their views are *not* widely shared. And so on.

The role of the news media in this spiral of silence can be quite dramatic. To the extent that people tune in to TV news and perceive that most people hold a particular opinion or viewpoint on a given issue, the spiral of silence can be off and running. Media researchers **William Eveland, Douglas McLeod,** and **Nancy Signorielli** found evidence supporting the spiral of silence theory when they conducted a sample survey on attitudes toward the Gulf War back in 1991.[17] In contrast to the strong consensus in favor of the war that the news media reported, the survey revealed that very few people actually expressed strong support in their answers to the questions. In fact, while less than 7% of the respondents expressed strong support for the war, over half of the respondents expressed either neutrality, disagreement, or strong disagreement. When the researchers examined how the supporters differed from the nonsupporters, they found that their perception of public opinion was a key variable. Those who thought that public opinion was running strongly in favor of the war tended to be the ones who expressed strong support themselves. Those who thought that public opinion was mixed or not so strongly in favor of the war were more willing to express neutrality or disagreement. This close link between how people perceive public opinion and the attitudes they are willing to express is a fundamental prediction of the spiral of silence. The fact that the media coverage of the war was decidedly distorted in favor of support may have contributed to the unwillingness of many to speak out publicly against the war effort. After people watched the news coverage, they carried away an interpretation of the events that suggested that public opinion was heavily in favor of what the United States was doing.

How Much of the News Do We Remember?

With a story like the Persian Gulf War that appears night after night, the public gradually comes up to speed on the basic facts and begins to comprehend and commit to memory certain details. When we speak of people "carrying away" an interpretation of a message that has been framed in a particular way, we are talking about memory. The question that is raised here has to do with how well people typically remember the information that they are exposed to in a newscast. As it turns out, the answer may be very different depending upon the nature of the newscast and how many times a person hears the story. In most cases, unlike coverage relating to the Persian Gulf War, we are exposed to a story just one time.

Not long ago, I was contacted by an attorney who wanted me to provide an expert opinion on a legal matter that arose out of a TV newscast. Her client, a TV station, had recently broadcast a story that clearly identified by name a young man who was in his late twenties. According to the report, which relied heavily upon information provided by the local law enforcement authorities, the man had gone to a suburban home, knocked on the door, and promptly shot a young teenager in the stomach. A day or two later, law enforcement authorities discovered that the man had an airtight alibi and could not possibly have been at the boy's home at the time the crime occurred. The young teenager who had been shot also confessed that he had lied about the incident. As it turned out, he was a very disturbed young boy who had, in fact, turned a gun on himself! In the aftermath, the man who had been identified in the TV news story decided to file a lawsuit against the TV station, charging that they had libeled his good name. The case was settled out of court and never went to trial. But if it had, I might have been called upon to give an opinion about the extent to which the man who sued the TV station had really been injured by the news report. Two of the issues that would have entered into my analysis would have been the extent to which people comprehend the news they are exposed to in an average newscast and the extent to which they retain information or remember it after the newscast is over. What does the research reveal about these two issues?

Two researchers, **John Robinson** and **Dennis Davis,** provided some insights on these issues in their article "Comprehension of a Single Evening's News." [18] In tracking the responses of a group of people who watched the evening news on one particular night, the authors used an 8-point coding scheme to assess how well the news was recalled. If a viewer's recall was rated as a "0," it indicated recall of the wrong story or information that was not even contained in the newscast. A "1" indicated the inability to recall a story, no reply, or a "don't know" response. On the other end of the scale, a "7" indicated recall of the central point of the story plus two additional important details. An "8" indicated recall of the central point plus three or more additional details. After coding the data the researchers noted that on the average, viewer response to stories fell between "2" and "3" on the 8-point scale. A "2" indicated that viewers could "recall something but then can give no details" from the specific news broadcast. A "3" indicated that viewers could provide only "vague, general responses related to the story."

If these results surprise you, think about the way most people probably watch the news. Only rarely do people sit down and glue their attention to the TV screen during a newscast. On many occasions, the news comes into the home amid a host of daily activities that might include meal preparation, conversations with family members, and other routine tasks. People are more likely to monitor the news audio and engage in the well-documented practice of **selective exposure** to news material. The principle of selective exposure emphasizes that people come to any communication message with their own attitudes, interests, beliefs, and values (see chapter 3). These attitudes and interests help to guide attention to particular messages. If a person is especially interested in the news story, attention will be high. But if a story is perceived as uninteresting, a person will be more inclined to tune out. During an average newscast, a person's attention may fluctuate from low to high and back to low many times as the stories change. Many news stories are simply not attended to very well because viewers find them to be irrelevant, uninteresting, or too demanding in terms of the effort required to fully comprehend the major points. Consistent with this point of view, **Hans Kepplinger** and **Gregor Daschmann** recently presented a model for how people process news content. In summarizing their understanding on this topic, they stated the following: "To put it more generally, much information is avoided, much is misunderstood, and only some is adequately retained." [19]

If I had been called upon to give testimony about the man who was concerned about his reputation after the TV news broadcast his name as a potential gunman, I might have pointed out that the chances are very high in the light of what we know from research on news that most of the viewers probably didn't even remember the alleged gunman's name. If this was the case, his reputation might not have been damaged nearly to the extent that he thought it was. On the other hand, a news story about a shooting incident might be a story of greater-than-average interest. And it might have had an unusual emotional impact on local viewers. In this type of situation, sorting out the effects of the messages on comprehension can be pretty difficult. Researchers have only begun to discover how emotions, vivid images, and standard news content might mix together to produce different results in terms of overall comprehension.

John Newhagen and **Byron Reeves** attempted to study how vivid or intense images might affect what people remember from a news story. Their findings were intriguing. When they asked people to recall news topics and facts from the news stories 6 weeks after exposure to a newscast, the researchers found that people were able to recall the facts and topics better if they had been presented without a vivid visual. However, when vivid visuals were included, people definitely remembered the visuals.[20] These results support a type of **dual-coding theory** of news content. Images might be processed differently than verbal information. When a vivid image is presented alongside of verbal information, it might actually tend to distract people from processing the verbal information efficiently. On the other hand, the vivid images themselves prove to be highly memorable and might even enhance memory for the information that comes right after the images appear. There is probably some practical wisdom that news directors can glean from these results. If, for example, a station wants to give verbal instructions about how to avoid the calamity of being killed in a tornado, it probably wouldn't be a good idea to show dramatic video footage of a tornado destroying buildings at the same time the instructions are being given. Newhagen and Reeves's results indicate that tornado footage offered at the same time as instructions might actually prevent effective processing of the instructions. However, it might be a good idea to catch viewers' attention with the tornado footage and then, after it was over, immediately follow up with the verbal instructions for safety. Recent research with children conducted by Barrie Gunter and his associates also found evidence for dual coding of news. Children learned more information from television news than they did from print or audio versions of the same material. However, this advantage was only found when the pictures on TV were completely redundant with the verbal information in the news story.[21]

THE ROLE OF EMOTION

One reason why vivid images may tend to be memorable is that they evoke more intense emotional reactions than spoken words or plain written text. Of course, there might be exceptions to this rule. If you were highly involved with a particular issue, mere words in the newspaper or words spoken by a newscaster might be more than enough to set your emotions stirring. But generally speaking, vivid images have a more direct pathway to the emotions. John Newhagen recently reported some new research from his program of studies on emotional media images. Using news images, he found that the ones that provoked anger in viewers were the most memorable, followed by images that induced fear. Finally, people had the worst memory for images that they had found to be disgusting. Newhagen pointed out that these findings may have practical implications for the way news stories are put together. As he stated, "[P]roducers can use such images to first draw attention to a story, and then insert information they think viewers will want to remember right after them. Images that elicit disgust, on the other hand, inhibit memory late in the stories" (pp. 274–275).[22]

The research on emotional news images and memory is becoming a well-developed literature. Newhagen's research findings are not the only ones that point to the memory-enhancing effects of some types of negative news stories. In a study reported by **Annie Lang,** John Newhagen, and Byron Reeves, negative news stories increased memory for news items.[23] Lang and her co-authors speculated that the primary function of negative news video may be to heighten the overall emotional impact of a story. The greater impact of the story shows up in a person as increased physiological arousal. That arousal results in increased memory. As I write this brief summary of Lang's research, the news media all across the state of Indiana as well as the CNN Headline news have been replaying the last lap of the 2001 Daytona 500 NASCAR race. You don't have to be a race fan to know what happened in this fateful contest. Racing star Dale Earnhardt Sr. was killed instantly when he crashed into the wall at 180 mph. The news footage of this crash was dramatic and highly emotional. I am certain that if I had been wired to sensors monitoring my physiological state, I would have showed clear signs of arousal upon watching the tragic crash footage. Thanks to new video technology, viewers were actually able to see what the crash looked like from Earnhardt's perspective from inside his car. According to the research findings, my heightened physiological response was probably typical. People who watched this coverage were probably very likely to remember the news material that was reported during the video footage and directly following it.

Nowhere is the role of emotion in news more important than in politics. One of the first demonstrations of the potential role of emotion from TV images in politics came from the first presidential debates between the Republican candidate, Richard Nixon, and the Democratic candidate, John Kennedy, in the election of 1960. Even though 90% of Americans had a TV set in 1960, radio was still a popular medium for political news. Many people decided to listen to the debates on the radio instead of watching them on TV. According to **Sid Kraus,** who may be the only communication researcher who has been in attendance at every presidential debate since they began in 1960, the people who listened to the debates on radio were more inclined to perceive Nixon as the winner. In contrast, those who watched the debates on TV thought that Kennedy had the upper hand. Although the integrity of the supporting data for this conclusion has been debated through the past few decades, Kraus concludes after his exhaustive review of the data that, "[M]y own observation on the night of the debate in 1960, and my consultations with scholars conducting debate research at that time convinced me that the finding was a credible one."[24] In support of Kraus's conclusion, the following excerpt from *Broadcasting* magazine, a leading trade journal in the broadcasting industry, states the finding clearly: "In answer to the question who won the debates, 48.7% of the radio audience named Mr. Nixon and only 21% picked Mr. Kennedy. Among those who watched the debates on TV, 30.2% named Mr. Kennedy the winner and 28.6% picked Mr. Nixon."[25] Since the TV audience was so much larger than the radio audience, the advantage that Kennedy had on TV presumably meant a narrow victory.

The fact that TV images of political debaters may exert greater influence on voters than the actual words spoken has been reinforced by more recent research by **Michael Pfau** and **Jong Kang.** These authors emphasized that on TV, political candidates with a "softer, warmer communication, similar to communication in an interpersonal context" will be more influential among the voters.[26] One of the first political ads that demonstrated how images may be more powerful than words was the now infamous *Daisy Girl* commercial that was designed by advertising genius **Tony Schwartz** for Lyndon Johnson's 1964 presidential campaign against Barry Goldwater. The ad began by showing a young girl picking petals from a daisy and counting (incorrectly) from one to ten. When she reached the number ten, the camera slowly zoomed in on the child's eye and then farther into the pupil of the eye as a cold, military-sounding voice began a countdown from ten to one. The pupil of the girl's eye became transformed into a window where the viewer saw a nuclear explosion. As the screen went black, an announcer's voice said, "These are the stakes, to make a world in which all God's children can live, or to go into the darkness. Either we must love each other or we must die."[27] The ad only aired one time, but it caused a national discussion about political advertising techniques. Most political analysts agree that it virtually ended Barry Goldwater's campaign without even mentioning him by name. Schwartz believes that the ad used powerful images to connect to the deep-seated emotions that people had about nuclear war. By surfacing the fears associated with the possibility that Goldwater might actually be inclined to use nuclear weapons to settle global conflict, the ad drove people to vote for Johnson in packs. In a documentary on political advertising made for public television, the news commentator Bill Moyers complained that he found it troubling to note that Johnson was portrayed as the peacemaker in the 1964 election and Goldwater the warmonger.[28] This image was effectively exploited with the *Daisy Girl* commercial. But, Moyers noted, it was Johnson who committed the country to the bloody conflict in Vietnam that we eventually lost. Not a single spot, according to Moyers' recollection, even touched on the Vietnam issue in 1964. The *Daisy Girl* ad may have been a triumph of image over issue, pictures over words, and emotions over deeper thinking. Study Box 9-1 focuses on the advertising philosophy of Tony Schwartz, who some refer to as a modern-day media guru.

When I was preparing my notes for this chapter, one of the things that struck me in the final analysis was how little attention research on news receives

---

STUDY BOX 9-1   Who Is Tony Schwartz?

Tony Schwartz has been using electronic media to influence the political process for several decades. He has worked for countless candidates and has created public service campaigns for police departments, fire departments, the American Cancer Society, and many others. He has also done numerous product campaigns. Schwartz believes that many people who use the media to influence others have a very poor understanding of how media work. Below, I have listed some of the key principles that Schwartz relies upon when he works on a political campaign.

1. **Use PRE-search—not research.** Schwartz believes that most politicians create campaign material and then test the effects of that material before they decide to put it on the air. This, according to him, is totally backward. He does not test ad material. Instead, he conducts research BEFORE he creates an ad to find out what people are thinking and feeling about the candidates in a campaign. Once he knows their feelings, he can design media that taps into those feelings easily. He feels no need to test his commercials. When his pre-search in the 1968 presidential campaign revealed that many people thought that Spiro Agnew as a vice presidential candidate was a joke, Schwartz made an ad that consisted of little more than a voice laughing in the background while viewing Agnew's name on a TV screen.

2. **Create "resonance" between the message and the audience.** Schwartz is a big believer in the notion that the audience has a lot to say about whether or not it is influenced by a message. The goal of a campaign message, he says, is to resonate with the feelings inside of voters. A good campaign ad will take advantage of these feelings, stir them up, and then use them ever so gently to nudge the receiver in the desired direction. Schwartz is no fan of "hard sell" advertising. He prefers the term "deep sell." The *Daisy Girl* ad discussed in this chapter is a good example.

3. **Use the audience as "workforce," not as a target.** Many practitioners of advertising treat the audience as a target. They just throw information at the receiver as if they were throwing darts at a dartboard. Schwartz rejects this practice. He wants to find out what is already inside of his audience members and then use his ads to draw that information out of them so that it can be put to work for his cause. For Schwartz, the feelings and information that exist in the hearts and minds of the audience are the most powerful forces that he has at his disposal. If he can draw those feelings out, then the audience begins to work for his cause. They become his "workforce." The goal of any commercial for Schwartz is not to put information inside of the audience. Instead, he tries to use commercials to draw information out of the audience. One way he knows what is inside of the audience is from news reports. If a jumbo jet crashes and kills hundreds of people, he might create a spot that asks people to think of that tragedy. Then he will follow by asking people to think about the fact that tobacco use annually kills the equivalent of three fully loaded jumbo jets going down each day.

---

from the popular press relative to research on topics like violence, sex, and fright. It is important to note, however, that popular press coverage is a relatively poor barometer for determining the importance of a research topic. Media messages about news and politics potentially help people to understand the world and how to respond to various social and political problems. Increasingly, media messages help shape the contours of leadership by determining who gets elected to public office. News content does not tend to be associated with the most dramatic and sensational effects. Since news is designed to inform readers, listeners, and viewers, its effects are generally taken to be functional rather than dysfunctional. This may predispose the press and even those of us who conduct research on media effects to deemphasize the topic. By reading this chapter, you should now have some sense for how important media effects in this area can be.

SUMMARY

In this chapter, we have examined a number of effects of media news content. As we have seen, certain types of news content (suicide stories) may actually trigger imitative behavior in the population. This effect emerges because some people ruminate about the news stories they have read or seen. People who are high in their need for cognition are particularly likely to ruminate and think about the things they have processed in the news. Agenda-setting theory postulates that the media actually affect what people think about. Research on the theory is supportive. Through the process of framing, the media may not only affect what people think about; they may also affect what we think. What we think helps to determine public opinion. The spiral of silence theory details one way the media may affect public opinion by giving sanction to the expression of certain viewpoints. Still, one of the issues that emerges in the study of news content has to do with how much people actually remember from their news exposure. Emotion may be one key variable that helps to determine what we remember. In politics, emotional reactions to debates and short commercial messages can often play a pivotal role in election outcomes.

KEY TERMS AND CONCEPTS

Werther effect 153

  repositioning or re-
  scheduling effect 153

  additive effect 153

Need for cognition 154

Political sophistication
154

Agenda-setting theory
155

Framing 156

The spiral of silence 157

Selective exposure 159

Dual-coding theory 160

KEY NAMES

David Phillips 152

Robert Cialdini 152

Elmar Etzersdorfer and
  Gernot Sonneck 153

John Cacioppo and
  Richard Petty 154

Elizabeth Perse 154

Mollie Condra 154

June Rhee and Joseph
  Cappella 154

Maxwell McCombs and
  Donald Shaw 155

Shanto Iyengar and
Donald Kinder
156

James Tankard 156

Em Griffin 157

Elisabeth Noelle-
Neumann 157

William Eveland,
Douglas McLeod, and
Nancy Signorielli 158

John Robinson and
Dennis Davis 159

Hans Kepplinger and
Gregor Daschmann
159

John Newhagen and
Byron Reeves 160

Annie Lang 161

Sid Kraus 161

Michael Pfau and Jong
Kang 162

Tony Schwartz 162

WEB LINKS

1. For a comprehensive bibliography on television news effects, try . . . http://www.wfu .edu/~louden/MEDIA.html

2. For a profile of Tony Schwartz, try . . . http://home.earthlink.net/~newsounds/

3. For a site of resources on the Kennedy-Nixon debates of 1960, try . . . http://www .beyondbooks.com/gop00/1b_link.htm or http://au.yahoo.com/Government/U_S_ Government/Politics/Elections/Presidential_Elections/History/20th_Century/1960/ Kennedy_Nixon/Debates/

To learn more about the topics in this chapter, enter the Key Terms and Concepts and Key Names found in this chapter as subject and keyword searches on your InfoTrac College Edition.

NOTES

1. Phillips, D. P. (1979). Suicide, motor vehicle fatalities, and the mass media: Evidence toward a theory of suggestion. *American Journal of Sociology, 84,* 1150–1174.

2. Phillips, D. P. (1978). Airplane accident fatalities increase just after newspaper stories about murder and suicide. *Science, 201,* 748–750.

3. Cialdini, R. B. (1988). Influence: Science and practice. Glenview, IL: Scott Foresman.

4. Phillips, D. P. (1982). The impact of fictional television stories on U.S. adult fatalities: New evidence on the effect of the mass media on violence. *American Journal of Sociology, 87,* 1340–1359.

5. Cacioppo, J. T., & Petty, R. E. (1982). The need for cognition. *Journal of Personality and Social Psychology, 42,* 116–131.

6. Perse, E. (1992). Predicting attention to local television news: Need for cognition and motives for viewing. *Communication Reports, 5,* 40–49.

7. Condra, M. B. (1992). The link between need for cognition and political interest, involvement, and media usage. *Psychology-A Quarterly Journal of Human Behavior, 29,* 13–18.

8. De Pelsmacker, P., & Geuens, M. (1998). Television viewing behaviour, program preference and individual differences: The role of affect intensity and need for cognition. *Communicatie, 27,* 2–19.

9. Rhee, J. W., & Cappella, J. N. (1997). The role of political sophistication in learning from news: Measuring schema development. *Communication Research, 24,* 197–233.

10. McCombs, M., & Shaw, D. (1973). The agenda-setting function of the mass media. *Public Opinion Quarterly, 37,* 62–75.

11. Cohen, B. (1963). *The press and foreign policy.* Princeton, NJ: Princeton University.

12. McCombs, M., & Shaw, D. (1973). The agenda-setting function of the mass media. *Public Opinion Quarterly, 37,* 62–75.

13. Iyengar, S., & Kinder, D. (1987). *News that matters.* Chicago, IL: University of Chicago Press.

14. Tankard cited in: Griffin, E. (1999). *A first look at communication theory.* Boston: McGraw-Hill.

15. Griffin, E. (1999). *A first look at communication theory.* Boston: McGraw-Hill.

16. Noelle-Neumann, E. (1991). The theory of public opinion: The concept of the spiral of silence. In J. A. Anderson (Ed.), *Communication Yearbook 14* (pp. 256–287). Newbury Park, CA: Sage.

17. Eveland, W. P., Jr., McLeod, D. M., & Signorielli, N. (1995). Actual and perceived U.S. public opinion: The spiral of silence during the Persian Gulf War. *International Journal of Public Opinion Research, 7,* 91–109.

18. Robinson, J., & Davis, D. (1986). Comprehension of a single evening's news. In J. P. Robinson & M. R. Levy (Eds.), *The main source: Learning from television news* (pp. 107–132). Beverly Hills: Sage.

19. Kepplinger, H., & Daschmann, G. (1997). Today's news—tomorrow's context: A dynamic model of news processing. *Journal of Broadcasting & Electronic Media, 41,* 548–565.

20. Newhagen, J. E., & Reeves, B. (1992). The evening's bad news: Effects of compelling negative television news images on memory. *Journal of Communication, 42,* 25–41.

21. Gunter, B., Furnham, A., & Griffiths, S. (2000). Children's memory for news: A comparison of three presentation media. *Media Psychology, 2,* 93–118.

22. Newhagen, J. E. (1998). TV news images that induce anger, fear, and disgust: Effects on approach-avoidance and memory. *Journal of Broadcasting & Electronic Media, 42,* 265–276.

23. Lang, A., Newhagen, J., & Reeves, B. (1996). Negative video as structure: Emotion, attention, capacity, and memory. *Journal of Broadcasting & Electronic Media, 40,* 460–477.

24. Kraus, S. (1996). Winners of the first 1960 televised presidential debate between Kennedy and Nixon. *Journal of Communication, 46,* 78–96.

25. Debate score: Kennedy up, Nixon down. (1960, November 7). *Broadcasting, 27*–28.

26. Pfau, M., & Kang, J. G. (1991). The impact of relational messages on candidate influence in televised political debates. *Communication Studies, 42,* 117.

27. Schwartz, T. (1973). *The responsive chord.* New York: Anchor Books.

28. CEL. (1984). The 30-second president. In *A walk through the 20th century with Bill Moyers.* Washington, D.C.: Public Broadcasting Service.

10

■

The Effects of
Media Stereotypes

WHAT'S IN A FACE?

In the fall of 1984, I was busy conducting research on people's emotional reactions to frightening mass media when I ran across an article that referred to a concept I had not heard of before. A researcher named **Dane Archer,** along with his colleagues, had published an article in the *Journal of Personality and Social Psychology* that was called "Face-ism: Five Studies of Sex Differences in Facial Prominence."[1] The title piqued my curiosity. What exactly was "face-ism?" The more I read in Archer's article, the more fascinated I became. As it turns out, **face-ism** refers to the tendency to represent people in terms of their face or head as opposed to their body. The face-ism index is a very simple computation that Archer and his colleagues describe as

> . . . the ratio of two linear measurements. The numerator of this index is the distance (in millimeters or any other unit) in a depiction from the top of the head to the lowest point of the chin. The denominator of the index is the distance from the top of the head to the lowest visible part of the subject's body.

Figure 10-1 shows the ratio visually and computes the face-ism index for two figures. Once I understood how the face-ism index was computed, the research findings uncovered by Archer and his colleagues seemed almost incredible.

For starters, the researchers examined over 1,700 published photographs in the news and advertising sections of five major U.S. periodicals. They computed

167

FIGURE 10-1:   Face-ism Ratios

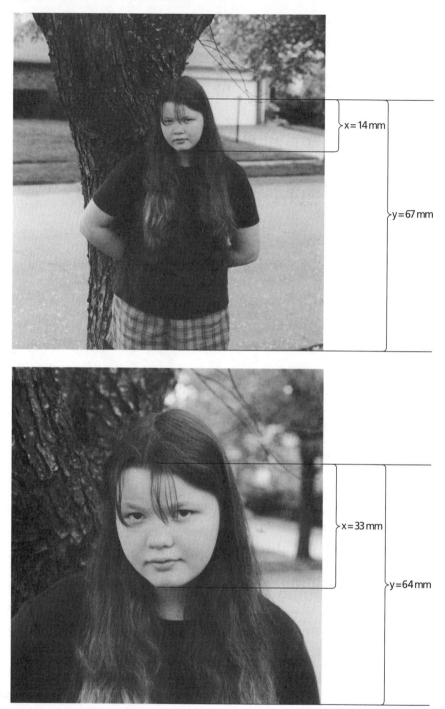

The face-ism ratio is computed by taking the distance from the top of the head to the bottom of the chin and dividing it by the distance from the top of the head to the bottom of the body. In the top picture, the ratio is 14mm/67mm, or .21. In the bottom picture, the ratio is 33mm/64mm, or .51. In general, media depictions of males are more likely to be like the bottom picture. Media depictions of females are more likely to be like the top picture.

the average face-ism index for the males depicted in the photos and compared it to the average face-ism index computed for the females. The results were startling. For males, the average index was .65. But for females it was over 30% less—about .45. Think about what these numbers mean. In photos of males, the head or face was depicted as about 65% of the entire male figure. But for females, the head or face was depicted as only about 45% of the entire female figure. Males were more likely to be represented in terms of their heads or faces, while females were more likely to be represented in terms of their bodies. It was unlikely that the difference in the face-ism ratio was due to chance. The probability of getting a difference by chance that was as large as the one documented in Archer's research was less than 1 in 1000 ($p < .001$).

As I started to think about what differences in face-ism might mean (the differences are referred to by the authors as the face-ism effect), Archer and his colleagues hit me with even more provocative findings. The face-ism effect is not limited to U.S. media. It was documented in publications from nearly a dozen countries across the globe. In addition to generalizing across countries, the effect apparently generalizes across centuries as well. The authors noted that in a study of nearly 1,000 portraits and self-portraits of art over a span of six centuries, the same face-ism effect emerged again and again. There was even some evidence that the size of the difference between male and female representations was increasing over time.

The authors also reported research that investigated the extent to which face-ism might be present in private representations as well as public ones. In drawings of college students that were requested from both males and females, the male images were repeatedly drawn with higher face-ism ratios than the images of females. I was intrigued with the factors that might lie behind this systematic difference in male and female representations. Of course, one obvious hypothesis is that the images simply reflect a real biological difference such that male heads are larger than females. However, this hypothesis turns out not to be true. As I searched for a less obvious explanation, Archer and his colleagues threw in the real kicker. In an experiment that manipulated face-ism ratios for photos of the same individual, naïve judges rated the people who were high on facial prominence in the photos as more intelligent, more ambitious, and better looking. Frankly, when I read about this research, I thought the potential effects of face-ism in the media were nothing short of staggering. If high facial prominence was associated with intelligence, ambition, and attractiveness, what impact were media depictions of females (who were characteristically low in facial prominence) having on the general way females were perceived in the culture at large—were females perceived as less intelligent? less ambitious? less attractive? These were potential effects that as far as I knew had never been explored by media effects researchers.

My intrigue with the face-ism effect might have taken a back seat to my other research had it not been for a graduate student, Christine Fehlner, who occupied an office nearby and happened to be working on a project that tracked news coverage of the presidential campaign of 1984. Just after I finished reading about face-ism, I came out of my office and saw a stack of newspapers that Fehlner had been collecting of campaign coverage. There on the front page was a picture of Walter Mondale, the Democratic nominee for president, along with his vice presidential running mate, the first female ever to occupy this role, Geraldine Ferraro. The idea to begin investigating the face-ism effect in the 1984 political campaign was born at that instant. Fehlner and I went on to conduct a study on this topic that was published 2 years later in the *Journal of Communication*.[2] We looked at the face-ism ratios of the two male Republican candidates, Ronald Reagan and George Bush, as well as those of Mondale and Ferraro. We looked at these ratios for all photos that appeared in *Time* and *Newsweek* during the months of the campaign. Our findings diverged a bit from Archer's. The face-ism ratios of the four candidates were essentially equivalent. But when we went back and looked at other males and females pictured in the same magazines, we found evidence of the same face-ism effect that had been reported in past research. Males were more likely to be depicted with higher levels of facial prominence than females.

We can't be certain exactly why we found no face-ism effect in how Geraldine Ferraro was represented compared to the male candidates. Perhaps the results of our study are best explained by a norm of equivalent representation for all candidates in a presidential campaign. We noted that in many of the pictorial layouts in magazines, the presidential candidates were presented in photos that were framed identically and appeared as off-setting, competing representations. It may be that in politics at the national level, the press is constrained to represent candidates in a photographically similar manner, regardless of gender.

In the end, the most interesting aspect of the face-ism effect is the fact that people's perceptions of those with higher facial prominence are more positive. Some scholars have suggested that this has to do with the fact that the head is where the brain is and that people associate the head or face as the center of an individual's intelligence. Whatever the reason, if the media represents males with higher facial prominence than females, the experimental data would suggest that this practice has negative implications for the evaluation of women. I would like to conduct a study in which people are asked to report their exposure to mass media and also asked to provide their own drawings of males and females. One hypothesis based on the current literature would be that heavy media consumers who spend more time processing faces that are systematically different according to the sex-biased face-ism effect might be more likely to show this effect in their own drawings. This is a study waiting to be done. In fact, as I write these words, an undergraduate student in my own department is planning to investigate this hypothesis by collecting data from fifth-grade students. We can hardly wait to see the results.

I am certainly not alone in expressing interest in the face-ism effect after reading the work of Archer and his colleagues. The face-ism effect has attracted some recent attention from two other researchers, **Miron Zuckerman** and **Suzanne Kieffer.** They examined pictures of Whites and Blacks that have appeared in paintings, periodicals, and on the face of postage stamps. Reasoning from the past literature that higher facial prominence was associated with impressions of power, they predicted that images of Blacks would have lower facial prominence than images of Whites. This is exactly what they found. More-over, they also found concrete evidence that people represented in photos with higher facial prominence were perceived as being more dominant.[3]

STEREOTYPICAL REPRESENTATIONS
IN THE MEDIA

The discussion of face-ism raises a number of issues about media depictions of people. When media representations tend to depict groups of people in particu-lar ways, they may play an important part in determining how media consumers come to think about individuals who are members of those groups. Social psy-chologists do not necessarily agree on how to think about stereotypes, but **Susan Fiske** and **Shelly Taylor** offer an approach that seems clear and sen-sible. They say that "One can think about stereotypes as a particular kind of role schema that organizes people's expectations about other people who fall into certain social categories."[4] If, for example, you tended to think that a male was more likely than a female to be an attorney, we might say that you had a **role schema** that was part of your thought processes when it came to think-ing about men and women. Schemas help to organize thoughts. In the case of a role schema, the thoughts and expectations you have for a specific person are guided by a general set of expectations that you might have for people who hold the same role as the specific person you're thinking about. If you think that females are not as likely as males to be attorneys, then your expectations for females are **stereotyped** in a particular way.

One's expectations about someone else's role may be based on accurate data. That is, it might be the case that males really are more likely to be attor-neys than females. However, one negative consequence of holding a stereotype, even if it is accurate, is that it might function to reinforce the status quo and unfairly restrict the diversity of social roles that individuals might hold. Think about the consequences of what might happen if most people held the stereo-type that males were more likely to be attorneys than females. To the extent that people had such expectations, females might not be socialized into career paths that would lead them to law school. In this way, stereotypes, even if accurate at a given point in time, can serve to perpetuate the status quo and be unduly restrictive for various groups of people. Of course, if stereotypes are inaccurate rather than accurate, they produce false expectations about others.

The media may generally depict people in stereotypical ways such that con-sumers are encouraged to adopt expectations about the roles that those people occupy. Following the example of female attorneys, if the media depicted very few females in the role of attorney, then consumers of the media might come to associate males as much more likely to be attorneys. The media would be engaging in a stereotypical depiction that has an impact on media consumers. If this is the case, then there are two fundamental issues to be addressed in any discussion of the media and stereotypes. First, one might ask about the par-ticular role expectations that the media encourage. In other words, how do the media actually depict certain groups of people? Second, once we know the answer to the first question, we might ask whether these depictions actually affect the role expectations that media consumers have for those same people. As it turns out, there is much more data available for the first question than the second. Nevertheless, both questions are important to examine.

Sex Role Stereotypes

One of the most repeated findings from content analyses of TV programs is that men far outnumber women. Summarizing across a number of different studies, **Tannis MacBeth Williams** observed: "[T]here are more than twice as many male as female models on TV, and when women do appear, they are most frequently found on comedy and light entertainment programs. Furthermore, this situation has remained constant over time."[5] One of the few consistent exceptions to the strong tendency to employ males more than females in the world of TV is found in the content of afternoon soap operas. Research by **Natan Katzman**[6] confirms that the proportion of male and female characters in the soap opera genre is roughly equal. In a review of some of the more recent content analyses on the frequency with which males and females appear in the media,[7] **Richard Jackson Harris** pointed out that males are three times more likely to appear in children's cartoons,[8] twice as likely to appear in music videos, and four to five times more likely to be featured as voice-over announcers—even though they aren't any more persuasive than female voice-overs.[9] For many researchers, the fact that males outnumber females in the TV world is a troubling finding that may suggest to viewers that males, by virtue of their greater presence, should be considered to be more important or more significant. Of course, researchers must be extremely careful at this point. Remember that in previous chapters, the point was made that media content cannot be assumed to cause any particular effect. It is important to distinguish carefully between the two questions about content and effect. Media effects researchers cannot speak about the effects of any particular stereotype without having evidence of an effect. The mere presence of a stereotype does not constitute evidence for an effect.

In addition to documenting the fact that females don't appear on TV as frequently as males do, researchers have found a full range of other stereotypical depictions. Tannis MacBeth Williams reviews evidence showing that married females on TV are far less likely to be employed than females in the actual population. Moreover, when females do hold jobs on TV, they tend to be restricted to a more narrow range of occupations than males. **George Gerbner** has also contributed some interesting insights about sex role stereotyping from his research on media violence. He maintains that women are much more likely to be depicted as victims of crime and violence than males. While males are depicted in violent scenarios more frequently as the perpetrators or the aggressors, females are depicted more frequently as the victims. To Gerbner, these sorts of systematic distortions communicate a strong message about who has power in the culture. According to him, the predominant message of TV is that males have power over females; males are relatively powerful, and females are relatively powerless.[10]

When all of the content studies are considered together, there seems to be little doubt about the appropriate conclusion when it comes to sex role stereotypes. Two researchers, **Jennifer Herrett-Skjellum** and **Mike Allen,** used a technique known as **meta-analysis** to examine this issue. A meta-analysis is a method designed to statistically summarize over a large number of studies so that researchers can reach a confident conclusion about what the literature actually reveals on a given question. They summarized the data in the following way: "Television programming generally portrays men and women in traditional gender stereotypical roles. . . . All content analyses illustrate the consistent finding that men are more often on TV, in higher status roles as characters, and are represented as having greater power than women."[11] The important question for our purposes is: So what? Why should stereotypical presentations of men and women be of concern? Are there any effects associated with these portrayals? That is, do the media stereotypes actually cause people's perceptions to change or cause them to act any differently? As it turns out, several researchers have attempted to answer the question of media impact with respect to gender role stereotypes. Let's take a look at some of the findings.

Effects of Sex Role Stereotypes

As I am writing this section, my daughter Jordan, a sophomore in high school, is preparing to attend a week-long computer camp at Purdue University. Over the course of the week, she will learn various things about computers and actually compete in some computer projects with the other campers. One day last week, we checked with the camp registration just to make sure things were in order, and we discovered a shocking statistic. There were 19 girls signed up for the camp along with 98 boys. While Jordan and her female friends may have found this statistic to be quite exhilarating, the camp leaders would probably have preferred a better balance of girls to boys. But recruiting girls to computer camp is quite a challenge. Somehow, adolescent girls just don't seem to be that attracted to computers. Why might this be? One likely reason has to do with the way young girls construct their social reality. Many have adopted beliefs about the social world around them that does not have much room for females being attracted to computer camps. Obviously, there are many things that might affect young people's view of their social world, but the media messages that are consumed might be one important factor. Two communication researchers who are concerned about how media messages influence the **construction of social reality** are Robert Hawkins and Suzanne Pingree. In one study that they reported with their coauthor, Ilya Adler, they surveyed more than 1,300 adolescents, most of whom were from Australia. The most important general finding from their investigation was that heavy TV viewers tended to have beliefs about the world that were consistent with the messages of TV.[12]

We might actually be able to get some insight into this question by looking at the natural experiment that Tannis MacBeth Williams conducted in Canada. You may recall reading about this study in chapter 4. Along with her colleague, **Meredith Kimball,** Williams examined what happened to boys' and girls' job expectations over a 2-year period in a town that initially had no access to television (Notel) and then received access to one TV channel. The results were enlightening. The researchers had two main hypotheses, both of which were confirmed.

First, Kimball and Williams believed that children who lived in Notel would hold fewer stereotypical attitudes about the appropriateness of various behaviors than would the children who lived in towns that did have TV access. The researchers measured stereotypical attitudes by having children in the sixth and ninth grades fill out the Sex Role Differentiation Scale. As expected, the results showed that the children in the town with no access to TV (Notel) did not differentiate behaviors according to sex to the same extent as the children in the TV towns. Given that the towns were chosen to be similar in almost every other respect except their TV access, the authors interpreted this as evidence in favor of the idea that children develop sex-stereotyped attitudes as a result of watching TV.

But the evidence is even more compelling when the second hypothesis is examined. Immediately after the first hypothesis was tested, the children who lived in the town with no TV gained access to TV reception. Two years later, when the researchers returned and administered the Sex Role Differentiation Scale once again to children in the same grades, they found that the pattern of the results had changed. In contrast to the scores 2 years earlier, now that the children in Notel had TV access, their scores on the Sex Role Differentiation Scale changed to show a dramatic increase in stereotyped attitudes. Given that the only major change over the 2-year period was access to TV, the researchers felt comfortable interpreting this evidence as a clear media effect. In drawing implications about these findings, the researchers stated the following:

> Several studies, including this one, have documented links between TV viewing and stereotyped sex-role attitudes. The evidence for same-sex preferences in viewing television, greater recognition of same-sex characters and behaviors, and the role of gender schemata in processing sex-role information probably account for the effects of TV viewing. In light of this information, we recommend that more female characters be portrayed in more varied roles on television. This may be particularly important for young children.[13]

It wouldn't be good science to conclude that the great disparity between males and females who registered for the Purdue computer camp was due to the impact of media messages. But could media images have contributed, in part, to this enrollment pattern? Extending the conclusions from this research, it certainly seems like a plausible idea.

Media Images of Thin Bodies
and Effects on Body Image

If sexual stereotypes in the media might make an impact on the socialization of young boys and girls such that enrollment patterns at computer camps might be affected, then perhaps there might be other important areas of media impact related to sexual stereotypes. One such area that has received a fair amount of research attention over the last decade is the way in which female bodies are represented and the impact of those representations.

In one of the most recent content analyses to address this topic, **Gregory Fouts** and **Kimberley Burggraf** studied 18 situation comedies from prime-time TV.[14] Their findings were striking. First, they discovered that the females in these programs were far more likely to be judged as being "below average" in weight as opposed to "average" or "above average." This finding is consistent with the results of other research that shows that media images of females tend to place a heavy emphasis on an idealized, overly thin standard compared to males.[15] Second, and even more important, the higher the weight of the female character depicted, the more likely it was that negative comments were made by other characters about her or directly to her. Moreover, these negative comments were often followed by a laugh track that suggested to the audience that these negative comments were funny. The authors speculated that the combination of programming that presents a disproportionate emphasis on overly thin female bodies and creates a context that explicitly reinforces the value and attractiveness of this standard may amount to a huge social problem. If young girls internalize the idea that females should be thin, then the media might have some role in creating **body dissatisfaction** or **body-image disturbance** among females. That is, because of their natural tendency to engage in **social comparison,** young female viewers may compare their own bodies with the ones that are frequently depicted and reinforced in the media. To the extent that there is a perceived mismatch, young girls might start down a road that could lead to various eating disorders like bulimia or anorexia nervosa. Such a path might jeopardize the health, or even the life, of young girls.

Of course, these effects are largely speculative. Is there any research to suggest that overly thin females in the media actually have an impact on the way young girls think or behave? The answer to this question is yes. Let's take a brief look at some of the studies that have been reported.

In one of the few published experiments on this topic, two researchers, **Eric Stice** and **Heather Shaw,** randomly assigned 157 female college students to view pictures in magazines that contained either thin models, average models, or no models.[16] Immediately after viewing the pictures, the students responded to a number of items on a questionnaire. The results revealed that the students who had viewed the thin models were more likely to report a variety of negative emotions like stress, shame, guilt, depression, and insecurity. They also indicated higher levels of body dissatisfaction. A second finding of the study was that, in general, students who reported high levels of body dissatisfaction, regardless of their experimental condition, were more likely also to report that they suffered from the symptoms associated with bulimia. More recently, **Kristen Harrison** and **Joanne Cantor** surveyed over 400 college students and asked questions about media consumption, body dissatisfaction, drive for thinness, and various symptoms related to eating disorders.[17] Their results, while not conclusive in terms of causality, were consistent with the experimental results reported by Stice and Shaw. For the female students, media consumption was related to higher body dissatisfaction, a drive for thinness, and reports of symptoms that suggest eating disorders. For the male students, media consumption was related to the tendency to endorse thinness and dieting for females. Harrison has recently reported the results of yet another study that replicates and extends these same findings.[18]

To summarize the research on this topic, it appears that a number of studies document that media images of females are stereotypical in that they tend to represent females with idealized, overly thin bodies. These depictions may be very important because a number of studies clearly point to the conclusion that they have negative effects on both males and females. Females are encouraged to internalize the ideal image and may strive to attain it even in the face of suffering from various eating disorders. Males are encouraged to reinforce the ideal image and thus may create additional social pressure on females to conform to this ultrathin body standard.

One question that has surely occurred to you by now is what one can do about a negative media effect such as this one. Researchers and scholars recommend teaching students to engage in **critical media consumption.** One of the hoped-for consequences of writing a textbook like this one is that college students will become more sensitive to media stereotypes and the possible effects of media exposure on attitudes and behavior. Many media scholars recommend that elementary and secondary schools explicitly teach children about these sorts of media stereotypes and their effects on viewers. Research on high school females strongly suggests that school curricula designed to expose sexual stereotypes in the media are effective in reducing the extent to which young girls embrace the idealized, overly thin body standard that consistently shows up in magazines, movies, advertisements, and TV shows.[19]

One organization that is dedicated to teaching students to consume media more critically is the *Media Education Foundation*. You can find their Web site in the Web Links listed at the end of this chapter. One aspect of their teaching mission is to produce videos that seek to reveal the way certain types of media depict stereotypes that are potentially harmful. For example, in a series of videos (*Dreamworlds*) on the way music television stereotypes males and females, Sut Jhally has presented brief clips that encourage the viewer to see these videos in a new light. Similarly, Jean Kilbourne's *Killing Us Softly* series examines how women are depicted in advertising in ways that are demeaning and stereotypical. While these videos are valuable instructional aids, their focus, like much of the research on stereotypes, is on the nature of media content—not upon the scientific investigation of the effects of that content. Consequently, some social scientists find these videos to be long on claims and short on supporting evidence.

Racial Stereotypes

Sex stereotypes are not the only area of research that should concern the student of media effects. Several years ago, the Frito-Lay company introduced a cartoon character in its advertising that was supposed to convey the message that Fritos corn chips are delicious. The character was dubbed the "Frito-bandito," and his role was to run around stealing bags of Fritos because he couldn't resist the taste. He wore a big yellow hat and a gun on either side of his waist. His long mustache and Mexican accent clearly identified him as a Mexican. The company thought that it had a smashing advertising campaign until the Mexican community began to protest. Their argument was very simple and reduced to two points: (1) The frequency of media depictions of Mexicans is so low that *any* depiction was critically important in terms of the overall image that it represented to the masses of media consumers, and (2) the image of the Frito-bandito, being one of the only media representations of Mexicans, was an image that encouraged consumers to adopt a very undesirable stereotype associating their ethnic group with crime and thievery. The storm of controversy surrounding the cartoon icon reached such a feverish pitch that the Frito-Lay company decided to put the Frito-bandito in his grave. They abandoned the use of the bandito in all of their advertising.

While the Frito-bandito certainly stirred controversy, perhaps the greatest concern over the years about stereotypes in U.S. media has been about the representation of African Americans. In his brief discussion of the history of how African Americans have been portrayed over the years, Richard Jackson Harris noted that "Until the 1960s, there were almost no African Americans as models in mainstream U.S. advertising . . . and the only African Americans in prime-time TV programming were limited to a few stereotyped and demeaning roles."[20] While the situation has certainly changed over the last three decades, and the presence of African Americans is now much more commonplace in advertising and serious dramatic roles, a recent content analysis, discussed in the next section, reveals that negative media stereotyping of African Americans is still taking place in a surprising and dramatic way.

Overrepresentation of
African Americans as Lawbreakers

In a fascinating study of TV news, two media researchers, **Travis Dixon** and **Daniel Linz,** carried out a major content study designed to reveal information about how TV newscasts in a major U.S. city represented African Americans and Latinos in stories about crime.[21] Using random-sampling procedures, these authors sampled news programs from TV stations in the Los Angeles area over a period of 20 weeks that extended from October 1995 to June 1996. Their final sample contained 116 news broadcasts and included examples from virtually every news program broadcast in the Los Angeles area during the selected time period. A team of coders viewed these newscasts and coded all stories that reported crimes. The race of the people who were shown as perpetrators of each crime was coded along with the race of the people who were shown as law defenders (police, judges, lawyers, etc.).

In reporting their results, Dixon and Linz relied upon three types of comparisons. First, they used the **intergroup comparison.** This is a very simple comparison of the percentage of one group compared to the percentage of another group. Intergroup comparisons have been used regularly in content analyses of racial representations. In Dixon and Linz's study, they found that the news coverage across all the programs in their sample included 129 perpetrators of criminal offenses. Of those 129, 69 were Black perpetrators and 40 were White perpetrators. Stated in ratio form, for every White perpetrator shown on the news, there were 1.72 Black perpetrators. When the analysis was restricted to felony crimes, the ratio was even higher. For every White perpetrator, there were 2.46 Black perpetrators. The intergroup comparison is a convenient way to report and compare data for different groups. In this case, the data show that Blacks were more likely to be shown as perpetrators of crime than Whites. Dixon and Linz also reported similar data showing that Latinos were also more likely to be shown as crime perpetrators than Whites—but not as likely as Blacks.

A second type of comparison utilized by Dixon and Linz was the **interrole comparison.** This comparison is used to compare the distribution of the same group of people according to particular roles. For example, in their study, they coded the race of the police officers depicted in the news stories as well as that of the perpetrators. There were 87 Blacks depicted in their sample of news stories. Of those 87, 69 appeared as perpetrators of crime while only 18 appeared as officers. In ratio terms, for every Black officer, there were 3.83 crime perpetrators. When the same analysis was conducted for Whites, a very different picture emerged. Of the 133 Whites who appeared in the crime stories, 93 appeared as officers and 40 appeared as perpetrators. In ratio terms, for every White officer, there were only .43 perpetrators. From this analysis, it seems clear that Blacks were more likely to be shown as perpetrators of crime than as officers; Whites were more likely to be shown as officers than as perpetrators.

Finally, Dixon and Linz utilized a comparison known as the **interreality comparison.** In this case, the authors were interested in comparing the percentages of Blacks, Whites, and Latinos who appeared in the TV crime stories with the percentages that showed up in actual crime statistics catalogued in the Los Angeles area. The interreality comparison is, perhaps, the most revealing of all three of the comparisons because it shows how the media depictions may distort reality. When the authors went to the actual crime data, the records showed that Blacks comprised 21% of all the criminal arrests in Los Angeles. Whites comprised 28%. Latinos comprised 47%. But when these percentages were compared to the percentages shown on TV newscasts, quite a difference emerged. While Blacks actually comprised the *lowest* percentage of arrests in the real crime statistics, they comprised the *highest* percentage of perpetrators represented on TV news. Compared to their actual arrest rate (21%), a full 37% of TV news perpetrators were Black. In contrast, compared to the actual arrest rate for Whites (28%), only 21% of the perpetrators shown on TV news were White. While Blacks were overrepresented as criminals on the news, Latinos appeared to be underrepresented. Compared to their actual arrest rate (47% of all arrests), only 29% of the criminal perpetrators on TV news were Latino.

In addition to providing a replication of some earlier studies on the depiction of Blacks and Whites as criminals on TV news, the study by Dixon and Linz is important because it is one of the first to report data on Latinos. It is also important in terms of the explanations that the authors advanced to explain their findings. Why might Blacks be overrepresented as criminals compared to Whites? The authors argued that TV news may be drawn to report blue-collar crime instead of white-collar crime. Blue-collar crimes like assault and robbery are more visually dramatic and attractive to TV reporters. They may also be more likely to be committed by Blacks. Whites, who have access to more economic resources and positions of power, may be more likely to commit white-collar crime. In comparison with the highly visual drama of a violent arrest or car chase, white-collar crimes like embezzlement don't offer very exciting news footage. This may partially account for the representational distortions that Dixon and Linz uncovered.

What about the effects of these representations? You have already been reminded several times in this text of the caution that media content does not equal media effect. Dixon and Linz studied the media content—not the way that content had an impact on viewers. Nevertheless, they did underscore the need for some systematic research on the impact of these depictions. At the end of their research report, they stated the following:

> We suggest that immediate work must be undertaken with regard to how these portrayals might encourage or discourage stereotyping and increase fear of African Americans. Cultivation theory as well as the mechanisms explicated in the social cognition literature suggest that these representations may have a powerful impact on viewers. (p. 151)[22]

You may want to review cultivation theory in chapter 8 and see if you can determine what Dixon and Linz are concerned about. Recall that the theory basically states that heavy consumers of media will tend to be cultivated in terms of their attitudes and values toward the view of reality depicted by the media. One of the "mechanisms explicated in the social cognition literature" that the authors may have in mind could be **priming,** a concept discussed in chapter 5. If the media continue to associate Blacks with the perpetration of crime and Whites with law enforcement, these associations may become so strong in a person's mind that merely thinking about one could prime thoughts of the other. Clearly, as Dixon and Linz suggest, future research efforts need to examine how these representational distortions may affect media consumers.

THE IMBALANCE IN MEDIA
RESEARCH ON STEREOTYPES

Countless content studies document representational distortions of various types. Such studies are so easy to conceive that if one of my graduate students seems lost in terms of a research idea for a seminar, as a last resort I will sometimes suggest a content analysis on the prevalence of some group or behavior that might be of interest in media messages. To give you a sense of what I mean here, consider just a sampling of the studies reported in the literature that use content analysis to study different media stereotypes.

In terms of different groups of people, the studies go far beyond the depictions of Blacks, Whites, and Latinos as studied by Dixon and Linz. As we have already seen, many studies have examined how women are represented in prime-time TV or in advertising. Other studies have examined the depictions of men and the types of behaviors that are deemed acceptable for men to perform. Harris documents studies on other groups as well, including Native Americans, Arabs, homosexuals, the disabled, police officers, lawyers, farmers, and college students. Often, groups of people are not the focus of content studies; instead, specific behaviors are the main interest. Content studies of media have examined cigarette smoking, alcohol use and abuse, seat belt use, a variety of aggressive behaviors, helping and prosocial behaviors, and so forth (see Study Box 10-1 for a focus on how some of these behaviors are depicted in movies). All of these studies have helped to contribute to our understanding of how the media may communicate subtle and not-so-subtle stereotypes. But as I reviewed the literature in preparation for this chapter, one thing was very apparent: There are far more studies on the *presence* of media stereotypes than there are on the *effects* of those stereotypes on media consumers.

There are some good reasons why the media literature reflects an imbalance between content studies and effects studies. First, while content studies are often more time-consuming and tedious than studies of media impact, they also permit the researcher to avoid a number of obstacles that inevitably appear whenever people are the units of analysis in a study instead of media messages. Researchers who need human subjects must worry about securing approval from a human-subjects committee about the procedures that are planned. And once approval is granted, people don't always show up for the study. Sometimes, they show up and then decide not to participate. Researchers must also be concerned about the ethics of subjecting subjects to potentially harmful media messages. In short, research with human subjects can be considerably messier than research with media messages. Often, beginning researchers will get their feet wet with a content study and never move on to research with human subjects, which is where we learn about media effects.

Another reason contributing to the imbalance may be the obligation to document the presence or absence of content *prior* to doing a study on media impact. For example, before I started to investigate how depictions of paranormal messages affected people's paranormal beliefs, I was concerned about the prevalence of paranormal messages in the media. It took a content study to

---

**STUDY BOX 10-1   Depictions of Unhealthy Behaviors
in the Movies**

Using data provided by *Variety*'s annual reports of the top-grossing movies, Terre, Drabman, and Speer conducted a major content analysis of 200 movies (the top-20 films of each year over the 10-year period from 1977 to 1988). They coded a number of unhealthy behaviors, using each 5-minute segment of the film as the unit of analysis. For each segment of each film, they coded whether characters were shown *possessing* cigarettes, drugs, junk food, or sports equipment. They also coded the *suggested use* of the things that were possessed. For example, if a cigarette was only being held but not actually smoked, its use was only suggested. *Overt action* was also coded. Taking drugs or drinking an alcoholic beverage counted as actual use. Finally, the *behavioral outcomes* of engaging in these actions were coded. The results of the content analysis revealed several significant trends over the decade, but there were two very important findings. First, the frequency of depictions of smoking and illegal drug use increased significantly. Second, none of the risky behaviors that were coded (smoking, drug use, alcohol use) were consistently associated with either positive or negative outcomes. The authors concluded that "These results present a disturbing picture of the health-relevant social norms being portrayed in recent, popular films. . . . Of particular concern is the trend toward increasing portrayals of health-detrimental behaviors" (p. 1316). The authors explicitly noted that their report did not permit them to assume that the depictions had any effects on consumers. However, they do speculate on the basis of media effects already documented and existing theory about media impact that depictions of risky behaviors in movies may very well have negative social consequences.

SOURCE: Terre, L., Drabman, R. S., & Speer, P. (1991). Health-relevant behaviors in media. *Journal of Applied Social Psychology, 21*, 1303–1319.

---

determine that the messages were prevalent enough to warrant concern. Sometimes content studies are produced that don't end up leading to studies of media effects.

Another reason for the imbalance in studies of content and studies of effects is probably the main one: Documenting media effects is considerably more difficult than documenting the presence or absence of media content. Even in the most carefully designed sample survey, evidence for a clear causal effect remains elusive. And the most carefully designed laboratory experiment still has significant limitations in what it can reveal about media impact. Most lab experiments reveal short–term effects but tell us little about media impact over the long term. Added to these inherent design limitations, there are a host of thorny procedural details that can easily confound the best-laid plans of a would-be media effects researcher. I don't want to be overly negative at this point. I have spent my career studying media effects, and I remain just as enthusiastic about doing effects research today as I was when I started over 20 years ago. But the point remains that solid conclusions about the content of the media are much easier to generate than solid conclusions about the impact of the media.

So, where does all this leave us? The research reviewed in this chapter leaves little doubt that media stereotypes do affect people. Nevertheless, the challenge for the research community is to begin taking some of the well-documented stereotypical depictions (e.g., sex and race stereotypes) and showing precisely how they affect people's attitudes and behaviors. It is one thing to speculate on the importance of media stereotypes; it is quite another thing to actually document the importance with a carefully executed study that shows evidence of media impact.

SUMMARY

This chapter began by documenting a curious effect that seems to exist in different sorts of images of males and females throughout the culture (photos, paintings, drawings, etc.). The face-ism effect is the tendency for males to be represented with higher degrees of facial prominence than females. This systematic variance in male and female images has possible implications, including development of stereotypes, that were discussed in the chapter. The remainder of the chapter reviewed research on various stereotypes in the mass media that have been documented by content analyses. Sexual stereotypes and racial stereotypes are two areas of research that have received the most attention. While some studies on the effects of stereotypes have been undertaken, it was noted that content studies are far more prevalent than studies of impact. One area of effects is in the study of female body images and their possible impact on eating disorders. The reasons for the existence of fewer studies on effects and more on content were discussed, and the important distinction between content and effect was again emphasized.

KEY TERMS AND CONCEPTS

Face-ism 167	Body dissatisfaction 175	Intergroup comparison 178
Role schema 171		
Stereotype 171	Body-image disturbance 175	Interrole comparison 178
Meta-analysis 173	Social comparison 175	Interreality comparison 178
Construction of social reality 173	Critical media consumption 176	Priming 179

KEY NAMES

Dane Archer 167	Susan Fiske and Shelly Taylor 171	Natan Katzman 172
Miron Zuckerman and Suzanne Kieffer 170	Tannis MacBeth Williams 172	Richard Jackson Harris 172
		George Gerbner 172

Jennifer Herrett-Skjellum and Mike Allen 173

Meredith Kimball 174

Gregory Fouts and Kimberley Burggraf 175

Eric Stice and Heather Shaw 175

Kristen Harrison and Joanne Cantor 176

Travis Dixon and Daniel Linz 177

WEB LINKS

1. For suggestions from the Media Awareness Network about how to talk to children about racial stereotypes, try . . . http://www.media-awareness.ca/eng/issues/minrep/getinvolved/talking.htm

2. For a recent news article on the increasing number of racial stereotypes in TV sitcoms, try . . . http://gabrielmedia.org/news/racialsitcoms.html

3. To listen to an important panel discussion on media stereotypes sponsored by the Simon Wiesenthal Center, try . . . http://www.broadcast.com/events/swc/antis/

4. For a short paper on the relationship between media use and healthy behaviors, try . . . http://www.medialiteracy.net/research/media_literacy.pdf

5. For information on stereotyping from the Media Education Foundation, try . . . http://www.mediaed.org

To learn more about the topics in this chapter, enter the Key Terms and Concepts and Key Names found in this chapter as subject and keyword searches on your InfoTrac College Edition.

NOTES

1. Archer, D., Iritani, B., Kimes, D. D., & Barrios, M. (1983). Face-ism: Five studies of sex differences in facial prominence. *Journal of Personality and Social Psychology, 45,* 725–735.

2. Sparks, G. G., & Fehlner, C. L. (1986). Faces in the news: Gender comparisons of magazine photographs. *Journal of Communication, 36,* 70–79.

3. Zuckerman, M., & Kieffer, S. C. (1994). Race differences in face-ism: Does facial prominence imply dominance? *Journal of Personality & Social Psychology, 66,* 86–92.

4. Fiske, S. T., & Taylor, S. E. (1991). *Social cognition.* New York: McGraw-Hill.

5. Williams, T. M. (1986). *The impact of television: A natural experiment in three communities.* Orlando, FL: Academic Press.

6. Katzman, N. (1972). Television soap operas: What's been going on anyway? *Public Opinion Quarterly, 36,* 200–212.

7. Harris, R. J. (1999). *A cognitive psychology of mass communication.* Mahwah, NJ: Erlbaum.

8. Dobrow, J. R., & Gidney, C. L. (1998). The good, the bad, and the foreign: The use of dialect in children's animated television. *The Annals of the American Academy of Political and Social Science, 557,* 105–119.

9. Bretl, D. J., & Cantor, J. (1988). The portrayal of men and women on U.S. television commercials: A recent content analysis and trends over 15 years. *Sex Roles, 18,* 595–609.

10. Jhally, S. (1994). *The killing screens: Media and the culture of violence* [video]. Northampton, MA: Media Education Foundation.

11. Herrett-Skjellum, J., & Allen, M. (1996). Television programming and sex stereotyping: A meta-analysis. In B. R. Burleson (Ed.), *Communication yearbook* (pp. 157–185). Thousand Oaks, CA.: Sage.

12. Hawkins, R. P., Pingree, S., & Adler, I. (1987). Searching for cognitive processes in the cultivation effect: Adult and adolescent samples in the United States and Australia. *Human Communication Research, 13,* 553–577.

13. Kimball, M. A. (1986). Television and sex-role attitudes. In T. M. Williams (Ed.), *The impact of television: A natural experiment in three communities* (pp. 265–301). Orlando, FL: Academic Press.

14. Fouts, G., & Burggraf, K. (2000). Television situation comedies: Female weight, male negative comments, and audience reactions. *Sex Roles, 42,* 925–932.

15. Malkin, A. R., Wornian, K., & Chrisler, J. C. (1999). Women and weight: Gendered messages on magazine covers. *Sex Roles, 40,* 647–655.

16. Stice, E., & Shaw, H. E. (1994). Adverse effects of the media portrayed thin-ideal on women and linkages to bulimic symptomatology. *Journal of Social & Clinical Psychology, 13,* 288–308.

17. Harrison, K., & Cantor, J. (1997). The relationship between media consumption and eating disorders. *Journal of Communication, 47,* 40–67.

18. Harrison, K. (2000). The body electric: Thin-ideal media and eating disorders in adolescents. *Journal of Communication, 50,* 119–143.

19. Irving, L. M., DuPen, J., & Berel, S. (1998). A media literacy program for high school females. *Eating Disorders: The Journal of Treatment & Prevention, 6,* 119–132.

20. Harris, R. J. (1999). *A cognitive psychology of mass communication.* Mahwah, NJ: Erlbaum.

21. Dixon, T. L., & Linz, D. (2000). Overrepresentation and underrepresentation of African Americans and Latinos as lawbreakers on television news. *Journal of Communication, 50*(2), 131–154.

22. Dixon, T. L., & Linz, D. (2000). Overrepresentation and underrepresentation of African Americans and Latinos as lawbreakers on television news. *Journal of Communication, 50*(2), 131–154.

11

■

The Impact of New Media Technologies

THE REVOLUTION IN
NEW MEDIA TECHNOLOGY

Over the last 75 years, media effects researchers have usually lagged behind in studying the impact of the very latest media. As late as 1960, when TV had exploded upon the scene, the prevailing wisdom among researchers was that electronic media had limited effects. You might recall from chapter 3 that this "wisdom" was mainly the consequence of a single study—a large survey conducted in 1940 during the presidential campaign and prior to the days of television. It wasn't until the mid-1960s, almost 25 years after the survey that ushered in the era of limited media effects, that researchers began systematic study of the effects of TV. Of course, it makes some sense that research on a given medium would lag a bit behind. Any new technology has to be in place and in use by a reasonable proportion of the population before the research community deems it worthwhile to focus on the impact of that new technology. Consequently, when we ask questions about the effects of new technology, it makes sense that the number of studies at our disposal are not nearly as numerous as when we ask questions about the effects of a well-established medium like TV or movies.

As I write these words, the music industry has dominated the headlines of the past week with articles about the problem of the *Napster* Web site. If you are a typical consumer, you might not regard *Napster* as a problem. Upon arriving at the site, you can make music files available to anyone else on the site

—files that you have copied from a CD onto your computer hard drive. You can also search through hundreds of thousands of other music files that are available from others who are on the site and copy whatever you wish. The problem, of course, is that the music industry is not very happy about what they regard as a violation of copyright law. Anyone can potentially download an entire album and avoid the purchase price that would otherwise have to be paid. A judge has already tried to shut down the site until some legal solution can be found, but her action was overturned. Now, an appeals court has upheld the basic judgment to shut the site down if the language can be changed in the initial injunction. As of this writing, *Napster* is still in business. At the rate things are changing in the realm of new media technologies, the situation might be different by the time you read this paragraph.

When we speak of the impact or effects of new media technology, there are a whole host of effects that one might potentially contemplate. Computers and the World Wide Web have certainly changed the way we behave in many domains. People shop online, trade stocks online, get their news online, initiate friendships online, and so forth. Children spend time playing the latest computer games. The potential effects that we could discuss might easily turn into a separate, book-length volume. What is all of this new technology doing to us? One thing that it is doing is encouraging traditional media–effects scholars to ask new questions and design new research paradigms.

Two media scholars, **Jane Brown** and **Joanne Cantor,** recently outlined a series of crucial questions surrounding new technology that researchers need to study in future years. They framed these questions in terms of the concept of **perpetual linkage,** the new tendency for youth to be constantly connected with each other through some type of technology. The authors asked the following questions:

> What is the impact of the connectedness that the newer media promote, i.e., the almost constant technological links that youth have with each other, using their cell phones, beepers, E-mail, and other devices soon to be developed? What about the relationships young people have with others they have met only via technological links? Do youth, for example, have stronger social ties to their peers because they are in virtual contact for so much more of the time? Or are they more alienated because this technological contact comes at the expense of potentially richer face-to-face interaction?[1]

These questions are ones that are just beginning to appear in the research literature, and there are no clear answers at the present time.

Another area of research that has caught the attention of researchers and public health officials in the past few years is the impact of video games on youth, particularly games that involve graphic violence and permit the player to take the role of a **"first–person shooter."** In these games, the player handles a gun and fires directly at characters on the screen in an attempt to "kill" them. Like the questions raised by Brown and Cantor, the questions that arise about the impact of these games still demand more research before a consensus emerges among scholars. Even though questions about computer use and video games have not yet yielded clear answers in the research literature, there have been studies published in the last few years that begin to address some of the issues. This chapter introduces you to the few studies that have been done in each of these areas and outlines some of the current controversies and issues that remain for future studies.

COMPUTERS AND THE INTERNET: CONNECTION OR ALIENATION?

Media Metrix, an organization that monitors Internet use, released a report in August 2000 that surprised many analysts and media researchers. For the first time in its brief history, the Internet was being used by more women than men. In addition, every day more women than men go online for the first time. The most dramatic change over the past year was in the demographic group of girls between the ages of 12 and 17. At the beginning of the year, slightly fewer than 2 million from that age group were Internet users. At the end of the year, nearly 4½ million were regular users—an increase of 125.3%.[2] Clearly, the late 1990s and early years of the new millennium will go down in media history as the years when the Internet exploded onto the scene, much like TV did between 1950 and 1960.

With such tremendous growth at such a rapid pace, the question of the effects of this new technology is obviously one that people are curious about. But because the technology is so new, the media–effects community is unable at this point to provide definitive answers. Nevertheless, there have been a few major studies that took aim on the Internet technology to try to figure out what was going on.

The Carnegie Mellon Study

In September of 1998, a research team at Carnegie Mellon University, led by **Robert Kraut** of the Human Computer Interaction Institute, published one of the first major studies on the impact of Internet use. The researchers titled their study with a provocative question: "Internet Paradox: A Social Technology That Reduces Social Involvement and Psychological Well-Being?"[3]

The question gives a strong clue to the answer that their research provided. One thing that emerges quite quickly upon reading the original research report is that studying the impact of the Internet is not a very easy proposition. The researchers had to put in a lot of effort to set up their study in a way that would yield meaningful results. And as you will see, even after all of this effort, the study has been severely criticized.

One of the positive features of the Carnegie Mellon study (sometimes referred to as the HomeNet study) was the fact that the researchers employed a longitudinal design. Recall from chapter 2 that a longitudinal study is one in which data is collected at several points in time. In this case, the study involved

256 people in 93 different households during their first 2 years of being online. Each family actually received a computer, a free telephone line, and a free Internet connection. The families who participated had a high-school student in the household or belonged to at least one community group in the Pittsburgh area. In return for the freebies, the families agreed that the researchers could track their Internet use with special software and periodically ask them survey questions during the time of the study.

Despite the fact that the researchers found that the people in the study used the Internet to engage in communication with others, they also found evidence of a rather alarming state of affairs. Use of the Internet was associated with a general decline in communication with family members who lived in the household. In addition, those who used the Internet more frequently tended to report that the number of people in their social circle declined over the years of the study. Finally, Internet users tended to report greater levels of depression and feelings of loneliness than they did before the study began.

If using the Internet is really associated with these negative psychological effects, what specifically is it about using the net that causes them to occur? According to Kraut and his associates, there are two main possibilities. First, the data might reveal an **activity displacement effect.** This sort of effect was discussed in chapter 4 in connection with TV. People have a limited amount of time during any day to engage in their various activities. Once family members are hooked up to the Internet, perhaps they tend to spend more time in isolation from others, using the Internet for private entertainment and Web surfing. Second, perhaps the data reveal that the Internet **displaces strong social ties.** According to this explanation, when people go online, they often end up talking to people in chat rooms and even occasionally make new friends. But overall, the kinds of relationships that are formed online tend to be more superficial and are characterized by weaker ties than the relationships that people tend to have with family members and significant others who appear in one's life face-to-face on a daily basis. When people use the Internet, they may be depriving themselves of the richness of their deeper, strong ties with family and other significant friends in favor of relationships that simply are not nearly as deep or involving.

After considering these two alternatives, the authors clearly seemed to prefer the second option to the first. The main reason that they reject the activity displacement explanation is because their data showed that so many people in their sample used the Internet for social purposes. Clearly, if the reason for increasing isolation and loneliness was the fact that the Internet was displacing social contact, the data would have to show that social contact on the Internet was much lower than it was before use of the Internet began. But the data didn't show that at all. People used the net for exchanging email, going to chat rooms, and so forth. Moreover, the authors claimed that some of their data actually showed that those who used the Internet for social purposes were more likely to suffer the negative social effects than those who used the net for less social purposes. If the negative effects were due only to social displacement, we probably wouldn't observe that particular pattern in the data.

Instead of displacing social activity, the authors prefer to focus on the possibility that Internet use tends to encourage a particular type of social relationship at the expense of another. They suggest that Internet users form more superficial relationships instead of connecting deeply to other human beings. If you take a moment to think about it, this view does make some sense. If the extent of your involvement with a person is through email, there is much about that other person that you don't know. Online relationships also don't tend to encourage the kind of mutual help and service that characterize most close friendships. When I think of the people in my own life who are closest to me, they all tend to be people who would feel comfortable calling me on the phone and asking me to run an errand for them. And I would feel equally comfortable calling them for the same. It may be that the deep intimacy that comes with relationships is built on a kind of involvement and mutual service that the online connections simply don't tend to produce. And if people spend time online in the more superficial relationships, they are using up time that they would have for relationships of the deeper variety.

You may be skeptical of the "weak ties" idea. We have all heard about people who met while using the Internet and eventually decided to get married. The popular movie *You've Got Mail* was based on this premise. But the stuff of Hollywood and media feature stories may not be the stuff of normal life. While there are some people who may have discovered deep intimate friendships while using the Internet, Robert Kraut and his colleagues point out that the best data seems to refute this pattern as normative. They note that their own data seem to converge with data collected by two other researchers, James Katz and Philip Aspden. In a national survey conducted by these authors, they found that only "22% of the respondents who had been using the Internet for two or more years had ever made a new friend on the Internet."[4] On the other hand, some new experimental work on Internet interaction suggests that even communicating with strangers can induce strong feelings. In one study, the amount of communication between participants in a chat room was positively correlated with the nature of the statements that people were making. The researchers examined both positive statements and negative statements made during chats. Positive statements were ones that complimented another person, expressed agreement with the other, expressed approval of some idea or behavior, expressed a positive emotion and so forth. Negative statements were ones that criticized another person, expressed disagreement with the other, expressed disapproval, or expressed a negative emotion. Intuitively, you might think that the more positive the comments, the more communication took place. Actually, the form of the correlation was directly opposite. The more negative the comments, the more communication took place. At least in chat rooms, positive comments don't seem to get many takers. People seem more willing to argue and engage in various forms of hostility.[5] Study Box 11-1 focuses on some new experimental work on Internet communication that confirms that people experience intense feelings in Internet interactions. Clearly, the research community is just beginning to scratch the surface in its attempts to discover the relational dynamics of Internet communication.

STUDY BOX 11-1   Virtual Relationships Can Induce Strong Emotions

The Internet is now being used by researchers to set up various kinds of experiments. While there are some limitations to this type of research, psychologists and communication researchers will undoubtedly use the Internet to collect valuable data in future years. In one recent experiment, three researchers set up an Internet study that had nearly 1,500 participants from 62 countries. When the participants arrived at the Web site, they were told that the purpose of the experiment was to see if computers could be used as a tool in mental visualization. They were asked to engage in a relatively simple exercise in which they would virtually toss a flying disk to one of two other players who they thought were playing the game online at the same time. Actually, the other two players were generated by the computer software and were controlled by the program. During the task, the players were asked to visualize themselves throwing the disk and catching it. No disk actually appeared on the screen. The computer program informed the players when the disk was tossed, who caught it, and who should throw it next. Each player was represented on the screen with a color. The participants had to push a button when they were in possession of the disk in order to throw it to one of the other players. They also could select which of the other players (colors) to throw it at.

After two throws, the computer program assigned each participant to one of four experimental conditions. In two of the conditions, the participants were ostracized—they were almost never on the receiving end of a throw from the other two players. In one of these conditions, they were *never* thrown the disk. In the other condition, they were thrown the disk only 20% of the time. In the other two conditions, participants were either included in the game at a rate equal to the other two players, or they were overincluded—receiving the throws 67% of the time. Following the game, participants reported their feelings. As levels of ostracism increased, so too did the respondents' reports of bad feelings, perceptions of less control, and feelings of a loss of belonging. Even though the supposed players could not be seen, were complete strangers, were unlikely to ever be engaged in future interaction, and were throwing a virtual disk that was only imaginary, the participants in the experiment felt a dampening of their mood when they were excluded from the game. The authors concluded, "As our global society moves closer to worldwide use of the Internet, opportunities for exacerbating these feelings through real or perceived ostracism clearly exist and demand our attention" (p. 760).

SOURCE: Williams, K. D., Cheung, C. K. T., & Choi, W. (2000). Cyberostracism: Effects of being ignored over the Internet. *Journal of Personality & Social Psychology, 79,* 748–762.

Applying the Lessons of History

You might recall from the chapter on media violence (chapter 5) that one of the earliest theorists who conducted research on the impact of televised violence was **Seymour Feshbach.** His theory of symbolic catharsis actually received some initial support from a few studies, and in the early 1960s many researchers thought that this idea would become a dominant one in the literature. But, alas, as often happens in science, some ideas that receive initial support turn out to be wrong. In interpreting the results from the Carnegie Mellon study, we should be careful. The study is not without its critics. **Donna Hoffman,** editor of the journal *Marketing Science,* was quoted shortly after the study's release as saying, "Speaking as an editor, if this had crossed my desk, I would have rejected it. . . . The mistakes are so bad that they render the results fairly close to meaningless."[6] What mistakes is Hoffman referring to? After all, the study was published in a major journal, *American Psychologist.* In the final analysis, the Carnegie Mellon study suffers from three key limitations that should lead us to at least be cautious in interpreting the study's results.

First, the sample of people used in the study was not chosen randomly. This is certainly an important limitation because it means that we can't be confident that the results pertain to any general population of people other than the specific people who participated in the study. Kraut and his colleagues acknowledge the fact that the sample was not random, but they defend their technique. In choosing families who were involved in a community group or had a high-school student living at home, they made sure that they had people in the study who already had some social connections with others in the community. By starting with a group who had connections, they had the possibility of observing some changes. Consequently, they had to control who participated to a much greater extent than a random sample would have permitted. True random samples permit no control at all about who gets into the study. The selection process is strictly by chance.

Second, there was no control group in the Carnegie Mellon study. Critics argue that the data would have been much more valuable if the results of those using the Internet could have been compared to a control group of people who did not use the Internet. Perhaps, the critics argue, there was some change across the entire society during the 2 years of the study such that even those without the Internet connections would have reported more depression and loneliness. Once again, Kraut and his colleagues counter that the use of a control group was simply not possible. There was simply no acceptable incentive to offer people in a control group for their continued cooperation in answering questions over a 2-year period.

Finally, critics have complained that Kraut and his colleagues went too far in suggesting that their data supported a **causal claim.** Recall from the earlier chapters on research methods and some of the other chapters on specific effects that surveys suffer from an important limitation. In principle, they simply cannot be used to argue unequivocally for causal relationships. The experiment is the only method that really solves that problem. Since Kraut's data is based on the survey method, it is always possible that the relationships observed are due to some other unmeasured variable.

So what's the bottom line? While it may be frustrating to encounter good arguments about why we shouldn't accept the findings of a particular study, it is a good lesson to learn that science can often be frustrating. But the flip side of that frustration is excitement. As we stand on the frontier of new research on the impact of the Internet and other new technologies, there is an excitement about doing more research and honing in on the ultimate answers to the important questions. Does Internet use cause more social isolation, depression, and loneliness? Perhaps you or one of your fellow students will go on for graduate work in communication and help us to answer these important questions with a greater sense of certainty. Or perhaps you are more attracted to another, equally controversial question: the effects of playing video games—particularly violent ones.

ARE VIDEO GAMES REALLY TRAINING KIDS TO KILL?

It doesn't seem like too long ago that my son and I carefully unpacked the newest and hottest toy in all the land—an Atari video game system. Together, we sat transfixed at the TV set and played game after game of *Pong*. We weren't sure that life got any better. What we couldn't have foreseen at the time was that *Pong* was the beginning of a video game revolution that seems to have no end in sight. Over the years, the graphics have become so advanced that it is sometimes difficult to tell whether the person on the screen is an animated image or a real human character off of a TV show. The game characters now move in ways that are so close to human movement that it almost seems miraculous.

While video games have provided hours of enjoyment and entertainment for those who own them, in the past few years the video revolution has shown a darker side. Many of the games seem to be little more than exercises in virtual killing. These games, known as "first-person shooters," equip the player with a video gun. The object of these games is to rack up the highest score by blasting various characters to smithereens. The improved graphic technology of these games has enabled the manufacturers to create scenarios that seem quite realistic. The games have fantastic appeal to adolescents—particularly males. They are so much a part of our culture that as you read these words, you are undoubtedly able to think of specific games and images that perfectly illustrate what I am describing. In fact, video game producers take in between 5 and 6 billion dollars each year. Recent titles that feature lots of violent action are *Quake, Doom,* and *Mortal Kombat*—but by the time you read these words, there will probably be others. While violent video games generated a certain amount of controversy in the public arena, things really started heating up after the violence at Columbine High School in Littleton, Colorado. The two teens, Eric Harris and Dylan Klebold, who attacked their classmates and teachers were supposedly quite fond of playing *Doom*. By this point, you should be able to recognize that a preference for playing a violent video game does not necessarily constitute a cause for violent behavior—even though the ones who prefer the game and the ones doing the violence are the same. It is quite possible that playing *Doom* had no impact at all on the Columbine murders. But once this controversy started, researchers began to show more attention to the issues surrounding the incident. Before we look at the academic research, let's briefly look at the rhetoric of **Lt. Col. Dave Grossman,** a military man who has gone on the record in the controversy about violent video games.

An Opinion on Video Games
from an Expert on "Killology"

In the 1950s, **Dr. Frederic Wertham,** a psychiatrist, became convinced that comic books were the ruination of the youth of America. He took his case straight to the public, shunning the peer review process of scholarly research articles. He wrote for popular magazines and published his own book, *The Seduction of the Innocent*[7] (see chapter 3). Although Wertham's analysis of the tremendous negative impact of comic books was never accepted or validated by the research community, he still played a significant role in the public arena and helped to shape standards in the comic book industry itself. When one reads the writings of Lt. Col. Dave Grossman, the similarities with Wertham cannot be ignored. It is almost as if the same basic story is being played out again 50 years later. Like Wertham, Grossman has a professional credential that gives him some authority with the public and government policy makers. Just as Wertham had a popular book in which he articulated his thesis, Grossman is the author of his own book on the subject of killing.[8] While Wertham published in popular magazines like *Colliers,* Grossman has a series of articles in the *Saturday Evening Post.*[9] Most importantly, Wertham's claims about the effects of comic books were based more upon his own private convictions than upon solid, scientific evidence. Likewise, Grossman seems to be convinced that violent video games are transforming young people into "homemade sociopaths who kill reflexively," a proposition that, as yet, scientists have been unable to confirm. Let's look briefly at Grossman's claims about violent video games.

Grossman claims that the urge to kill is unnatural. He explains that the whole purpose of the military is to use brutalization and desensitization techniques to overcome the natural aversion to killing. He insists that through **desensitization,** the media have trained children to associate violence and killing with pleasure. Video games that require the player to shoot a gun and react reflexively with the shooting response are, he claims, teaching an entire generation of children to associate shooting with pleasure. He argues that the increases in murder and assault around the world are due largely to violent mass media—and especially to violent video games. You may have heard from news reports over the past few years that violent crime is actually decreasing. Grossman counters that this is only an illusion. Modern medical technology is now so efficient that thousands of assaults that would have ended up as murders years ago never make it into the murder column of today's statistics. Grossman contends that violent assault is increasing because of the increasing violence in our media. As a good student of media effects, how should you respond to Grossman's contentions? Is it really true that violent video games are transforming our youth into a culture of sociopaths? Grossman is so convinced that this is the case that he has even given a name to what he considers a psychological epidemic. Instead of

AIDS (Acquired Immune Deficiency Syndrome), Grossman calls this epidemic **AVIDS** (Acquired Violence Immune Deficiency Syndrome).

What Does the Research Say?

In attempting to evaluate Grossman's position, the first thing that we need to know is whether there are published scientific studies on the effects of violent video games. While the literature at this point would certainly have to be described as limited, some published studies do exist. Back in 1988, **Nicola Schutte** and her colleagues reported the results of a very simple study that was reminiscent of the early research of **Albert Bandura** on social learning theory[10] (see chapter 5). Working with young children between 5 and 7 years old, she randomly assigned them to play either a violent or nonviolent video game. The violent game was called *Karateka* and involved a protagonist who was controlled by the player and had a mission to hit, kick, and kill enough villains so that a damsel in distress would be saved. The nonviolent game, *Jungle Hunt,* involved a character who would swing from vine to vine in such a way that he would not fall and perish.

After the children played one of the two games, the researchers observed the children's free play in a large room that was equipped with several toys. One of the toys was a jungle swing with small men attached to vines; another toy was a "bobo" doll that was dressed in a karate-type robe that resembled characters in the violent video game. There were two main findings of the study. First, the children who had played *Jungle Hunt* tended to play with the jungle swing toy while children who played *Karateka* tended to play with the karate bobo doll. Second, as the authors had predicted, the children who had played *Karateka* tended to play in a more aggressive fashion than the children who had played *Jungle Hunt.* They had significantly higher scores on pushing, hitting, and kicking another child in the playroom as well as higher scores on hitting or kicking the bobo doll.

If you remember the results of Bandura's studies from chapter 5, these results really shouldn't surprise you very much. They are consistent with some of the first studies on the effects of televised violence. The results also suffer from some of the same limitations as those early studies. We have to be careful about generalizing the results broadly from a single study that used one particular violent game. We also have to be careful about drawing too much from the fact that the children who played the violent video game acted more aggressively toward a bobo doll. Play aggression may have little to do with aggression toward real people. However, the authors did note that these same children were also more aggressive toward other children who played in the room.

Two other researchers who studied video games in the late 1980s, **Craig Anderson** and **Catherine Ford,** reported the results of an experiment in which college students played either a high-aggression game (*Zaxxon*) or a mild-aggression game (*Centipede*).[11] Other students were randomly assigned to a no-game control group. Instead of measuring aggressive behavior, the researchers had the students assess their feelings by checking off words that described how they felt after playing the games. The results showed that both of the video games produced higher feelings of hostility than the control group. In addition, the group that played the high-aggression game reported significantly higher levels of anxiety than either of the other two groups. The authors concluded that "The results indicate that playing aggressive video games can have short-term negative effects on the game-player's emotional state."

An important limitation in Anderson and Ford's study was that aggressive behavior was not measured directly. Placing check marks next to adjectives may have little to do with what someone actually does after playing a violent video game. Anderson tried to address this limitation in a more recent study that he authored with **Karen Dill.** The authors actually conducted two different types of studies and reported them together in an article in one of the leading journals in psychology, the *Journal of Personality & Social Psychology*.[12] At the time this book was published, Anderson and Dill's studies were the two most recent ones to appear in the literature.

In their first study, Anderson and Dill had college students respond to some questions about the extent to which they played video games of various types as well as the extent to which they had been involved in aggressive delinquent behaviors in the past. They found that these two variables were significantly related. Students who reported more playing time with violent video games also reported more aggressive delinquent behaviors. Of course, once again, we must be careful in interpreting this evidence. A relationship of this sort does not necessarily mean that playing the games caused increases in aggression. Perhaps some unmeasured variable was causally related to both playing aggressive video games and the tendency to commit acts of delinquent aggression. In fact, the authors gathered some evidence for this possibility. They also had students respond to a number of items that formed a measure of trait aggressiveness. For those students who scored high on trait aggression, the relationship between playing aggressive video games and delinquent acts of aggression was even stronger. One way to interpret these results is that some people are, for whatever reasons, inclined to behave aggressively. They score high on the trait of aggression. These people are also more likely to play violent video games, and they are also more likely to be involved in acts of delinquent aggression when compared to people who do not possess the trait of aggression.

While the kind of survey data that Anderson and Dill gathered in this first study is certainly informative, it still doesn't help very much in gaining understanding about the impact of playing violent video games on actual aggressive behavior. To address this issue more precisely, the authors set up a second study that used an experimental design. Some college students were randomly assigned to play a violent video game (*Wolfenstein 3D*), and some were randomly assigned to play a nonviolent game (*Myst*). These two games were chosen because in laboratory pretests, they both generated the same amount of physiological arousal during playing even though they differed significantly in terms of their levels of violence. After the game-playing sessions, the students participated in another phase of the experiment that they thought was unrelated to the video game session. They were placed in a situation where they had to react to a stimulus faster than their opponent. If they won the reaction time test, they could blast their opponent with a loud noise. Not only that, they got to choose within a certain range how loud the noise could be and how long the noise would blast.

Imagine that you were in this study and had just lost one of the reaction time competitions. In the next competition, you win and are now allowed to blast the person who just beat you the time before. You might suspect that under these circumstances, you would send out a particularly loud blast of noise for a relatively long duration. In this respect, the students in the experiment reacted the same way regardless of which video game they had played. All students tended to blast their opponent louder and longer after having lost a reaction time competition just prior to winning one. But those who had played the *Wolfenstein 3D* game blasted louder and longer than those who had played *Myst*. To the extent that this blasting behavior can be regarded as aggressive, the results of this experiment might be interpreted as evidence that playing a violent video game actually causes more aggressive behavior. Anderson and Dill certainly believe that these two studies, taken together, provide some insight about the relationship between playing violent video games and actual aggression. They stated:

> In the laboratory, college students who played a violent video game behaved more aggressively toward an opponent than did students who had played a nonviolent video game. Outside the laboratory, students who reported playing more violent video games over a period of years also engaged in more aggressive behavior in their own lives. Both types of studies . . . have their strengths and weaknesses. The convergence of findings across such disparate methods lends considerable strength to the main hypothesis that exposure to violent video games can increase aggressive behavior.

John Sherry, a researcher who also happens to be my colleague at Purdue University, has recently attempted to summarize all of the known studies on violent video games.[13] Using the technique of **meta-analysis** that was mentioned in the last chapter, Sherry was able to estimate the statistical effects uncovered across the entire published literature on this topic. As he notes in his analysis, the sample of studies to draw from is actually pretty small—only about 30 independent investigations—so we should be careful about drawing firm conclusions. Nevertheless, he reports that the data do show "a small but significant overall effect of video game play on aggression." However, he also notes that this effect is smaller than the effect of violent television on aggression. Sherry also concludes that one important variable in the relationship is the type of violence contained in the game. When the violence is related to sports or fantasy, the effect on aggression is smaller than when the violence involves virtual depictions of aggression toward human beings.

If you are like me, by this point you might be asking what we are to make of the research. That question may still be premature. One thing we can say for certain is that we need more studies. This is inevitably the case with almost any question about the effects of a new communication technology. But we might be able to say a little more. At this point, the existing data on violent video games look pretty familiar to researchers who have carefully studied the pattern that emerged with TV over 30 years ago. While the effects might not be quite as strong, it is beginning to look like there may be a causal relationship between playing violent video games and behaving aggressively—just as there is between viewing TV violence and committing aggressive acts.

Of course, the question that we would really like to know the answer to is how worried we should be about violent video games. Should we let our children play any violent games? Which ones are okay and which ones should be avoided? Definitive answers to these questions will emerge more clearly when researchers continue to report the results of new studies during the next several years. For now, it looks like there is some reason to be concerned that playing violent video games might be associated with the same sorts of effects that are well documented with movies and TV shows. Remember from chapter 5 that these effects are definitely causal effects—but they are modest from a statistical standpoint. There are a host of other variables that contribute to aggressive behavior in the real world. It would be a mistake to focus exclusively on any type of media as the sole cause or even the primary cause of aggression in society. Human behavior is complicated and caused by hundreds of factors, only some of which we know about. Given this state of affairs, we shouldn't expect to be able to find easy solutions to the causes of a behavior like aggression.

Some reports out of Littleton, Colorado, have noted that Eric Harris was fond of playing a modified game of *Doom* that had extra weapons, more than one shooter, and a special feature that rigged the game so that the characters on the screen could not shoot back. Some observers suggested that when Harris played the game, he was actually acting out the sort of attack on his classmates that he eventually implemented on that fateful day in April 1999. No amount of evidence from media-effects studies will be able to permit us to conclude that the specific acts of a given individual were caused by exposure to violent media. But given what we know so far about the effects of playing violent video games, it surely seems as though Harris's video game habits could have placed him in a high-risk category for translating some of those habits into real-world behavior.

In terms of evaluating the rhetoric of Col. Grossman, it seems that the current research evidence would hardly support the sweeping claims that he makes about the impact of violent media. His rhetoric may be successful in motivating politicians to pay attention to the problem of media violence, but ultimately, the sorts of "magic bullet" claims of media impact that he suggests are not likely to be supported by scientific research. His claims are probably best thought about in terms of rather gross exaggerations.

SUMMARY

This chapter has examined some of the newest research on the impact of two new technologies, the Internet and video games. One of the central questions being explored concerning the Internet is whether this technology increases social alienation, depression, and loneliness. The Carnegie Mellon study suggested that this was the case. But the study is not without its critics. In the coming years, we can expect to see more research that will help to provide insight on this question and clarify the impact of the Internet on individual relationships. In the case of violent video games, the limited research to this point suggests that playing these games produces effects that are similar to the effects of watching movies and TV programs. So far, the data suggest that the effects may not be quite as strong as those associated with TV, but there may be certain variables that can enhance the effects (e.g., lifelike human representations). Like the research on the impact of the Internet, the studies on the impact of video games will almost certainly proliferate in the coming years, and our understanding will progress as a result.

KEY TERMS AND CONCEPTS

Perpetual linkage 186

"first-person shooter" 186

Activity displacement effect 188

Displacement of strong social ties 188

Causal claim 191

Desensitization 193

AVIDS 194

Meta-analysis 196

KEY NAMES

Jane Brown and Joanne Cantor 186

Robert Kraut 187

Seymour Feshbach 190

Donna Hoffman 191

Lt. Col. Dave Grossman 193

Dr. Frederic Wertham 193

Nicola Schutte 194

Albert Bandura 194

Craig Anderson and Catherine Ford 194

Karen Dill 195

John Sherry 196

WEB LINKS

1. For one of the most recent articles on the effects of violent video games, try . . . http://www.apa.org/journals/psp/psp784772.html

2. For a discussion of violent video games and health on WebMD, try . . . http://onhealth.webmd.com/family/in-depth/item/item%2C88849_1_1.asp

3. For information on an ordinance in Indianapolis that seeks to legislate children's exposure to violent video games, try . . . http://www.ci.indianapolis.in.us/mayor/vvg/index.htm

To learn more about the topics in this chapter, enter the Key Terms and Concepts and Key Names found in this chapter as subject and keyword searches on your InfoTrac College Edition.

NOTES

1. Brown, J. D., & Cantor, J. (2000). An agenda for research on youth and the media. *Journal of Adolescent Health, 27*(2) (supp.), 2–7.

2. Media Metrix. Press release [Online]. Available: http://www.mediametrix.com/press/releases/20000809.jsp

3. Kraut, R., Patterson, M., Lundmark, V., Kiesler, S., Mukhopadhyay, T., & Scherlis, W. (1998). Internet paradox: A social technology that reduces social involvement and psychological well-being? *American Psychologist, 53*, 1017–1031.

4. Katz, J. E., & Aspden, P. (1997). A nation of strangers? *Communications of the ACM, 40*, 81–86.

5. Rollman, J. B., Krug, K., & Parente, F. (2000). The chat room phenomenon: Reciprocal communication in Cyberspace. *Cyberpsychology & Behavior, 3*, 161–166.

6. Caruso, D. (1998, October 28). Critics pick apart study on internet and depression. *America Online: Poptatari.*

7. Wertham, F. (1954). *Seduction of the innocent.* New York: Rinehart.

8. Grossman, D. (1996). *On killing: The psychological cost of learning to kill in war and society.* Boston: Little, Brown.

9. Grossman, D. (1999, July/August). We are training our kids to kill. *The Saturday Evening Post,* 64–71.

10. Schutte, N. S., Malouff, J. M., Post-Gorden, J. C., & Rodasta, A. L. (1988). Effects of playing videogames on children's aggressive and other behaviors. *Journal of Applied Social Psychology, 18*, 454–460.

11. Anderson, C. A., & Ford, C. M. (1986). Affect of the game player: Short-term effects of highly and mildly aggressive video games. *Personality and Social Psychology Bulletin, 12*, 390–402.

12. Anderson, C. A., & Dill, K. E. (2000). Video games and aggressive thoughts, feelings, and behavior in the laboratory and in life. *Journal of Personality & Social Psychology, 78*, 772–790.

13. Sherry, J. L. (2001). The effects of violent video games on aggression: A meta-analysis. *Human Communication Research, 27*, 409–431.

12

■

Meet Marshall McLuhan: A Less Scientific Approach to Media Impact

IS THERE ANY VALUE TO CONSIDERING MARSHALL MCLUHAN?

Some researchers who study media effects may raise an eyebrow of curiosity or feel some confusion about finding a chapter on **Marshall McLuhan** at the end of this text. From the very beginning, this book has taken great pains to introduce you to the scientific perspective of studying media impact. Each of the preceding chapters has emphasized empirical evidence collected in a systematic fashion as the most reliable way to learn about how media affect us. In contrast to the many other researchers mentioned in the earlier chapters, Marshall McLuhan didn't collect any research data. He never did content analyses, surveys, or experiments to test his ideas. Instead, he simply proclaimed what he thought about the effects of the mass media. To make matters worse, from the scientific perspective, most of his ideas seem to be unfalsifiable (see chapter 1) and beyond scientific scrutiny. Why should his ideas be presented in a text of this sort?

I believe there are three good reasons for including a chapter on McLuhan's ideas about the media. First, whatever approach one might take to the study of media effects, McLuhan's ideas about media influence have stirred discussion and analysis from media scholars for nearly 40 years. Some would argue that his ideas are enjoying a resurgence as we enter the digital age of communication. Students of media effects, regardless of their commitment to the scientific approach, should at least be familiar with McLuhan's analysis. Second, his ideas are so provocative and far reaching in their implications that students of media effects ought to at least consider what he has to say. Finally, McLuhan's "theory" provides a great contrast to scientific thinking. In the end, while you may find his ideas fun to think about, you should also see the frustration that comes with a body of theory that defies testing by recourse to empirical procedures. Ultimately, we simply can't test very much of what McLuhan said. You may recall from chapter 1 that when an idea can't be tested and shown to be false, it can't be shown to be true, either. Such ideas have limited value to the scientific community. Rather than inventing such an idea for illustrative purposes, why not consider a very provocative one that already exists?

MEET MARSHALL MCLUHAN

One way to begin to understand what Marshall McLuhan was referring to when he talked about the impact of electronic communication is to stop reading this book and pick up your pencil. Draw a horizontal line across the width of an 8½″ × 11″ piece of paper. Imagine that the line represents all of human history (roughly 40,000 years). The far left side of the line represents the beginning of that period of time and the far right represents this exact moment. If we wanted to locate the point in human history where electronic communication really started, we would have to move to the far right and go nearly to the end of the line. Electronic communication is new. One communication scholar, Don Pember, expressed the historical record of communication in this way:

> Imagine those 40,000 years of modern human history as a single calendar year. And right now it is midnight on December 31st, the last day of that year. Mechanical printing first occurred on December 27th, not quite five days ago. Newsbooks, the precursors of newspapers, first appeared in 1610, or about three-and-half days ago. Radio and motion pictures emerged as viable media in the early 1900's, about 9 o'clock this morning. And television first appeared in the United States at the end of the 1930's, or about 3:00 P.M. today. Despite its short existence, mass communications has come to truly dominate our lives today.[1]

It is difficult for people to comprehend a world without electronic media, and yet most of human history has been without it. Most people can't imagine what life would be like without newspapers, radio, or TV. Consequently, there aren't many people who would feel comfortable issuing proclamations about how the electronic media have changed the very fundamentals of the human experience. Proving such claims would be next to impossible. And how could anyone really be sure of these changes unless they had actually lived in the past?

Marshall McLuhan didn't seem to mind the fact that he couldn't *prove* any of his claims. He thought of himself as a **prober** or an explorer and found that there was a certain luxury in thinking about things that eluded clear-cut **proofs.** True, he might never be able to prove that his analysis was right, but others could never prove that he was wrong, either. McLuhan found this state of affairs to his liking. The genius of McLuhan (if there was any) was in his ability to stimulate thought about the exact nature of those changes that the move to electronic media had triggered. Even though he had never lived in the past, that didn't stop him from talking as if he knew exactly what the media were doing to us.

Marshall McLuhan was a Canadian scholar, born in Edmonton in 1911. After earning bachelor's and master's degrees at the University of Manitoba, he won a scholarship to Cambridge where he earned a second bachelor's degree, a second master's degree, and a doctorate. He taught English literature at St. Michael's College of the University of Toronto. He died in 1980 after suffering a series of strokes. In the early 1960s, his reputation as a provocative new thinker about mass media started to grow (it was McLuhan who coined the term "the media"). **Harold Innis** and **Walter Ong** influenced him, but it was McLuhan who wrote books like *The Gutenberg Galaxy* and *Understanding Media,* books that propelled him into the limelight.

It was not so much that his books caused people to write rave reviews. In fact, reviewers often complained that the writings were dense, complex, and difficult to digest. Teachers often express reluctance about suggesting that their students begin their quest to understand Marshall McLuhan by reading his books. A popular anecdote about McLuhan illustrates this point well. Upon arriving to campus one morning, McLuhan expressed irritation when he discovered that a student had parked her car in his parking space. Before finding another space for his car, McLuhan dashed off a note and placed it on the student's windshield, "Please do not park in my space in the future." He signed the note "Professor McLuhan." At the end of the day, when McLuhan returned to his car to leave campus, he noticed that a note was attached to *his* windshield. It read, "Dear Professor McLuhan, the note that you left me on my windshield this morning was the first thing you've written that I've been able to understand." There is no doubt that some of McLuhan's ideas were difficult to understand. But this notwithstanding, many sensed something deeply provocative about much of what he had to say.

The best way to begin to grasp the importance of McLuhan's ideas is to consider his view of human history. In a way, his major thesis is historical in nature. If McLuhan was right about human history, then we are all currently living in one of the most amazing times to ever come upon the earth.

THE ERAS OF COMMUNICATION HISTORY

The Tribal Age

McLuhan saw the history of the human race in terms of **eras of communication.** When he looked at the dawn of human history, he saw people who lived in a **tribal** state. They communicated with each other orally, and they didn't have a well-developed alphabet or system of writing. In this period of history, there was a heavy reliance upon acoustics, or sound. Since most communication took place through speech and other vocal sounds, the sense of hearing was very important. McLuhan liked to point out that the ear did not need to process information in any particular order to make sense out of it. That is, sounds from the environment come to one's ears in an "all-at-once" fashion, and it usually doesn't matter which ones we process first. It is true that the order of spoken words does matter in most languages. But McLuhan believed that in the tribal age, the order of spoken words was a very small part of the meaning that people derived in the communication process.

If you are not in a totally quiet environment as you read these words, take a minute to close your eyes and see how many different sounds you can hear. How many were you able to identify? In order to appreciate McLuhan's point about the all-at-onceness of processing sound, ask yourself this question: "What difference would it have made if the sounds you identified had occurred in a different order?" The answer to this question is quite likely "not much difference at all." In fact, some of the sounds that you heard were probably happening simultaneously. As you will see in the rest of the chapter, McLuhan believed that this quality of acoustical information was very important.

McLuhan also believed that processing of information went beyond acoustics. He believed that people relied heavily on the other senses as well. Sight, smell, touch, and even taste were all important sources of information to the tribal peoples. McLuhan pointed out that they lived in a state of **sensory balance;** the five senses were all important sources of information.

Moving from the Tribal Age to the Print Age

In terms of human history, the tribal age was the longest. Speech and the oral tradition persisted over thousands of years as the most important form of communication. By around 1500 B.C., however, the beginning of the end of the tribal age was evident when the phonetic alphabet emerged. This emergence signaled the beginning of a major transition period to a new medium of communication and a new age of human history, according to McLuhan. The invention of the printing press allowed documents to be mass produced. This invention ushered in the formal **print age.**

McLuhan noted several things about the transition to the print age. First, he pointed out that the move to print was a move that altered the sensory balance of the tribal age. McLuhan argued that the sense of *sight* became completely dominant in the print age in terms of processing important information. It now became possible to detach one's self from the tribe and still have access to the important information of human culture. One could read books in a private place. One could process important information without being in the physical presence of other people. The senses of hearing, touch, smell, and taste became less necessary in the age of print. The print age disrupted the sensory balance of the tribal state as the eye became the central mechanism for processing information.

A second important consequence of the move to the print age, according to McLuhan, was that human beings started to think differently. Unlike the

all-at-onceness of the old acoustical processing, the age of print forced people to process information in a **linear** fashion. You can see what McLuhan meant by the linear nature of print by doing a simple exercise. Close your eyes and drop your finger at random on this page. Write down the word that your finger lands upon. Now do it again. Do it five more times. Now look at the string of seven words that you have written. The chances are good that they don't form a coherent sentence. In the age of print, we must process our information in a particular order. If something scrambles that order, the message becomes lost. Even the essential ingredients of words, the letters, must appear in a particular order before we can make sense out of them. The particular order of words or letters (left to right in English or top to bottom in some oriental languages) is not important. The important thing is that we have to assemble them in a linear order before we can derive meaning from them. McLuhan thought that the shift to linear information processing altered people's basic thought patterns. Thought became more linear than it had been in the tribal state. This shift brought about an emphasis on deductive logic and upon making sure that every thought connected well to the one that had come before. Messages that reflected the less linear pattern of the tribal age seemed increasingly strange and incoherent. Over time, they diminished in value.

Moving on to the Current Electronic Age

According to McLuhan, the great technology of print completely transformed human culture. Then, in the late 1800s, Marconi's invention of the wireless telegraph gave rise to a new age in human history. The age of electronic communication had arrived. Just as print transformed the old tribal age, electronic media would transform the great culture of print. McLuhan pointed out that the transition from the print age to the **electronic age** would be similar to the earlier shift away from the tribal state. Both changes would occur over several hundreds of years. According to McLuhan, then, you and I are living at a most unprecedented time in human history. We are living on the cusp of two great communication technologies—print and electronics. If McLuhan is right, then a very provocative thesis presents itself for our consideration. McLuhan asks us to consider the possibility that much of the social upheaval and change over the last 50 years is directly due to the shift toward electronic media.

It was in talking about the various consequences of the move to electronic media that McLuhan came into his own as a media guru. He enjoyed the attention he received from TV talk shows and movie celebrities (he made a brief appearance in Woody Allen's film *Annie Hall*). All of the media attention, combined with the obscurity of some of his ideas, caused him to lose favor in the eyes of academic types. Still, he had some interesting things to say about what was happening to our culture with the steady rise of electronic communication forms.

First, McLuhan believed that, in the electronic age, human culture was returning to a form of communication that was much more similar to that of the tribal age. He often talked about the **global village** produced by electronic media. This was a reference to the power of instantaneous communication to unify the world into a massive, modern-day, tribal community. Almost everyone who was alive at the time remembers exactly where they were on November 22, 1963. On this date, John Kennedy died at the hand of an assassin. McLuhan often explained that the media coverage that followed an event of this magnitude allowed people to experience "one big group emotion." Since 1963, we have often seen the power of the electronic media to unite large portions of the world by drawing their collective attention to the same event. Think about the space shuttle *Challenger* exploding in midair, the first night of fighting in Operation Desert Storm, the Berlin Wall tumbling to the ground, the death of Princess Diana, the O. J. Simpson car chase on the L.A. freeways, or the tragic shootings at Columbine High School. On occasions like these, it is not hard to appreciate what McLuhan meant when he said that electronic media bring about the experience of the global village.

Since television is the dominant medium of the electronic age, McLuhan often used it to illustrate his basic points. Unlike the linear processing of print, television encourages a kind of information processing similar to the acoustical principle of the tribe. Processing a message from television is much more like the all-at-once processing of the ear than the linear processing of the eye when it reads a printed page. McLuhan was fond of pointing out that most people were in error in believing that television is a visual medium. On the contrary, he argued that television is fundamentally an acoustic medium. To make this point clear, he invited people to try a simple experiment. First, turn the sound down on the TV set for 1 minute during your favorite program. Now, for another minute, adjust the TV so that you can hear the sound but you can't see any picture. Which condition was more frustrating? Which condition gave you less information? McLuhan believed that, invariably, people who tried this little exercise would report more frustration in the condition where the picture was visible but the sound was inaudible. So, even though we think of television as a visual medium, McLuhan argued that it was primarily a medium of sound.

Second, McLuhan argued that the electronic communication forms were in direct opposition to the great technology of print. Linear thinking, deductive logic, and the private, information-packed experience of reading would gradually give way to the new electronic experience of radio and television. And the familiar things would gradually give way to a mode of thinking that was less linear, less logical, more spontaneous, and more like the thinking of our tribal ancestors. As far as McLuhan could tell, there was no way to stop these changes from occurring. The power of instantaneous electronic information would overwhelm the great culture of print in a matter of time. Although McLuhan claimed that he was almost always against the changes that he saw the electronic media instigating, he remained determined to understand exactly what was happening to us.

In his determination to communicate what he thought, McLuhan often relied on pithy sayings. His most famous of these, **"the medium is the message,"** was really an attempt to summarize his view of human history outlined above. A closer look at this saying will reveal a key principle of McLuhan's analysis of the media age.

THE MEDIUM IS THE MESSAGE

Part of McLuhan's popular appeal was his habit of coining slogans and phrases that he eventually referred to as "McLuhanisms." It was this same habit that often got him into trouble with scholars, who typically wanted more depth and explication of ideas than a simple slogan could provide. Nevertheless, McLuhan seemed to sense that these slogans were important tools of communication, and he churned them out with some regularity. As noted above, perhaps his best known phrase was "the medium is the message." McLuhan seemed to realize that one of the advantages of a phrase or slogan like this one is that it could mean different things to different people at different times. He took full advantage of this feature and provided a number of different twists on the meaning of the phrase. It is no wonder that scholars often strongly disagree about exactly what McLuhan meant when he uttered these words. Some scholars have even given up trying to understand what he meant and tend to dismiss all of McLuhan's ideas as little more than creations of an intellectual charlatan.

But if we understand how McLuhan viewed human history, it is possible to get some insight from the idea that the medium is the message. The first thing to understand in considering this phrase is that it plays off the common notion that people change as a result of processing persuasive messages. When we think of television affecting a person's behavior, we usually think in terms of a particular program or particular message that provoked the change. Such thinking has good support from research studies. There are hundreds of research studies that lend credence to the fact that human behavior changes from processing messages. Almost every chapter in this book revolves around the idea that some particular type of media message has a specific effect on human attitudes, feelings, or actions. McLuhan realized that most people tend to think of the messages in a given medium of communication as the agents of change. He didn't deny that messages have impact, but he wanted to get across what he believed was a much loftier and far-reaching proposition. In claiming that the medium is the message, McLuhan was saying that the thing that really changed people the most was not the message in any given medium of communication, but the medium itself. Hence, the medium *is* the message.

McLuhan believed that most people would find his concept to be a little strange and difficult to think about. His reason for this belief may seem stranger than the belief itself. McLuhan thought that all media were extensions of people. The wheel is an extension of the foot. The book is an extension of the eye. The electronic circuit is an extension of the central nervous system. McLuhan believed that these various extensions of ourselves intensified the particular organ or sense that found itself extended. In response to this intensification, he argued that the affected sense or organ would act to protect itself and engage in a numbing process that he equated with Freud's concept of repression. The result of this process in the case of electronic media would be to make people quite unaware of the media's effects. If we are unaware of the media's impact on our culture, the slogan that declares that the medium is the message is likely to sound a little strange.

Look back at McLuhan's view of human history. He claimed that the invention of print brought about cataclysmic change in human culture and that the invention of electronic media started a major revolution that we have yet to complete. McLuhan saw the important changes in human life arising from the changes in the dominant communication medium at given points in human history. This view stands in sharp contrast to the one that asserts that change arises from messages within a given medium. As he once said, "Societies have always been shaped more by the nature of the media with which people communicate than by the content of the communication."[2] This is probably the best way to understand the well-known slogan "the medium is the message."

THE EFFECTS OF ELECTRONIC
MEDIA ON HUMAN BEINGS

McLuhan liked to emphasize that the dominant medium of communication changed human behavior more than the individual messages that the medium contained. He played with his own slogan a bit and changed it to **"the medium is the *massage*."** By this he meant to underscore the fact that communication media are not neutral. They affect people. He once commented that media "rough people up" and act "chiropractically." Comments like these prompted some to charge that McLuhan's mind could only think in metaphors, and that he would make a metaphor even when there wasn't need for one. But despite this criticism, McLuhan actually had quite a bit to say about the specific ways that electronic media were changing us. That is one reason why this chapter is included in this text. The remaining portion of the chapter presents some of McLuhan's thoughts on the effects of electronic media. Keep in mind that he couldn't really prove that any of these effects were actually taking place. He did try, though, to point out the things that were consistent with his claims. And while many scholars scowled at McLuhan's inability to offer hard evidence for the effects he talked about, there was always that nagging doubt that maybe, just maybe, he was on to something. As author Tom Wolfe put it in one article, "Suppose he is what he sounds like, the most important thinker since Newton, Darwin, Freud, Einstein and Pavlov? What if he is right?"[3] Since little hard evidence presents itself one way or the other, most scientists throw up their hands when it comes to a serious consideration of McLuhan's ideas. They harken back to the notion of falsifiability of theory (see chapter 2) and note that since the ideas can't be falsified, their validity cannot be established. Below, I present McLuhan's ideas on several topics that he talked about frequently. To what extent do you find McLuhan's thinking about the media effects outlined below to have the ring of truth? Can you think of ways that they could be subjected to scientific test?

Education in the Electronic Age

During the 1960s, it became clear that television had completely changed the typical household in the United States. Almost every home had a TV set and viewing time was increasing daily. Interestingly, something else was also starting to happen at around this same time. The scores that students earned on standardized educational tests started to drop slightly. That decline has remained almost steady ever since. Since the 1960s, scores on the verbal portion of the SAT have dropped 50–60 points. Educators often bemoan the fact that many of today's college students demonstrate reading and writing skills that are far below the levels of their predecessors.[4] The critical question that demands an answer is "Why?" Without a carefully controlled study (which is practically impossible in this case), the answer seems to be beyond our definitive grasp. Many things have changed in society since the dawn of TV. There are more single-parent homes, there is more drug abuse, political instability has increased, and the quality of schools in the inner cities has declined. Any one of these things might be partially responsible for a decline in standardized test scores. But according to McLuhan, none of these things are the real cause. According to him, declines in test scores were very predictable in the age of television. He argued that it has to do with the fact that the traditional educational system thrives on the great print technology. Since television took over as the dominant medium of communication, the print-based educational system is a system under siege. By the time today's children arrive in the classroom, they have spent thousands of hours processing electronic information in a nonlinear, acoustic fashion. When they encounter the print-based educational system of the typical classroom, there is a huge incompatibility. Print-based education finds it difficult to win out over the instantaneous acoustic form of television.

McLuhan had a very interesting way of articulating one of the dilemmas of traditional, print-based education in the electronic age. Prior to the mid-1900s, he argued, a person knew that when he or she entered the classroom, the information level inside that room was always going to be *higher* than the information level outside the room. Think about that for a minute. Before electronic media, people simply couldn't find out about the workings of government or foreign affairs or almost anything else of importance, unless they went to school and spent time *reading*. Books were literally the only window on the world. But today, this is no longer true. In fact, McLuhan said that when today's children enter the classroom, they soon realize that, because of electronic media, the information level outside the room is *higher* than the information level inside. In a sense, McLuhan said that today's children know that going to school is an interruption of their education.

McLuhan was very fond of pointing out all of the various signs of the failing educational system. Elementary school teachers who had taught for 20 years prior to the rise of television frequently reported that the children raised on TV were more difficult to teach. They were more impatient, less well behaved, and more eager for entertainment than learning through books. McLuhan argued that we should come to expect such reports. It made perfect sense to him that the rise of electronic media would throw the old print-style educational system into crisis.

McLuhan once noted that we are "playing the old story backwards." In ancient Greece, he pointed out, a well-educated person was someone who had memorized the great epic poems like Homer and could sing them to his harp. This style of learning was consistent with the old acoustic form of the tribal age. The rise of literacy completely wiped out this definition of an educated person. McLuhan said that literacy wiped out Homer. And, he argued, if literacy could wipe out Homer, rock-and-roll music could wipe out literacy. He believed rock and roll was a new acoustic form of education that threatened the entire print establishment. He predicted that rock-and-roll music would thrive, while the traditional educational establishment would falter and grope for a way to survive. McLuhan empathized with frustrated parents of the old print culture who thought that something profoundly disturbing was taking place when rock music captured the imagination of their children. But these parents probably received little comfort in McLuhan's explanation of what was happening. He made one famous remark that combined his belief about rock and roll with his notion that the electronic media ushered in a communication environment similar to that of the tribal age. He said that parents of the Western world were in the process of watching their children become "third world" kids.

If he were alive today, McLuhan would not express surprise upon learning that many describe our educational system as being in disarray. Yet, simultaneously, the music industry is thriving. I remember thinking about McLuhan's analysis as I watched the first feature-length film on an Omni-Max projection system as it enjoyed its second holdover for a longer run at Chicago's Museum of Science and Industry. The Omni-Max system uses over 70 speakers for the sound track and projects the film's images on a domelike screen. The entire projection system complete with sound equipment costs around $2 million. McLuhan would probably smile confidently upon learning that the film that people were flocking to see at $15 per person was about the infamous rock group the Rolling Stones.

McLuhan believed that education would only be successful in the electronic age to the extent that it adapted to the new electronic forms. This process of adaptation would not be easy because the ways of print die slowly. As in almost every other area of human life, McLuhan saw turmoil and struggle as the two great communication technologies clashed in the 20th century. While he believed that successful adaptation was possible, he wasn't sure how it would emerge—or if it would emerge at all.

War in the Electronic Age: Not So "Hot"

For most of the latter part of the 1960s, Americans witnessed a real war on television for the first time in history. World War II, in contrast to Vietnam, was a radio war. Yes, there were movie newsreels that people could see weekly in the local movie theaters before the feature film began. But these didn't have the same impact on our emotions as watching and hearing our favorite news anchor (in most cases, Walter Cronkite of CBS) narrating the details of the latest battle each night. And the war went on and on . . . and on . . . and on. Each Thursday evening in the New York area, one of the local news stations would play the Vietnam "honor roll." This honor roll consisted of a list of all of the soldiers from the New York/New Jersey area whom officials had pronounced dead due to the Vietnam conflict during the week. The list of white names on a blue background scrolled slowly up the TV screens of hundreds of thousands of viewers. On some evenings, it would take many minutes for the list to finish. On a daily basis, news reporters from the fields of Vietnam sent back film footage of live conflict. The images were often deeply disturbing.

As Americans experienced the steady diet of images of war, they grew increasingly uncomfortable. More and more people came to believe that the United States had become involved in a conflict that was hopeless. The war became a political hot potato. In 1968, Lyndon Johnson refused to run for a second presidential term, and many speculated that he couldn't win anyway because of his unpopular Vietnam policy. Richard Nixon won the White House by promising an honorable end to the war in Vietnam.

Why was the Vietnam war so unpopular? Marshall McLuhan thought he knew the answer to that question. He argued that people experiencing the war through television found the brutal images to be most unpleasant and ultimately unbearable. Television, McLuhan argued, was a cool medium. **Cool media** were those that allowed high levels of participation and involvement. **Hot media** were those that had higher information definition and, consequently, did not involve the recipient of the message as intensely. Newspapers and radio were relatively hot media. Film was also a hot medium. According to McLuhan, hot media could tolerate higher levels of violence since people could not become actively involved in the processing of their messages. Newspapers and film thrive on violence, but television must be more careful in its portrayal of violent events because it is very involving.

If the distinction between "hot" and "cool" media seems a little vague to you, you are not alone. McLuhan never really explained the difference between hot and cool media in a way that made it easy to grasp. On some occasions, he would simply say, "Cool is involving—hot is not." But on other occasions, he would launch into a much more technical explanation.

For example, he argued that the reason television was highly involving was because there was never really a complete picture on the screen at any given instant. This is because the television picture consists of hundreds of lines that the screen fills in over fractions of a second. At any given instant, the screen contains only a partial picture. Consequently, McLuhan argued that the viewer had to work to fill in or complete the screen's image. This process of filling in the picture with one's mind was highly involving and helped to make television a very intense experience. Film, in contrast, consists of individual frames. Each frame is a total picture when it flashes by the projection bulb and appears on the movie screen. It does not require the viewer to fill in anything. Thus, the level of participation in processing film images is much lower than for television. Film is a hot medium relative to TV.

It is difficult to appreciate how this technical difference between the television image and the film image could make such a huge difference in the psychological experience that viewers have with TV and film. McLuhan's critics asked questions such as "What happens when you take films and put them on television? Is the result a hot medium or a cool one?" McLuhan might answer, perhaps in frustration, that the result was lukewarm. These sorts of answers did not satisfy very well.

McLuhan's distinction between hot and cool media may confuse as much as it enlightens. But it is difficult to argue with McLuhan's general thesis that Americans found a television war to be most unpleasant. Consider the nature of war on television since Vietnam. The recent crisis in Kuwait was over in a matter of weeks. The nature of the news coverage was very controversial. The government argued that strict control of the press was necessary in order to protect strategy and tactics. But critics argued that these controls went too far and were unnecessary. In any case, there were few TV shots of real human suffering. Some observers compared the typical news footage to a video game. We saw exploding buildings—but little more. More of the same type of coverage followed when NATO bombed Serbia over the crisis in Kosovo. McLuhan would probably say that the government learned to adjust to the electronic age. They learned their lesson from Vietnam: War does not play well on TV. So when it does occur, someone must take steps to sanitize the images and get it over with quickly.

Politics in the Electronic Age:
Was Bill Clinton "Cooler" Than George Bush?

In the 1960s, when McLuhan was enjoying his peak in media popularity, he offered his own political analysis of the presidential campaigns. John Kennedy, McLuhan explained, was the first television president. In a most insightful interview that McLuhan granted to *Playboy* magazine (the entire interview is available at the second Web link listed at the end of this chapter), he remarked:

> TV is an inherently cool medium, and Kennedy had a compatible coolness and indifference to power. . . . Any political candidate who doesn't have such cool, low-definition qualities, which allow the viewer to fill in the gaps with his own personal identification, simply electrocutes himself on television—as Richard Nixon did in his disastrous debates with Kennedy in the 1960 campaign. Nixon was essentially hot; he presented a high-definition, sharply defined image and action on the TV screen that contributed to his reputation as a phony. (p. 61)[5]

If McLuhan had been observing the 1992 political campaign, he would undoubtedly have seen Bill Clinton as the cooler of the two presidential candidates. Clinton was eager to stand up and step forward during one of the presidential debates and talk more conversationally to the live audience. He communicated more relaxation, casualness, and "coolness" than George Bush (Senior). McLuhan, who was a fierce critic of the standard debating format, would have viewed the more spirited and spontaneous exchanges that marked the 1992 debates as more consistent with the "coolness" of the television medium. He argued that the usual debating format had the candidates standing behind elaborate podiums in some of the "hottest" stuff that television was capable of producing. This style of debating was, in McLuhan's view, totally incompatible with the cool medium of television.

Drugs in the Electronic Age

When George Bush Sr. became president, he launched a war on drugs. Four years later, although his administration would claim some success, the drug problem that plagued the United States was worse than ever before.[6] McLuhan would not be at all surprised. In the same *Playboy* interview, he commented on the drug problem:

> The upsurge in drug taking is intimately related to the impact of the electric media. Look at the metaphor for getting high: turning on. One turns on his consciousness through drugs just as he opens up all his senses to a total depth involvement by turning on the TV dial. Drug taking is stimulated by today's pervasive environment of instant information, with its feedback mechanism of the inner trip. The inner trip is not the sole prerogative of the LSD traveler; it's the universal experience of TV watchers. . . . The attraction to hallucinogenic drugs is a means of achieving empathy with our penetrating electric environment, an environment that in itself is a drugless inner trip. (p. 68)[7]

McLuhan would probably be very sympathetic to what some scholars have called "television addiction." Although the evidence for a true physical addiction to TV is relatively scant, some believe that there are those individuals who have a literal addiction to the tube. In support of their claim, they point to people who seem to suffer the familiar symptoms of withdrawal—anxiety, physical nervousness, and depression—when deprived of TV viewing.[8]

MCLUHAN'S INFLUENCE

Because McLuhan's ideas seem to defy direct empirical testing, his theory has been of little value from a scientific perspective. But scientists often give high marks to a theory that instigates new discussion and controversy—even though the theory itself may not enjoy much direct support. If we use this standard to evaluate McLuhan's contribution, perhaps there is some shred of scientific value.

McLuhan started writing about the media more than 30 years ago. Communication scholars still use his ideas and extend them to new areas. McLuhan's basic perspective of **"technological determinism"** (the medium, not the message, determines changes in human behavior) is particularly evident in two books that have received wide acclaim. In his book *Amusing Ourselves to Death: Public Discourse in the Age of Show Business,* **Neil Postman** argues that television has trivialized public discourse. He states that:

> There is no more disturbing consequence of the electronic and graphic revolution than this: that the world as given to us through television seems natural, not bizarre. For the loss of the sense of the strange is a sign of adjustment, and the extent to which we have adjusted is a measure of the extent to which we have been changed. (p. 80)[9]

Another scholar, **Joshua Meyrowitz,** has written a very provocative book, *No Sense of Place: The Impact of Electronic Media on Social Behavior.* The following excerpt from the book's introduction sounds like McLuhan himself:

> [T]his book suggests that the widespread use of electronic media has played an important part in many recent social developments, including the social explosions of the 1960s, the many "integration" movements (blacks, women, elderly, children, disabled, etc.), the rise of malpractice suits, the development of "halfway" houses for prisoners and the mentally ill, the decline of the nuclear family. . . . The theory suggests that a broad, seemingly chaotic spectrum of social change may be, in part, an orderly and comprehensible adjustment in behavior patterns to match the new social situations created by electronic media. (p. 9)[10]

To be sure, both Postman and Meyrowitz go well beyond McLuhan's notions in advancing their own thoughts on electronic media. But McLuhan's influence on these widely read scholars and others writing about media impact is quite evident and openly acknowledged. There is no escaping the fact that McLuhan's basic ideas about media impact are at least worthy of some attention.

SOME FINAL REFLECTIONS

You should recognize McLuhan's perspective on media effects as qualitatively different from the ones represented in the other chapters in this volume. In the case of Marshall McLuhan, there is very little, if any, evidence of the scientific type to support his ideas. And yet, no book on the effects of mass media is able to ignore McLuhan. The media effects that he talked about were not trivial ones. If his assertions are right, the effects documented in the preceding chapters should take a second seat to the kind of sweeping cultural effects that he claimed the electronic media initiated. If you are like most people, you found some of McLuhan's thinking to be provocative and full of insight. But you may have reacted with skepticism to other parts of his analysis. In the end, media effects scholars don't really know what to do with McLuhan because his ideas fall short of the testability criterion that scientists embrace. Nevertheless, we must credit

---

STUDY BOX 12-1 McLuhan's Failed Experiment:
The Wonders (?) of Prohtex

If you are on the fence about how to evaluate the ideas of Marshall McLuhan, perhaps this little tidbit will push you over. One of the themes in the "theory" of Marshall McLuhan is that when the print age supplanted the tribal age, the sensory balance of communication was disrupted. According to McLuhan, tribal communication involved all the senses—including the olfactory. The sense of smell was an important and valued commodity in the tribal state. If, as McLuhan argued, the electronic age was a return to the acoustic communication environment of the tribal era, then it was also a return to an environment where more of the senses would once again become involved in communication. Consequently, McLuhan thought that the electronic age would be an age where the sense of smell would become increasingly important.

McLuhan was a person who was not afraid to invest in his own theoretical ideas. According to Gary Wolf, who wrote in *Wired* magazine, McLuhan announced a new product in 1971. In collaboration with his nephew, Ross Hall, who was a chemist, McLuhan actually patented a unique chemical solution that was designed to be applied to people's underpants. That's right, there was no misprint in that last sentence. It was designed to be applied to people's underpants. It gets even better. The secret formula, registered under the trademark Prohtex, worked marvels. It removed the smell of urine from one's underpants while leaving the more interesting body aromas associated with perspiration. McLuhan was convinced that natural body aroma was an important part of communication in the tribal state. According to Wolf, McLuhan really believed that "when electronic technology turned the world into a global village, tribal odors would make a comeback too." Needless to say, Prohtex didn't make McLuhan rich. Perhaps it was ahead of its time. Maybe the coming revolution that will usher us into the electronic age will pave the way for this odd formula to become an everyday best seller. Then again, maybe not.

SOURCE: Wolf, G. (1996). The wisdom of Saint Marshall, the Holy Fool [Online]. Available at: http://www.wired.com/wired/archive//4.01/saint.marshal.html?person=marshall_mcluhan&topic_set=wired people

---

McLuhan with stimulating the entire scholarly community to think about the power of the electronic media. If he was right, we may only be at the dawn of the full realization of the electronic age.

SUMMARY

Some media effects scholars may question the extent to which a chapter on Marshall McLuhan belongs in a book of this type. Three arguments for including such a chapter were presented. McLuhan saw the field of communication historically. He described at least three major eras in communication history: the tribal age, the print age, and the electronic age. His observations about the fundamental nature of communication in each era formed the core of his "theory." He made his fame in applying his insights to all sorts of modern-day phenomena, including drugs, education, politics, and war. Many of his ideas were difficult to grasp, and he disliked scholarly criticism. His perspective is nearly impossible to test scientifically. While this fact did not ultimately endear him to the scholarly community, it permitted him to roam freely with his speculations. No one could really prove him wrong. In the final analysis, McLuhan's perspective on the impact of the electronic media is worth thinking about—even while recognizing that gathering empirical evidence in favor of it seems unlikely.

KEY TERMS AND CONCEPTS

"Prober" versus "proofs" 201

Three eras of communication history 202

   tribal age 202

   print age 203

   electronic age 204

Sensory balance 203

Linear information processing versus all-at-once processing 204

The "global village" 204

"The medium is the message" 205

"The medium is the massage" 207

"Hot" vs. "cool" media 210

Technological determinism 213

KEY NAMES

Marshall McLuhan 200

Harold Innis and Walter Ong 202

Neil Postman 213

Joshua Meyrowitz 213

WEB LINKS

1. For a Web site dedicated to Marshall McLuhan, try . . . http://www.angelfire.com/ms/MediaLiteracy/McLuhan.html

2. For the full text of the interview that McLuhan did with *Playboy* Magazine in 1969, try . . . http://omni.cc.purdue.edu/~sparks/Playboy.htm

3. For Web links to articles mentioning McLuhan in *Wired* magazine, try . . .http://www.wired.com/wired/archive//4.10/dekerckhove.html?person=marshall_mcluhan&topic_set=wiredpeople

4. For the complete text of a lecture that McLuhan delivered on the move to the electronic age, try . . . http://www.videomcluhan.com/lectures.htm#top

To learn more about the topics in this chapter, enter the Key Terms and Concepts and Key Names found in this chapter as subject and keyword searches on your InfoTrac College Edition.

IMPORTANT SOURCES ON MARSHALL MCLUHAN

Innis, H. A. (1972). *Empire and Communication* (Rev. ed.). Toronto: University of Toronto Press.

Canadian Broadcasting Corporation. (1984). McLuhan: The man and his message [Video].

McLuhan, M. (1951). *The mechanical bride: Folklore of industrial man.* New York: Vanguard Press.

McLuhan, M. (1962). *The Gutenberg galaxy: The making of typographic man.* Toronto: University of Toronto Press.

McLuhan, M. (1964). *Understanding media: The extensions of man.* New York: McGraw-Hill.

Ong, W. J. (1982). *Orality and literacy: The technologizing of the word.* New York: Methuen.

Playboy interview: Marshall McLuhan. (1969, March). *Playboy,* 53–54, 56, 59–62, 64–66, 68, 70, 72, 74, 158.

NOTES

1. Pember, D. R. (1992). *Mass media in America.* New York: MacMillan.

2. Playboy interview: Marshall McLuhan. (1969, March). *Playboy,* 53–54, 56, 59–62, 64–66, 68, 70, 72, 74, 158.

3. Public Broadcasting Corporation [Video]. Marshall McLuhan: The man and his message.

4. Shanker, A. (1992, January 6). The higher education crisis. *New Republic,* 200, 2.

5. Playboy interview: Marshall McLuhan. (1969, March). *Playboy,* 53–54, 56, 59–62, 64–66, 68, 70, 72, 74, 158.

6. McKernan, V. (1992, September 21). The real war on drugs. *Newsweek, 120,* 14.

7. Playboy interview: Marshall McLuhan. (1969, March). *Playboy,* 53–54, 56, 59–62, 64–66, 68, 70, 72, 74, 158.

8. Smith, R. (1986). Television addiction. In J. Bryant and D. Zillmann (Eds.), *Perspectives on media effects* (pp. 109–128). Hillsdale, NJ: Erlbaum.

9. Postman, N. (1985). *Amusing ourselves to death: Public discourse in the age of show business.* New York: Penguin.

10. Meyrowitz, J. (1985). *No sense of place: The impact of electronic media on social behavior.* New York: Oxford University Press.

Names Index

Adler, Ilya, 173
Agnew, Spiro, 163
Alioto, Joseph, 35
Allen, Mike, 173
Anderson, Craig, 194–196
Archer, Dane, 167–170
Aronson, Elliot, 132
Asner, Ed, 138
Aspden, Philip, 189
Atkin, Charles, 140

Babbie, Earl, 11
Bagwell, Marilyn, 24, 32
Ball-Rokeach, Sandra, 137, 138
Bandura, Albert, 9, 43, 76–79, 194
Banner, David, 113, 114
Baran, Stanley, 15
Berelson, Bernard, 20, 48
Berkowitz, Leonard, 35, 83–84, 99
Berrenberg, Joy, 76
Blumer, Herbert, 43–45, 112
Blumler, Jay, 58
Brown, Jane, 186
Bryant, Jennings, 50, 96
Bundy, Ted, 44
Burggraf, Kimberley, 175
Bush, George, Sr. 170, 211, 212

Cacioppo, John, 132, 143, 154
Cadeau, Leslie, 21
Cantor, Joanne, 7, 39, 85, 111–114, 120, 186
Cantril, Hadley, 46, 47
Cappella, Joseph, 154–155
Centerwall, Brandon, 81
Chaiken, Shelly, 144
Chambers, Marilyn, 95
Cheung, C. K. T., 190
Choi, W., 190
Cialdini, Robert, 141, 142, 152
Clinton, Bill, 1, 2, 155, 211
Cohen, Bernard, 155
Condra, Mollie, 154
Copernicus, 3, 9
Court, J. H., 94
Cousins, Norman, 129
Creel, George, 41
Cronkite, Walter, 210

Dale, Edgar, 42, 90
Darwin, Charles, 9, 207
Daschmann, Gregor, 159
Davis, Dennis, 15, 159
Davis, Stacy, 24
Dean, W. W., 112
DeFleur, Melvin, 41, 45, 46
Dill, Karen, 195, 196
Dixon, Travis, 177–179, 180

Dobson, James, 99
Donnerstein, Ed., 96, 97, 98, 99, 106
Doob, Anthony, 134–135
Drabman, Ronald, 85, 181

Eagly, Alice, 144
Earnhardt, Dale, 161
Einstein, Albert, 207
Eisenhower, Dwight, 143
Eron, Leonard, 79–81
Estling, Ralph, 16
Etzersdorfer, Elmar, 153
Eveland, William, 158

Fehlner, Christine, 169, 170
Ferraro, Geraldine, 170
Feshbach, Seymour, 81–83, 190
Fiske, Susan, 171
Ford, Catherine, 194–195
Fouts, Gregory, 175
Freud, Sigmund, 129, 206, 207

Gaudet, Hazel, 48
Gerbner, George, 74, 133–135, 172–173
Goethe, Johann von, 152
Goldstein, Jeffrey, 85
Goldwater, Barry, 162
Greenberg, Bradley, 58–59, 102
Greenwald, Anthony, 130
Griffin, Em, 9, 14, 144, 157
Grossman, Dave, 193–194
Grube, Joel, 137, 138
Guildford, J., 31
Gunter, Barrie, 160
Gurevitch, Michael, 58

Hall, Ross, 214
Handford, A. Gordon, 65
Harris, Richard, 172, 177
Harrison, Kristin, 7, 176
Hawkins, Robert, 173
Hearst, William Randolf, 40
Hebb, Donald, 61
Herrett-Skjellum, Jennifer, 173
Himmelweit, Hilde, 112
Hippler, Fritz, 50, 143
Hitler, Adolph, 143
Hockett, A. B., 112
Hoffman, Donna, 191
Hoffner, Cindy, 111
Homer, 209
Houseman, John, 45
Hovland, Carl, 142
Huesmann, Rowell, 79–81
Humphrey, Hubert, 155

Innis, Harold, 202
Iyengar, Shanto, 156

Jhally, Sut, 176
Jo, Eunkyung., 83
Johnson, Lyndon, 93, 162, 210

Kang, Jong, 162
Katz, James, 189
Katzman, Natan, 172
Kennedy, John, 161–62, 211
Kepplinger, Hans, 159
Key, Wilson Bryan, 128, 129
Kieffer, Suzanne, 170
Kilbourne, Jean, 176
Kimball, Meredith, 174
Kinder, Donald, 156
Klapper, Joseph, 49
Kraus, Sid, 161
Kraut, Robert, 187, 188, 189
Krueger, Freddy, 118–119
Kunkel, Dale, 102–103
Kutchinsky, Berl, 94

Lang, Annie, 161
Lazarsfeld, Paul, 48
Lefkowitz, Monroe M., 79
Leonard, Kenneth, 97, 98
Lewis, Dorothy, 44
Lieberman, Joseph, 24
Liebert, R., 52
Linz, Dan, 177–179, 180
Lowery, Shearon, 41, 45, 46

Macdonald, Glenn, 134–135
Malamuth, Neil, 106
Marconi, G., 204
Mares, Marie-Louise, 24
McCombs, Maxwell, 155–157
McIlwraith, Robert, 60
McLeod, Doug, 158
McLeod, Jack, 53
McLuhan, Marshall, 200–216
Meese, Ed, 99
Meyrowitz, Joshua, 213
Milgram, Stanley, 97
Minow, Newton, 74
Mondale, Walter, 170
Moore, Timothy, 21
Moyers, Bill, 50, 143, 162
Mutz, Diana, 64
Myers, David, 65

Nass, Clifford, 60
Nathanson, Amy, 7
Newhagen, John, 160, 161
Newton, Issac, 207
Nimoy, Leonard, 141
Nixon, Richard, 93, 155, 161, 210, 211
Noelle-Neumann, Elizabeth, 157

Ong, Walter, 202

Palmer, Edward, 112
Palmgreen, Phillip, 70
Pavlov, I., 207
Pember, Don, 201
Perloff, Richard, 146
Perse, Elizabeth, 61, 154
Petty, Richard, 132, 143, 154
Pfau, Michael, 162
Phillips, David, 152–154, 155
Piaget, Jean, 112, 113
Pingree, Suzanne, 173
Postman, Neil, 213
Potter, James, 66
Pratkanis, Anthony, 130–131
Diana, Princess of Wales, 205

Randi, James, 15
Reagan, Ronald, 170
Reeves, Byron, 53, 60, 160, 161
Reeves, Rosser, 143
Remington, Frederic, 40
Reynolds, Patrick, 142–143
Reynolds, R. J., 142
Rhee, June, 154–155
Roberts, Donald, 64
Robinson, John, 159
Rokeach, Milton, 137, 138
Roosevelt, Franklin, 48

Rubin, Alan, 59
Rubin, Rebecca, 61

Saba, Walter, 145
Schick, Theodore, Jr., 13
Schutte, Nicola, 194
Schwartz, Tony, 142, 162, 163
Serling, Rod, 72–73, 111, 116
Shaw, Donald, 155–157
Shaw, Heather, 175
Signorielli, Nancy, 158
Simpson, O. J., 73, 205
Smith Robin, 60
Sonneck, Gernot, 153
Sparks, Cheri, 85
Speer, P., 181
Sprafkin, J., 52
Stice, Eric, 175

Tankard, James, 156
Taylor, Shelly, 171
Taylor, Stuart, 97, 98
Terre, L., 181
Thomas, Margaret, 85
Tucker, Larry, 24, 27

Valente, Thomas, 145
Valkenburg, Patti, 66

van der Vort, Tom, 66
van Vuuren, D. P., 64
Vaughn, Lewis, 13
Vicary, James, 128–129
Vince, P., 128

Wakshlag, Jacob, 50
Walder, L., 79
Ward, Monique, 102
Weaver, James, 78, 95–96
Weiss, Walter, 142
Wells, H. G., 45
Welles, Orson, 45–46, 47
Wertham, Frederic, 51, 193
Wilkie, Wendell, 48
Williams, K. D., 190
Williams, Tannis MacBeth, 65, 172, 174
Wilson, Barb, 111
Wilson, Paul, 44
Wilson, Woodrow, 41
Wolfe, Tom, 207

Zillmann, Dolf, 50, 78, 86, 96, 98, 101, 122, 123, 124
Zimbardo, Phillip, 140
Zuckerman, Marvin, 61
Zuckerman, Miron, 170

Subject Index

Acquired Immune Deficiency Syndrome (AIDS), 76
Acquired Violence Immune Deficiency Syndrome (AVIDS), 194, 198
ACT (Action for Children's Television), 140
Action for Children's Television (ACT), 140
Advertising, 139–140, 163
Agenda-setting theory, 155–157, 164
Aggressive behavior. *See* Violence, and aggressive behavior
AIDS (Acquired Immune Deficiency Syndrome), 76
Alice in Wonderland, 121
American Academy of Pediatrics, 70, 87
American Psychological Association, 74
Annie Hall, 204
Anorexia Nervosa, 175
Arousal, 100, 101–102, 107, 122–123, 161. *See also* Television viewing, arousal
Attitude, 127
Attitude change, 53–54
Authority, 3–4, 16, 141
AVIDS (Acquired Violence Immune Deficiency Syndrome), 194, 198

Basketball Diaries, 11
Batman and Robin, 51
Beyond Reality, 136
Body dissatisfaction, 175–177, 182
Body Mass Index, 68. *See also* Television viewing, obesity
Bulimia, 175–176
Burning Bed, The, 73

Carnegie Mellon study, 187–192
Case study, 12
Catharsis, 81–83, 86, 190
Causal relationships, 27–32, 34, 37, 76–85, 99–100, 134–135, 181, 191
Censorship. *See* Control of media content; Sexual content
Center for Media & Literacy, 87
Central route to persuasion, 132–133. *See also* Content analysis
Coder, 20. *See also* Content analysis
Coefficient of determination, 31
Cognitive coping, 120–121
Columbine High School, 1, 11–12, 16, 40, 192, 205
Comic books, 51–52, 54, 55, 193
Commercials, 21–23

Commitment. *See* Persuasion, commitment in
Committee on Public Information, 41
Committee for the Scientific Investigation of Claims of the Paranormal, 126n. 13
Computers. *See* Internet
Consistency. *See* Persuasion, consistency in
Content analysis, 19–23, 107, 133, 177, 200
  categories, 22
  coding agreement, 22
  of comic books, 51–52
  manifest vs. latent content, 20–21
  objectivity, 20
  racial stereotypes, 177–179
  sample for, 21–22
  of sexual content on TV, 100–101, 103
  systematic, 20
  units of analysis, 22
  quantitative data from, 20
Control group, 48, 191. *See also* Experiment, control groups
Control of media content, 104–106
Conversion, 48
Cool media, 210–212
Copy-cat behavior, 72–73, 111. *See also* Television viewing, imitation
Correlation, 27–32, 37, 99–100, 134–135
Credibility, 142–143
Cry Rape, 132

Daisy Girl commercial, 162, 163
Day After, The, 132
Deathwish, 84
Debates, Kennedy–Nixon, 161–162, 165
Dependent variable. *See* Experiment, dependent variable
Description, 19
Desensitization, 15, 84–85, 87, 193, 198
Displacement hypothesis, 64–67, 69, 188. *See also* Time spent with media
Domino's Pizza, 75–76
Doom, 192, 197
Doomsday Flight, The, 72
Dreamworlds, 176
Driving Miss Daisy, 78
Dual-coding theory, 160, 164

Eating disorders, 175–176
Ecological validity, 98

Elaboration likelihood model, 132
Electric shock, 97, 98
Electronic age, 204–206
Emotion, 160–164
Empiricism, 2
Ethics of research, 115–116, 180
Excessive Force, 78
Excitation transfer, theory of, 101–102, 122–123
Exorcist, The, 111, 117, 119
Experience, 2, 16
Experiment, 19, 32–36, 38, 52, 130, 136, 181, 190, 200
  control groups, 34–35
  dependent variable, 33–35
  experimental realism, 99
  identical treatment of conditions, 33–34
  independent variable, 33–35
  random assignment to conditions, 33, 35
  violent video games, 192–198
Expertise. *See* Credibility
Explanation, 5–6

Face-ism, 167–171, 182
Falsifiability, 9–10, 15, 16, 200, 207
Fantasy vs. reality, 112–114, 116–117, 120–121, 124
Fear. *See* Persuasion, fear in
Fear of victimization, 133–134
Federal Communications Commission, 129
Focus on the Family, 99
Framing, 156–157, 164
Frightening media, 39, 109–124, 135

Galvanic skin response, 42
Gender role socialization, 123–124
Global village, 204–205
Goals of science, 4–8, 16
  control, 6–8, 16
  explanation, 5–6, 8, 16
  how to achieve, 8–9, 16
  prediction, 4–5, 8, 16
  understanding, 6, 8, 16
Godfather, The, 84
Guilt. *See* Persuasion, guilt in

Happy Days, 131–132
Harpers, 45
Health campaigns, 145–146
He-Man, 77
Hitman, The, 78
Hot media, 210–212
Human Subjects Committee, 114, 115–116, 180

Humor
in entertainment, 50
in persuasion, 143, 145
Hypodermic needle model, 47.
See also Magic bullet model
Hypothesis, 9, 10, 16

Illusory placebo effect, 130
Imitation. See Television viewing,
imitation
Incredible Hulk, The, 112,
113–114, 115–116
Independent variable. See
Experiment, independent
variable
Internet, 59, 60, 104–105,
187–190, 198

Jackass, 73
Jaws, 111
Jerry Springer Show, The, 24

Kaiser Family Foundation, 63–64,
70, 71, 103, 107, 108
Killing Us Softly, 176

Legacy of fear, 45, 47, 51, 54
Liking. See Persuasion, liking in
Limited effects model, 47–51, 54,
58
Linear thought, 204, 205,
208–209
Little Man Tate, 78

Magic bullet model, 47, 52, 54.
See also Hypodermic needle
model
Mainstreaming, 134
Mattel toy company, 140
"Mean world" syndrome, 134
Media Awareness Network, 183
Media cultivation, theory of,
133–135, 147, 179
Media Education Foundation,
176, 183
Media Education Site, The, 107
Media Effects
types of, 52–54
Media Metrix, 187, 199
Meese Commission Report on
Pornography, The, 99–100,
106
Mercury Theatre, 45
Meta-analysis, 173, 182, 196
Micromhos, 43
Motion Picture Association of
America, 7
Movie ratings, 7, 124
Movies, 41–45. See also Payne
Fund Studies
Mundane realism, 98–99

Napster, 185, 186
National Association of
Broadcasters, 129
National Commission on
Obscenity and Pornography,
93–95, 99, 106

National Council of Churches, 90
National Television Violence Study,
7, 74–75
Need for cognition, 154–155, 164
News, 151–164, 211
imitative suicide, 151–154,
155, 164
recall of, 158–160
stereotyped images in,
177–179
vivid images in, 160–161
New York Journal, 40
Nielsen ratings, 85
Nightmare on Elm Street, 118–119
Noid, the, 75–76, 88. See also
Domino's Pizza
Nonlinear correlation, 31
Nonpermissive cues, 98
Northwest Mutual Life Insurance
Company, 139

Obscenity, 91, 105. See also
Sexual content
101 Dalmatians, 124
Origin of Species, The, 9

Paranormal beliefs, 135–137, 180
Paranormal content, 109, 111,
112, 114, 116–117, 119,
124, 135–137
Parasocial relationships, 60–61
Payne Fund studies, the, 42–45,
47, 54, 60
Penthouse, 105–106
People's Choice study, The, 48–49,
54
Perfect Strangers, 136
Peripheral-route persuasion, 133
Permissive cues, 98
Perpetual linkage, 186
Persuasion, 127–147
commitment in, 141
consistency in, 141
definition, 127–128
elaboration likelihood
model, 132–133
fear in, 143–144
guilt in, 143–144
illusion of personal
invulnerability, 140
liking in, 141
scarcity in, 141
subliminal, 128–131, 147
values, 137–139
Phonetic alphabet, 203
Picnic, 128
Placebo effect. See Illusory placebo
effect
Playboy, 95, 105, 211, 212
Political sophistication, 154–155
Poltergeist, 117–118
Pornography, 44, 92–100, 107
Postcards from the Edge, 78
Prediction, 4–5, 16
Priming, 83–84, 87, 179
Print age, 203–204, 205, 207,
208, 209, 214
Prohtex, 214

Propaganda, 41, 50
Protection motivation theory, 144
Psychics, 14–15
Punishments, 77

Racial stereotypes, 177–180, 182,
183
Rambo, 84
Random assignment, 33, 35
Random sample, 21, 191
Rating system, 73
Reality vs. fantasy, 112–114,
116–17, 120–21, 124
Reciprocity, 141
Reinforcement, 49
Relativism, 13–14
Repetition, 143
Replication, 36
Resonance, 134–135
Rewards, 77
RoboCop, 84
Role schema, 171

Safety valve theory, 94
Scarcity. See Persuasion, scarcity in
Science, 4
is general, 11–12
goals of, 4–8, 10, 16
hypothesis, 9
as a way of knowing, 4, 16
methods of, 10
content analysis, 19–23,
36, 37
experiment, 19, 32–36
survey, 19, 23–27, 37
nature of, 10–16
research, 12
theory, 8–9
Scientific questions, 15
Seduction of the Innocent, 51, 193
Selective exposure, 51, 50, 159
Self-report data, 43–45, 62–63
Sensation seeking, 61
Sensory balance, 203, 214
Sesame Street, 5, 50
Sex Role Differentiation Scale, 174
Sex role stereotypes. See
Stereotypes, sex role
Sexual content
censorship, 91
on the Internet, 104–105,
107
obscenity, 91, 105
political controversy, 90–92
sex crimes, 94–95
in subliminal ads, 128–129
on TV, 100–104, 107
See also National Commission
on Obscenity and
Pornography;
Pornography
Silence of the Lambs, 111
Simplicity, 143
Skepticism, 14–15
Snow White, 113
Soap, 90
Soap operas, 102, 152, 172
Social comparison, 175

Social learning theory, 43, 75, 77–79, 194
Social proof, 141
Social reality, 173
Sorrows of Young Werther, The, 152
Spiral of silence, 157–158, 164
Star Trek, 141
Statistical importance, 31
Statistical significance, 29–30, 37
Stereotypes, 171–182, 183
    and body dissatisfaction, 175–177
    in cartoons, 172
    racial, 177–179, 183
    sex role, 172–174
    of victims, 172–173
    voice-overs, 172
Subliminal persuasion, 128–131, 147
Suicide. *See* News, imitative suicide
Superman, 51
Surveys, 19, 23–27, 30–32, 37, 134, 200
    types of, 26–27
        cross-sectional, 26
        longitudinal, 26, 48, 65, 187; trend study, 26; cohort study, 26; panel study, 27, 48, 64–65
"Swing, The," 8
Systematic observation, 4, 16

Talk shows, 24–26
Technological determinism, 213
Television viewing
    academic achievement, 66
    addiction to, 60, 212

arousal, 61
crime, 79–81 (*see also* Violence)
dawn of, 52
imitation, 52, 73, 77–79
obesity, 24, 27–32, 67–69, 70 (*see also* Body Mass Index)
reading, 66–67
Terminator The, 2
Theory, 8–10, 16
    critical, 15
    normative, 15
Third-person effect, 140. *See also* Persuasion
Threshold effect, 66
Time spent with media, 63–67, 74
Tribal age, 202–203, 204, 205, 209, 214
Trigger hypothesis, 94
Trustworthiness. *See* Credibility
Truth, 13–14, 16
TV Guide, 138
Twilight Zone, The, 72, 109–111, 116

Under Siege, 78
Understanding, 6
Universal Soldier, 78
Uses and gratifications perspective, the, 58–62
    arousal, 59, 61
    children's TV viewing, 58–62
    companionship, 59, 60
    escape, 62
    habit, 60
    learning, 59–60

pass time, 59, 62
relaxation, 59, 61

V-chip, 43, 73
Video games, 11, 12, 186–87, 192–197, 198
Violence
    and aggressive behavior, 2, 5, 6, 35–36, 52, 73, 76–85, 111, 190, 192–197
    amount in the media, 74–75
    attraction to, 85–86
    catharsis, 81–83, 86
    desensitization, 15, 84–85, 87
    electric shocks, 35
    guns, 20
    media images, 6, 52, 74–75
    prolonged exposure to, 78
    realism, 35–36, 75
    sex differences, 77–78
    video games, 12, 186–187, 192–197, 198
Visualization, 190
Voter volatility, 51

War of the Worlds, 45–47, 54, 55
Ways of knowing, 2–4
    authority, 3–4, 16
    empiricism, 2
    experience, 2–3, 16
    science, 4, 16
Werther effect, 153
Wizard of Oz, The, 112

You've Got Mail, 189